IMAGES
of America

PLOVER

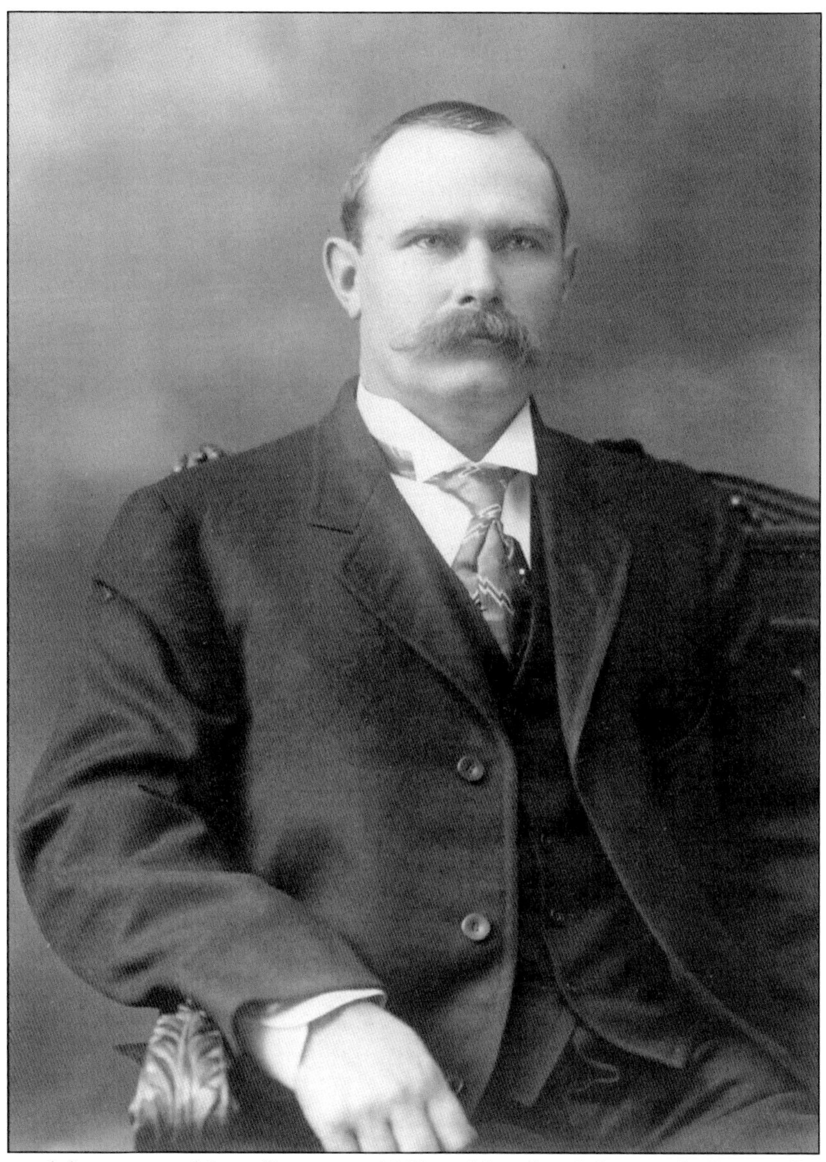

Walter Barnsdale emigrated from Britain in 1885 and lived with his uncle George Barnsdale in Plover for a short time. He then worked as a lumberjack and engineer in other cities, returning to Plover in 1891. In 1896 and 1897, Walter's interest in motion pictures was piqued by entertainers traveling through the area showing early motion pictures. He created improvements to the Edison machine by adding a sprocket with gears to provide for proper timing and perfecting the take-up reel, and is believed to be the first person to put the device into use. He also made his own gasoline-powered electric generator to supply power for his motion picture projector in rural areas. Barnsdale traveled the state for 20 years showing motion pictures, and after 1914, he began making his own. By 1926, larger theaters had their own machines and leased the pictures, bringing an end to Barnsdale's Vivorama. (Portage County Historical Society.)

On the Cover: This c. 1916 photograph shows the old Plover Post Office. Plover rural mail carriers Clint Moss (left) and his son John Moss are shown with their mail carriages. In 1916, John took over his father's route, abandoning his original Route 1. (Portage County Historical Society.)

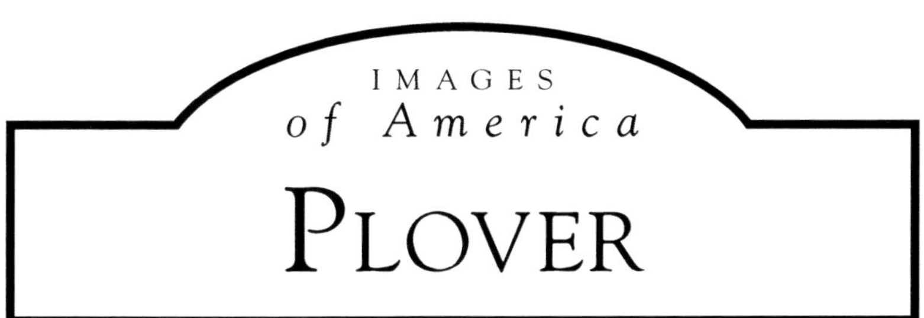

Plover

Brad Casselberry and Diane Lang

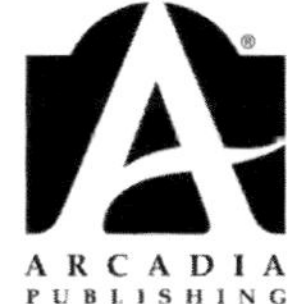

ISBN 978-1-4671-2545-1

Published by Arcadia Publishing
Charleston, South Carolina

Printed in the United States of America

Library of Congress Control Number: 2016958696

For all general information, please contact Arcadia Publishing:
Telephone 843-853-2070
Fax 843-853-0044
E-mail sales@arcadiapublishing.com
For customer service and orders:
Toll-Free 1-888-313-2665

Visit us on the Internet at www.arcadiapublishing.com

This book is dedicated to the memory of Walter Barnsdale,
without whom it would not have been possible.

Contents

Acknowledgments

Like any project, this book would not have been possible if it were not for the help of a variety of people. The authors would like to thank Mark Seiler for bringing this idea to us. We would also like to thank Ryan and Wayne Berrend and Gordon Fox for donating photographs and providing information for this book. Thanks also to Joyce Slack, who took the time to show us the Meehan Church and School and provided us with a sense of the Meehan community.

Thanks to the University of Wisconsin–Stevens Point (UWSP) Nelis R. Kampenga University Archives and Area Research Center and archivist Ruth Wachter-Nelson for providing photographs and an endless supply of historical information to identify people, places, and events depicted in the photographs. The resources of the Portage County Public Library, including digital materials, pamphlet files, and staff such as Wendell Nelson were indispensable to our research.

We thank the Portage County Historical Society (PCHS) for providing the vast majority of photographs. Anton Anday and Timothy Siebert were especially helpful in clarifying details of Plover's history and providing ample stories about people, events, and buildings. PCHS has preserved a number of Plover's early buildings at Heritage Park, located at the corner of Willow Drive and Washington Avenue in Plover. Without its dedication to preserving the history of Portage County, many of these buildings would have been lost. PCHS has also preserved the glass-plate negatives of Walter Barnsdale, the source of many of the photographs in this book. He was a prolific photographer in the early 1900s in and around the village of Plover. The voluminous collection of more than 1,400 glass-plate negatives and lantern slides were sold at an estate auction and later acquired by Timothy Siebert of the Portage County Historical Society. They are invaluable in discovering the history of Plover.

Unless otherwise noted, all images appear courtesy of the Portage County Historical Society.

INTRODUCTION

There is no certainty as to why it was named Plover, but legend has it that it was named after the ringed plover, a migratory bird that once graced the shores of the Wisconsin River at Plover in large numbers. Long before the white man came to the area, what would become known as Plover was originally used by Native Americans as a staging point for portaging to the Wolf River from the Wisconsin River and as a means to bypass the rapids of the Wisconsin River. Once lumbering began along the Wisconsin River north of Plover, the area was a convenient stopping point for those traveling on the main north-south road from Portage to the pineries.

When Portage County was first divided on January 9, 1849, the county board created three townships: Plover, Middletown, and Bull Falls. Plover's borders changed again in 1850, 1852, 1859, 1869, 1870, and 1908. There are several communities within the Town of Plover that we have chosen to include in this book, including Meehan, Springville, and Whiting, the latter being incorporated as a village on November 13, 1947. Because these areas at one point existed within the borders of the Town of Plover, we felt it was appropriate to include their stories in a history of the area.

The village of Plover was the first to be platted after being chosen as the Portage County seat in 1844, likely before a community had even developed. A post office was established on January 14, 1845, called Plover Portage, as the area had been known; the name was changed to Plover on January 14, 1850. The original village plat was set east of First Street (today's Post Road), extending four blocks and stretching north from Union Street (today's Plover Road) for eight blocks and a fraction. In 1857, Plover was incorporated as Algernon, and in 1858, the name was changed to Stanton. In 1864, the village returned to Plover. The village's incorporation was dissolved around 1870 shortly after a vote on August 1, 1868, which moved the county seat from Plover to Stevens Point. This created great tensions between the two cities, and newspapers from both towns seized on the opportunity to throw accusations of cheating, underhandedness, and ineptness at one another. In 1912, the village of Plover was once again reincorporated, only to be dissolved in 1931. In 1971, the village was incorporated for a third time and has remained ever since.

In 1845, the first court was held in Plover, attracting lawyers, businessmen, and others who were drawn to the newly formed county seat, including settlers and farmers. In the early days of the village, the most important businesses were taverns and hotels. Other early businesses that were integral to the development of the community were the general stores, blacksmiths, and Plover's first newspaper, the *Plover Herald*, which was started in 1856 by James S. Alban and Jervis W. Carter and published by H.G. Ingersoll. In 1872, the Green Bay & Lake Pepin Railroad (later the Green Bay & Western) came to Plover, which was an east-west road, and later, the Wisconsin Central, known as the Portage Line or P-Line, was a north-south road that ran through Plover. Many prominent Portage County residents lived in Plover. Among them are Luther Hanchett, James S. Alban, Miner Strope, S.A. Sherman, Walter Barnsdale, Walt Wilmot, James Pierce, Frank Halladay, and Sheriff Joseph Baker. Other prominent residents originally settled in Plover, but after several years moved to Stevens Point for other opportunities; these included George Cate, Gilbert Park, A.E. Bourn, and John Curran.

The lumber/logging and mill companies also brought a lot of people to the area and helped build commerce and a sense of community. Just north of the village, sawmills and gristmills that harnessed the power of the Wisconsin and Plover Rivers were erected. Meehan sprang up in the Town of Plover as a community just south of the mill that brothers Patrick and James Meehan had constructed across the river in Linwood. In the 1890s, large paper mills built by George A. Whiting, including the Plover Paper Company ("lower mill") and the Wisconsin River Paper and Pulp Company ("upper mill"), moved into the area, creating hundreds of jobs in the north end of the township. The paper industry in the northern part of the Town of Plover grew into an important industry in the area leading to the creation of the village of Whiting as northern Town of Plover residents felt the industries' tax money was unequally distributed to the southern part.

Plover has a proud tradition of serving the country, and during the Civil War, sent more men to fight than any other town of its size in Wisconsin. After the war, a post of the Grand Army of the Republic (GAR) was organized, which was integral to the community for decades to come. Other organizations and societies included Sons of Veterans, the Freemasons, Independent Order of Odd Fellows, the 1001 Club, Plover Camp of the Modern Woodmen of America, Busy Stitchers, and numerous religious organizations.

Beginning in the 1950s, Plover began a regrowth largely due to the boom created by increased potato production in the area. Improved irrigation methods led to an increased use of the land, which led to a boost in agricultural production, attracting large corporations to the area such as Ore-Ida and Del Monte. From its first incorporation in 1857, Plover has seen several declines, but it has also seen resurgences and has proven itself irrepressible. The growth of Plover during the late 20th and early 21st century highlights the need for a history of this community that has often been passed over.

At times, the history of Plover has been difficult to piece together. As you will see in some of these photographs, almost all of the early downtown landmarks have since been removed. Those that remained, such as the Cash & Carry (later St. Vincent de Paul), Springville Wharf, and various houses were removed within the last two years. Regardless, great effort has been made to accurately identify each photograph.

One

Street Scenes

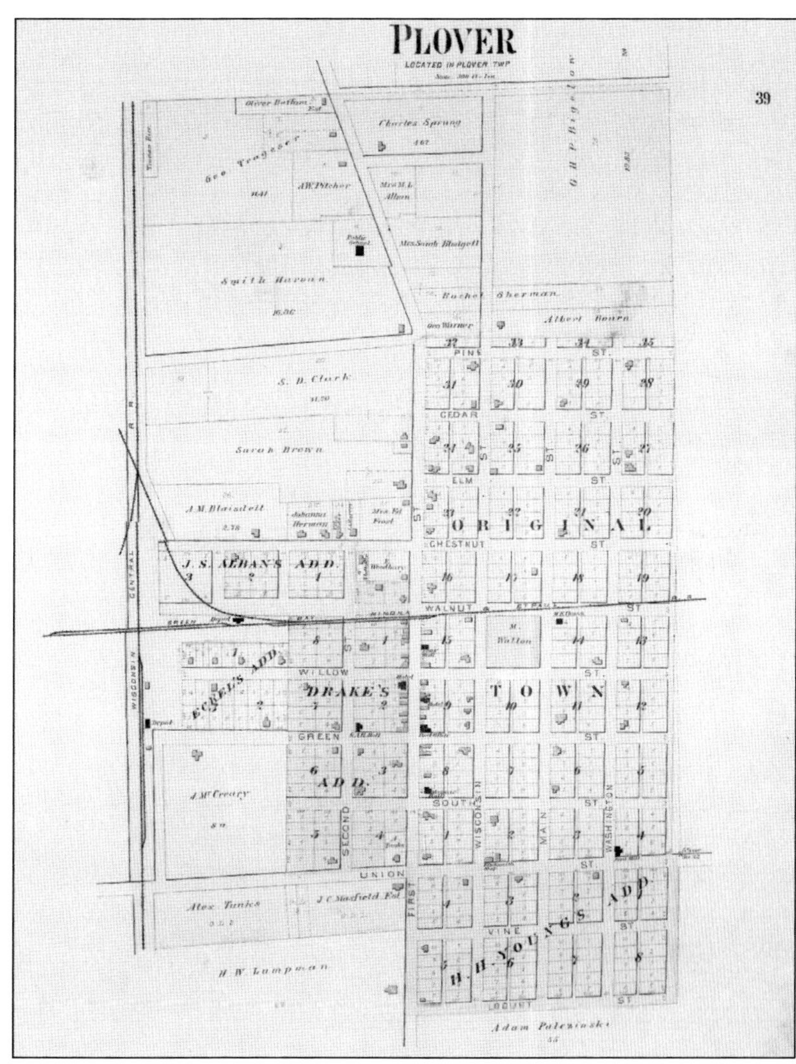

This Plover village plat of 1895 shows the concentration of businesses on First Street. In the 1960s, First Street was changed to Post Road; captions to earlier photographs in this book use the former name. (UWSP Archives.)

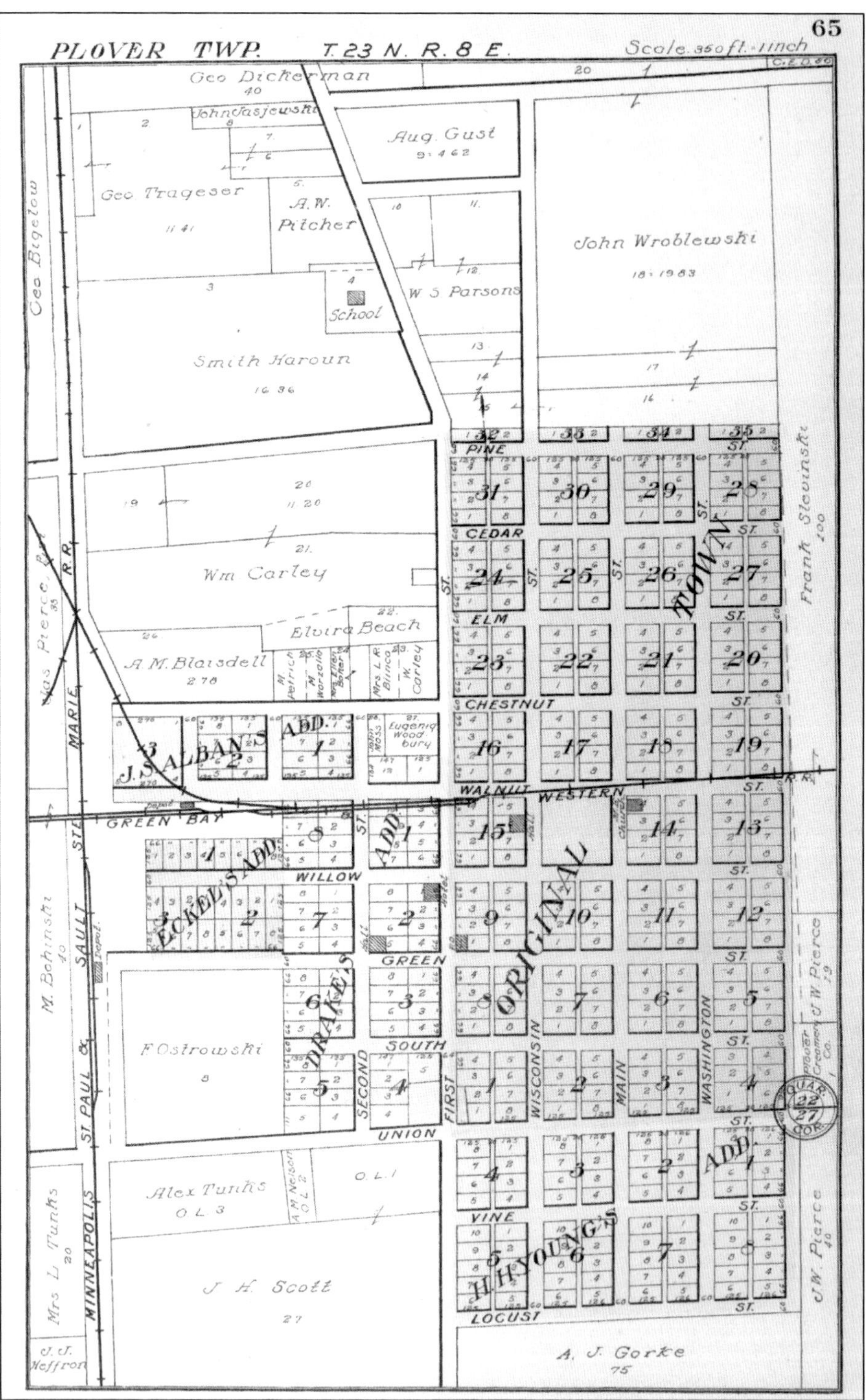

A plat of the village of Plover in 1915 is shown here. Most roads in the downtown area have been changed from street to drive since that time. Some captions in this book use the older name to reflect the time period in which the photograph was taken. (UWSP Archives.)

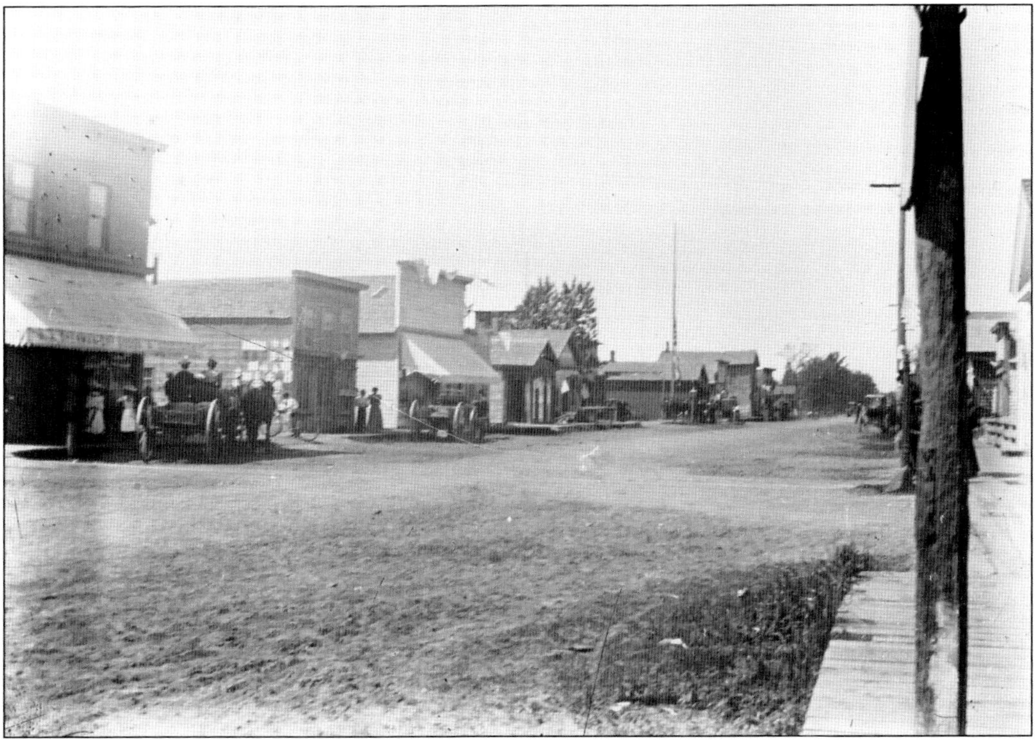

Looking north on First Street in this c. 1900 photograph taken just south of the Plover Post Office, Sherman's Dry Goods (later Pierce's grocery store) can be seen on the left at the northwest corner of Green and First Streets. The liberty pole can be seen near the center, which indicates where the Warner House was located.

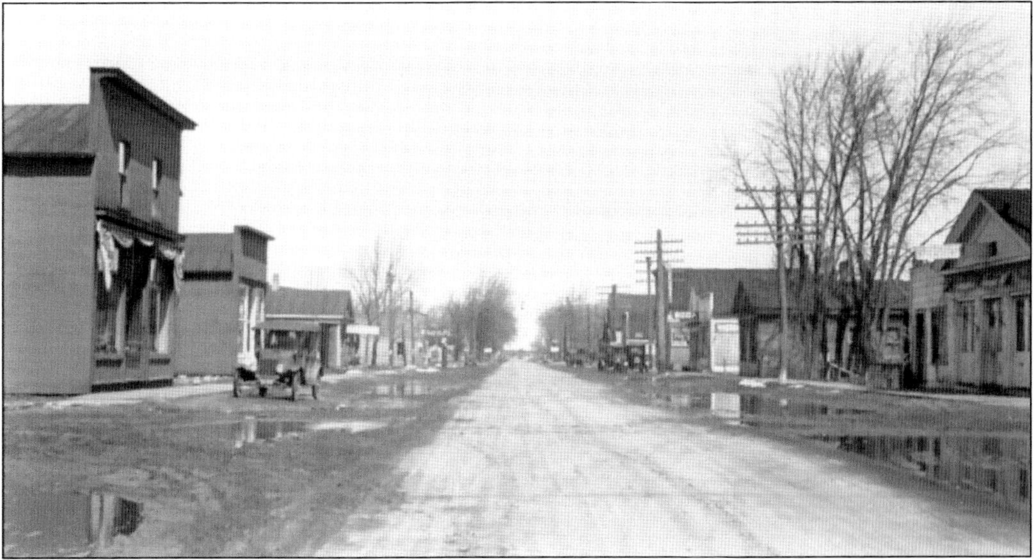

This photograph from 1925 looks north from the intersection of Green and First Streets. Pierce's grocery store is on the left, and the former post office, having since been converted into a restaurant, is on the right. Farther down the street, also on the right, is Lila's grocery store, which has a "soda" sign out front.

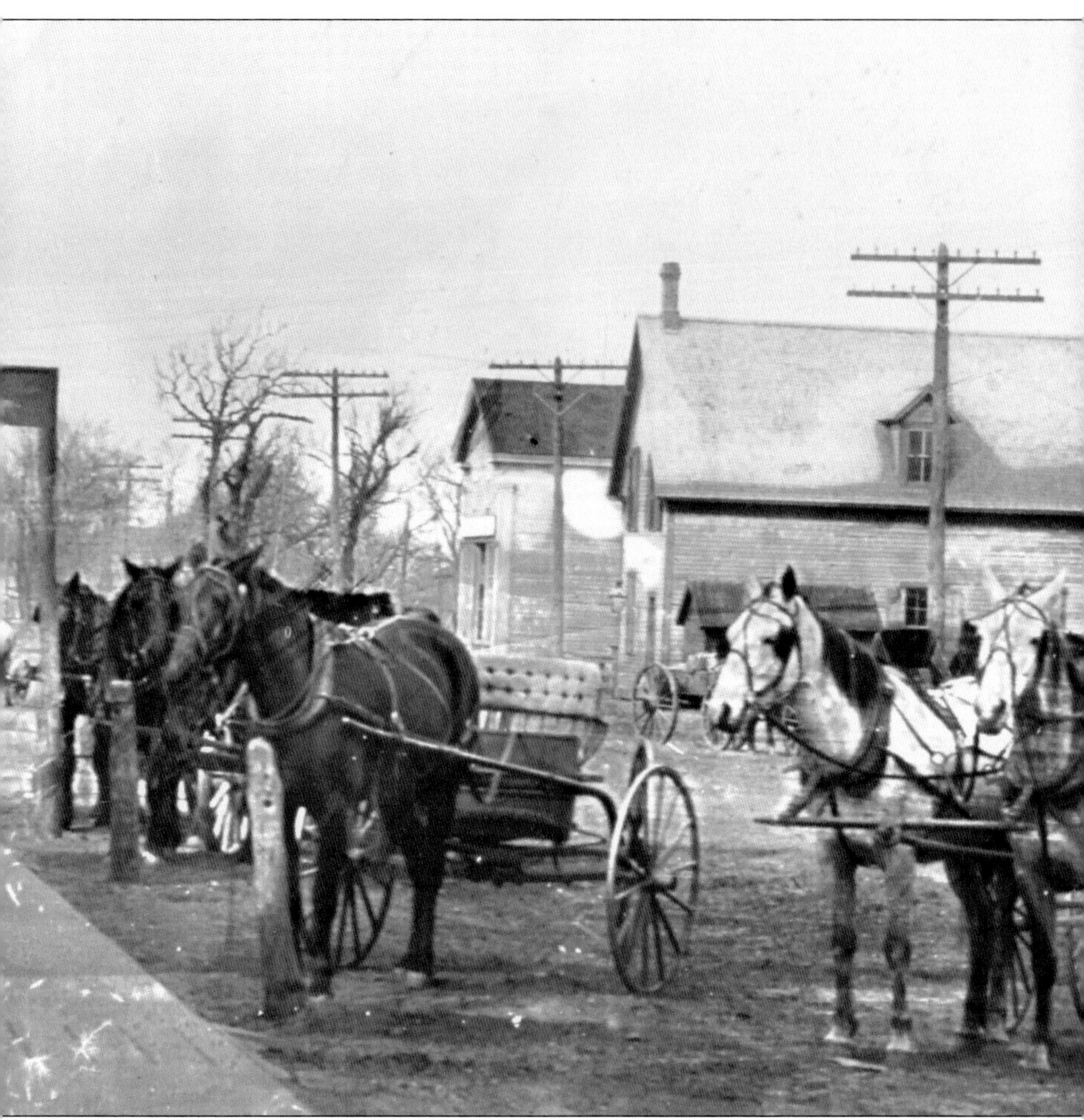

This street scene of Plover looks northeast toward the east side of First Street. The buildings are, from left to right, Plover Produce Company, the Odd Fellows Hall, a tavern owned by Adams & Rosenthal (formerly J. Waters' Saloon), Frank Lila's Dry Goods and Notions, and Frank Lila's

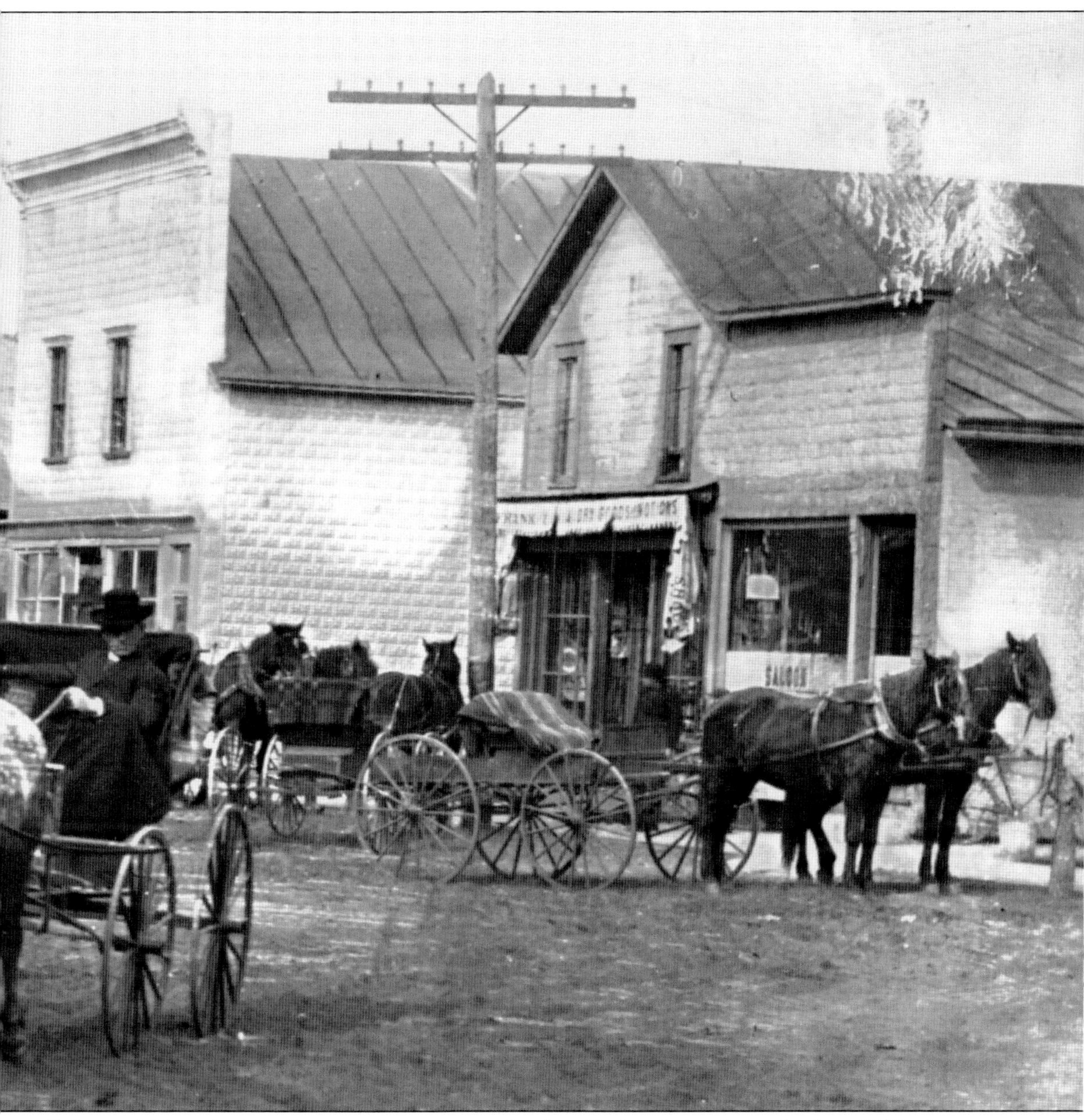

Saloon. Although this photograph is commonly identified as being from the late 1800s, it was most likely taken after 1909 because Adams & Rosenthal completed significant remodeling after purchasing J. Waters' Saloon.

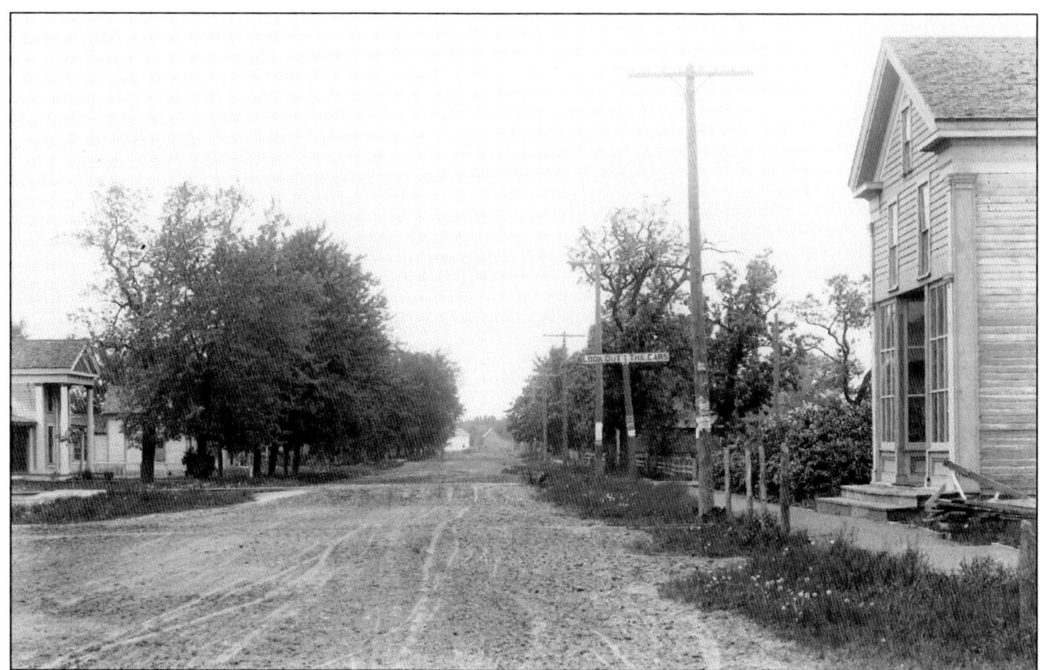

The Cate/Potts house can be seen on the left just north of the railroad tracks and Walnut Street. The building on the right side of First Street was purchased by the Plover Produce Company in 1906 from Walter Barnsdale. The group used the building as a potato warehouse and meeting place until 1911, when it was purchased by Alois Firkus, a buyer, seller, and grower of potatoes.

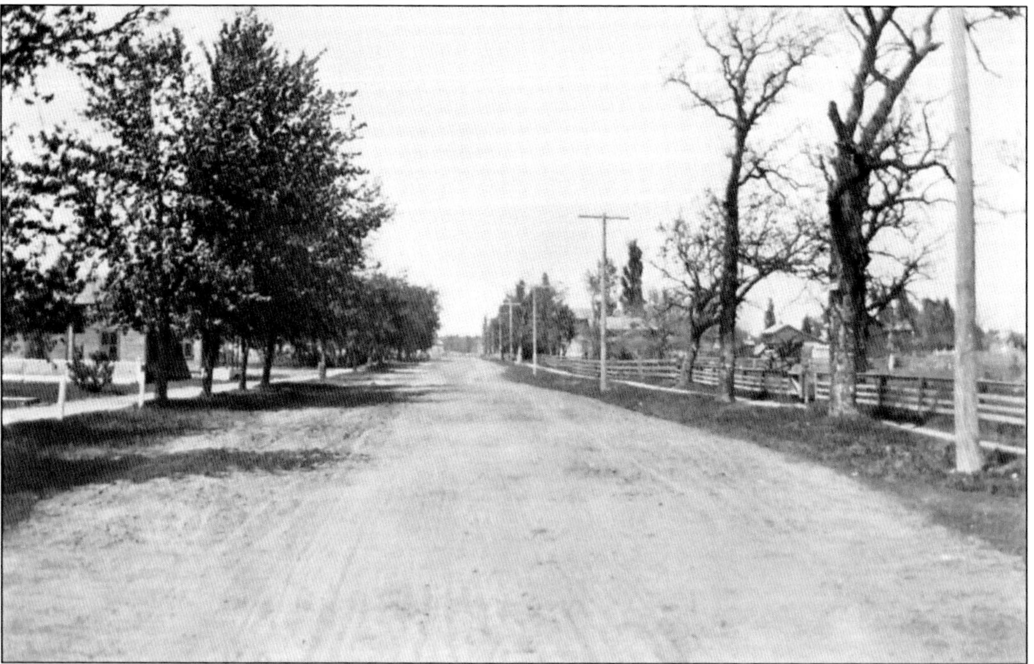

The area north of the railroad tracks on First Street was primarily residential in the early 1900s. Schoolchildren living near downtown Plover would walk this stretch of road to the schoolhouse, which is just around the bend down the road.

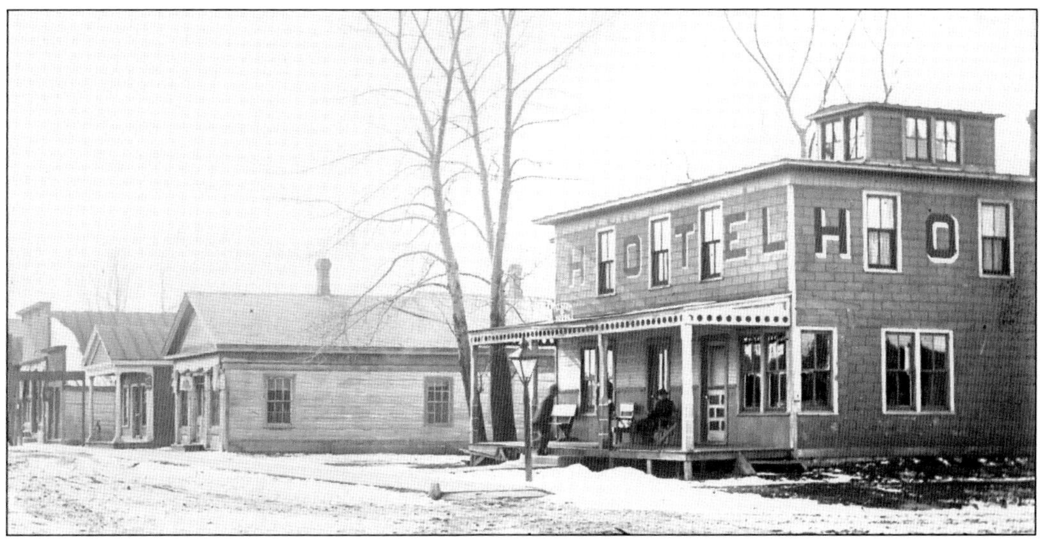

The conspicuous building on the right is the Tremont House, a hotel located on the southwest corner of Willow and First Streets. In previous years it was known as the Empire House and Warner House until it was renamed the Tremont House by C.J. Chapel after he bought it 1903. Chapel sold the hotel to George Yorton in 1911. The building next to the Tremont House was owned by William Carley and has since been moved to the Portage County Historical Society's Heritage Park.

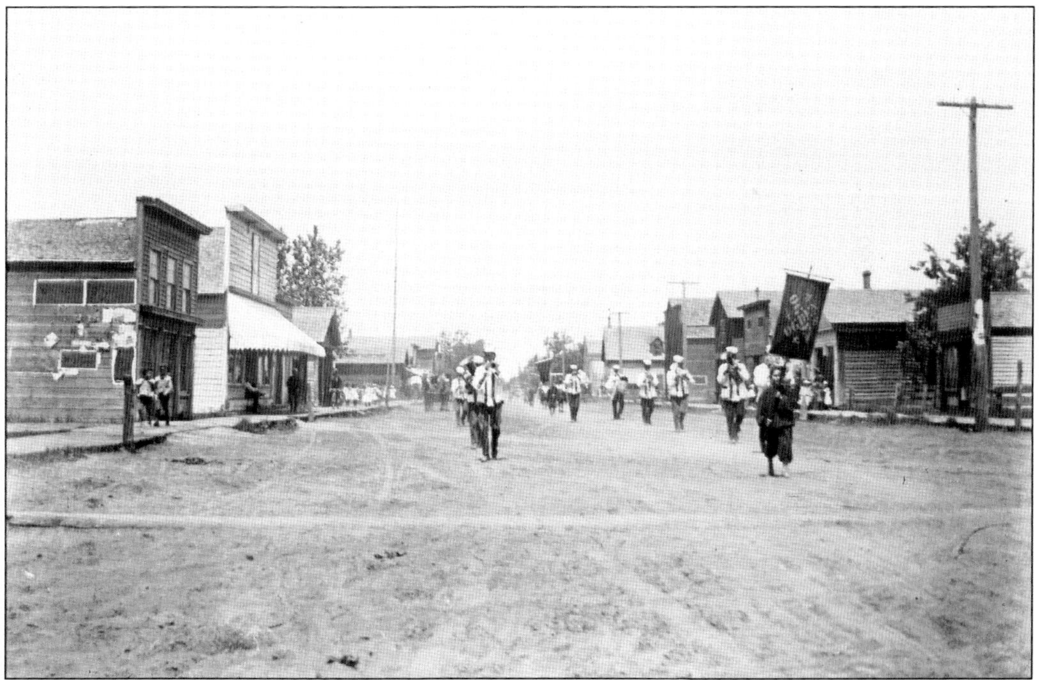

The Ogden traveling show parades south on First Street crossing the intersection with Green Street. The troupe traveled throughout central Wisconsin between 1902 and 1903, billed as "Ogden's World's Greatest Uncle Tom's Cabin Company" and "Ogden's Ten Nights in a Bar Room," putting on plays for local residents.

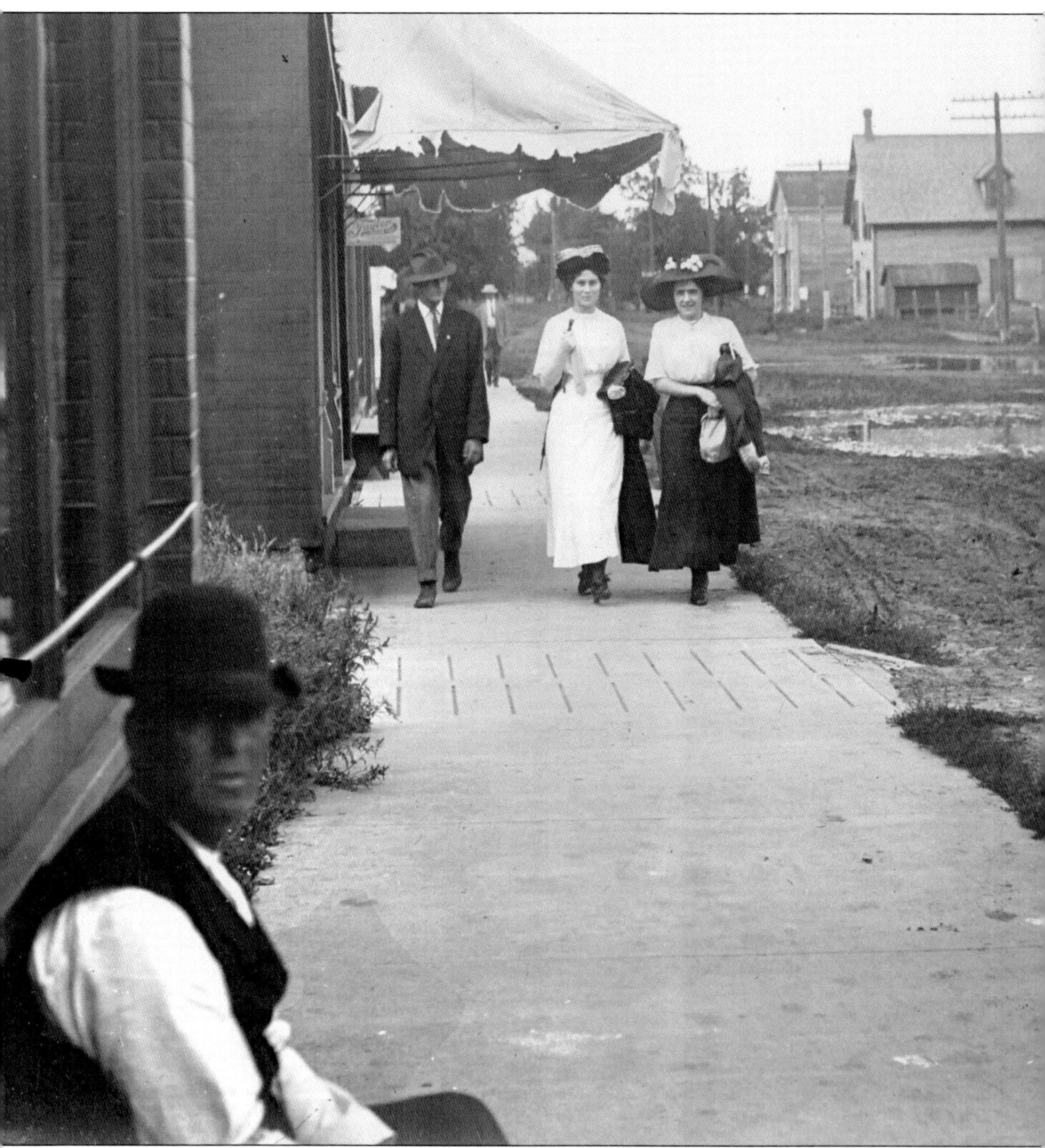

Three Plover residents walk south on the west side of First Street past Taylor's Tailors around 1910. In the background on the right is the Odd Fellows Hall. The man turning his attention to the photographer is likely sitting in front of Pierce's grocery store.

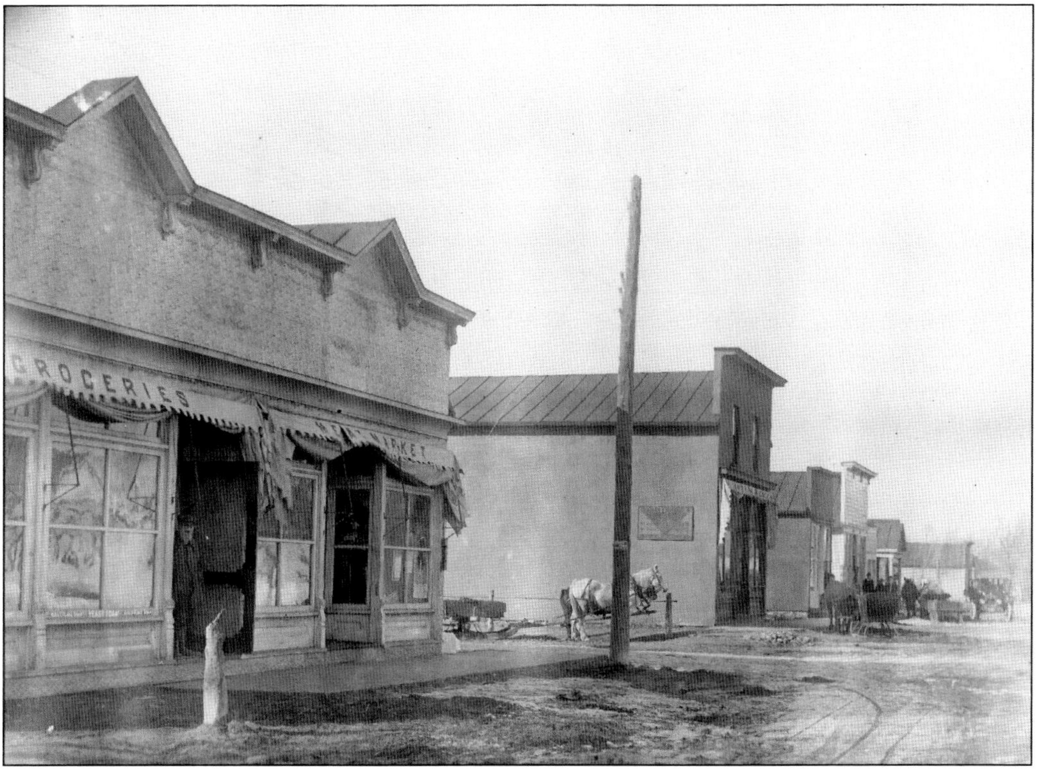

In this view looking north on First Street, two grocery stores are visible; the one on the left is Byron Rogers' Meat Market and Dry Goods, and the other is James W. Pierce's grocery store. There is an automobile in the background, while others are using horses and sleighs, which indicates early spring or winter.

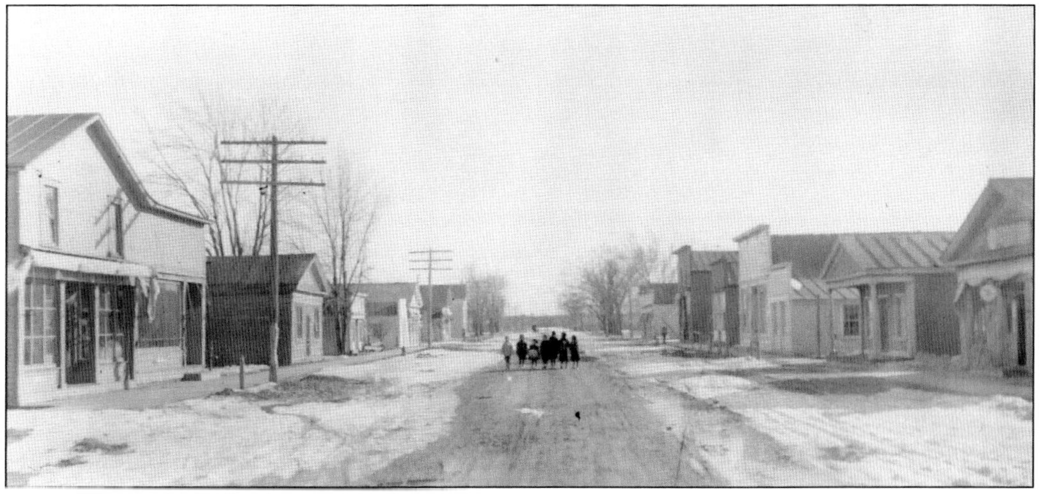

This scene looks south as a group of children walk down the middle of First Street toward Willow Street. On the left is Frank Lila's grocery store, and on the right is William Carley's building.

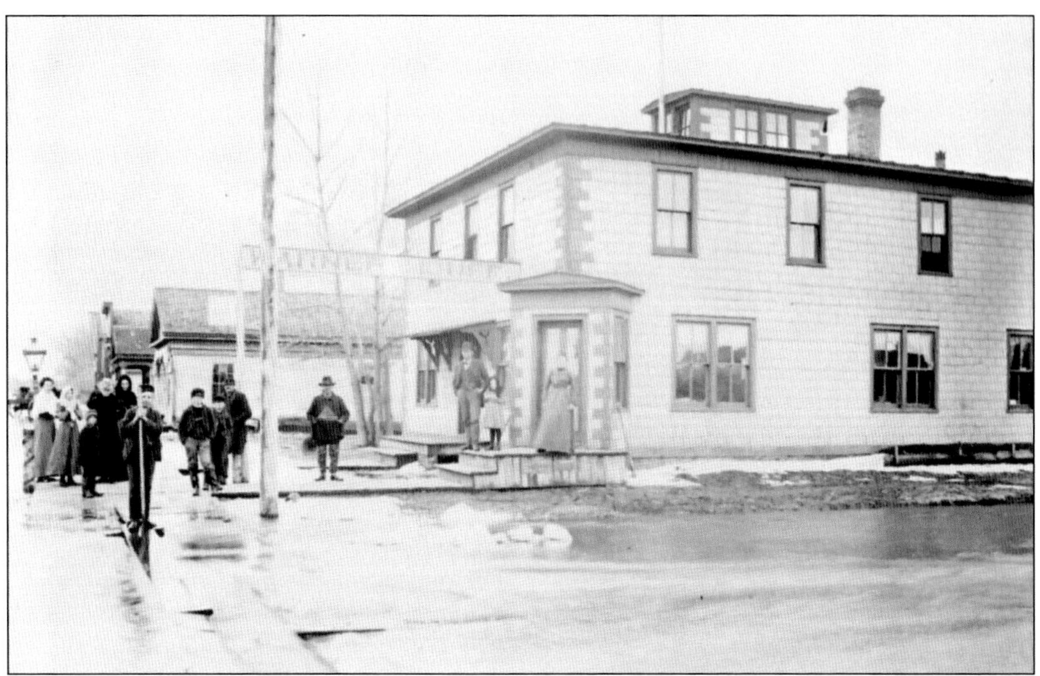

A crowd gathers in front of the Warner House at the southwest corner of Willow and First Streets. The Warner House was previously owned by T.F. Cooley and was known as the Empire House. The original Empire House caught fire in 1885 and was rebuilt in the same year. Horace Warner later bought the hotel and operated it under the name Warner House until 1903.

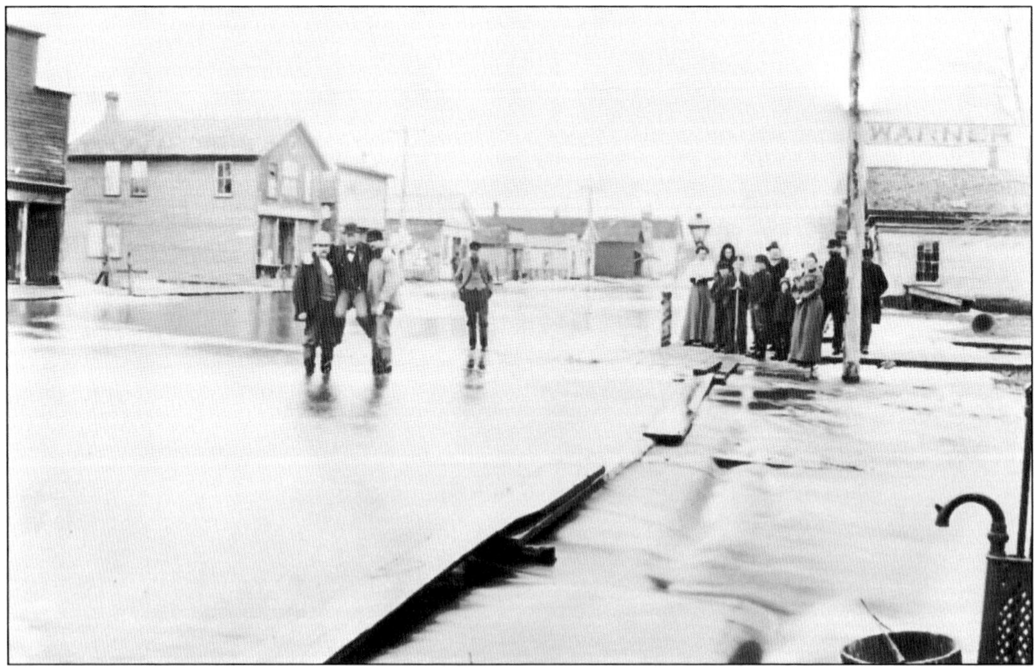

This image looks south as two men hold another out of the floodwaters on First Street. The water has filled First Street, rushing past the Warner House and onto Willow Street. The Warner House was a place where the community gathered for various holidays, events, and apparently, floods.

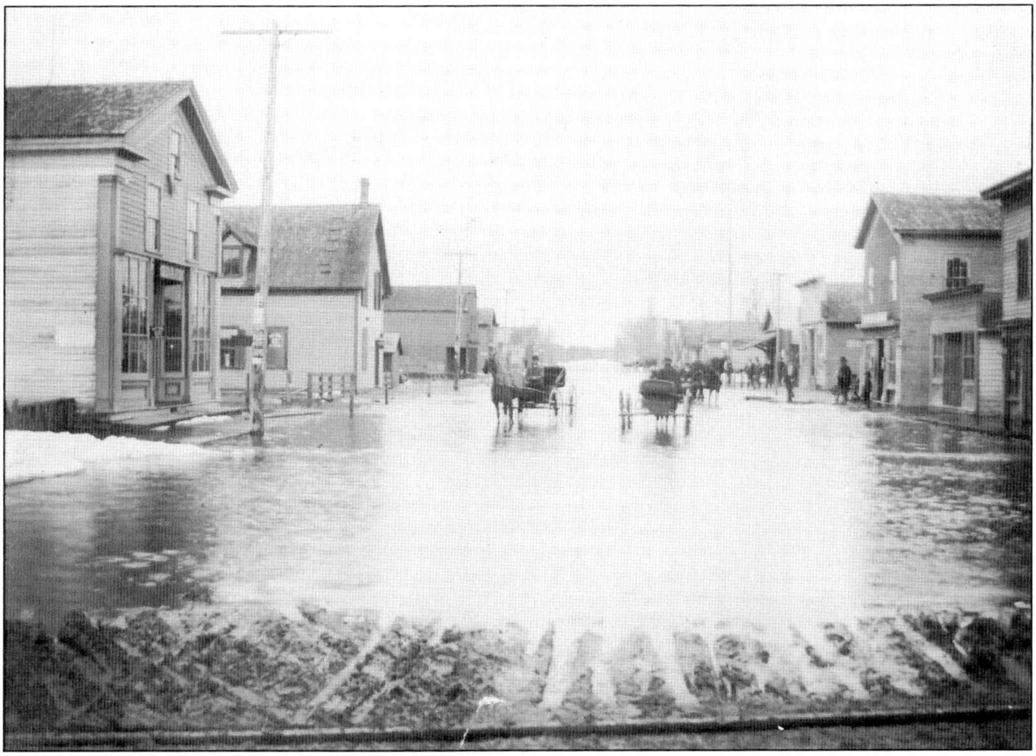

This image is looking south as First Street floods during a spring thaw. The building on the left bears George B. Fox's name, an insurance salesman from Plainfield who held an office in Plover. Next to that is the Odd Fellows Hall and J. Waters' Saloon. Frank Singley's Saloon can be seen across the street on the corner, with the awning.

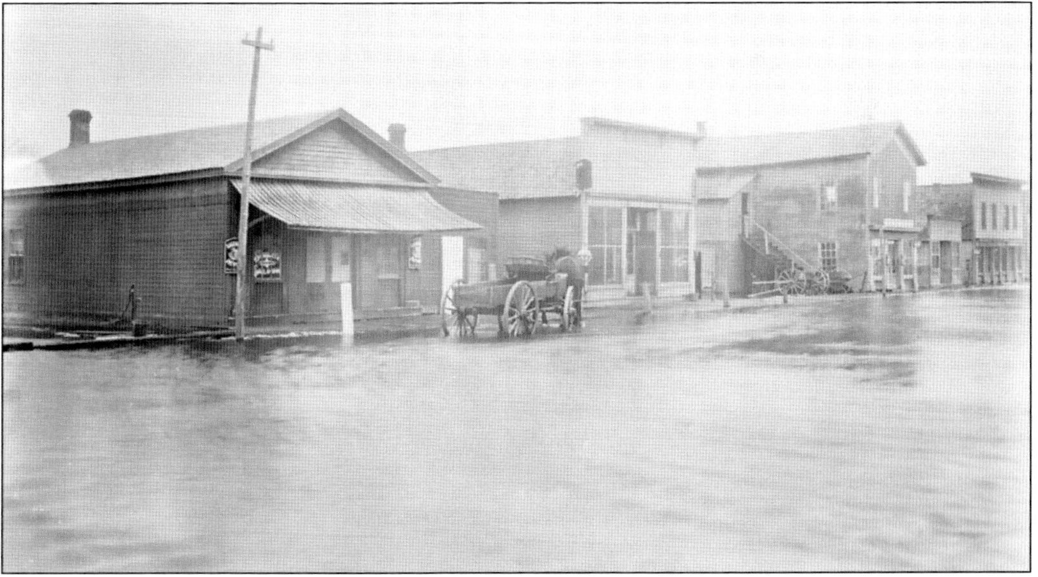

This view of Plover's flooded streets due to spring melt is looking northwest on First Street from the corner of Willow Street. The business to the left is Singley's Saloon owned by Frank Singley. This photograph is believed to have been taken prior to Singley's death in 1909.

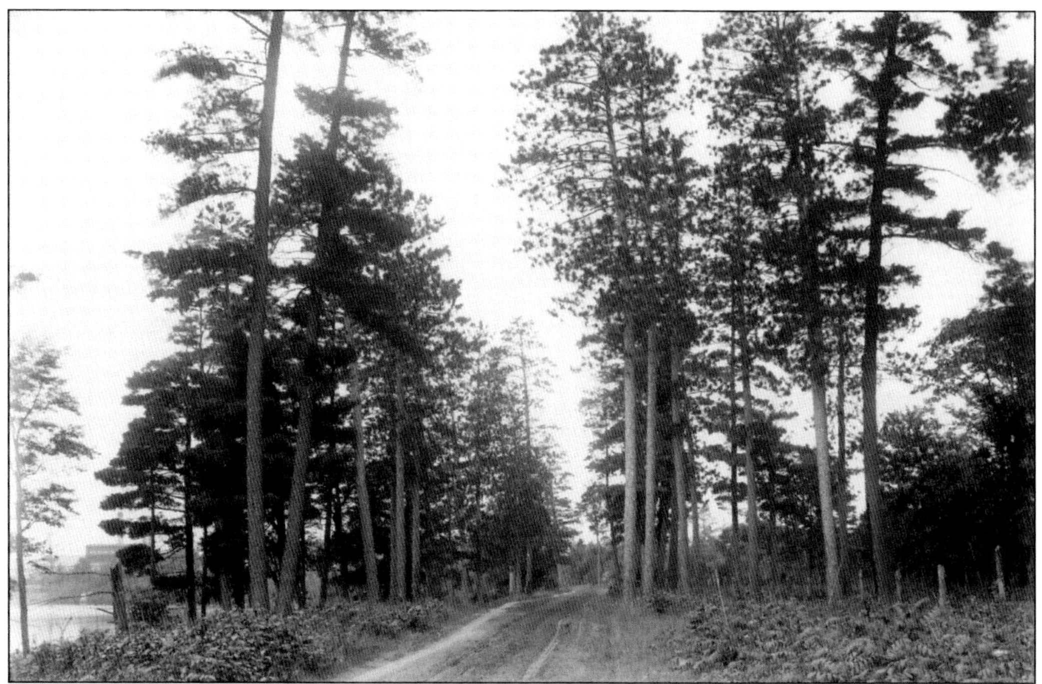

This picture looks northwest on Whiting Road toward the Wisconsin River Paper & Pulp Company in what would become the village of Whiting. The Wisconsin River Paper & Pulp Company can be seen in the distance on the left.

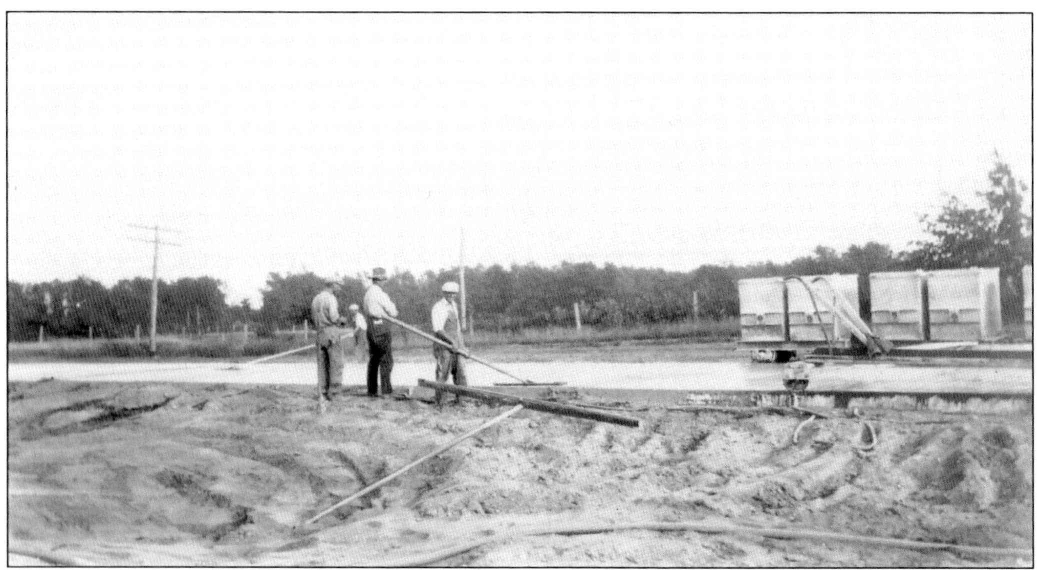

Highway 54/Plover Road was originally part of the Old Pinery Road, which ran from Fort Winnebago to Grand Rapids and then south to Portage. In this picture, taken in the summer of 1929, workers pave the road to accommodate the increasing automobile traffic through the area.

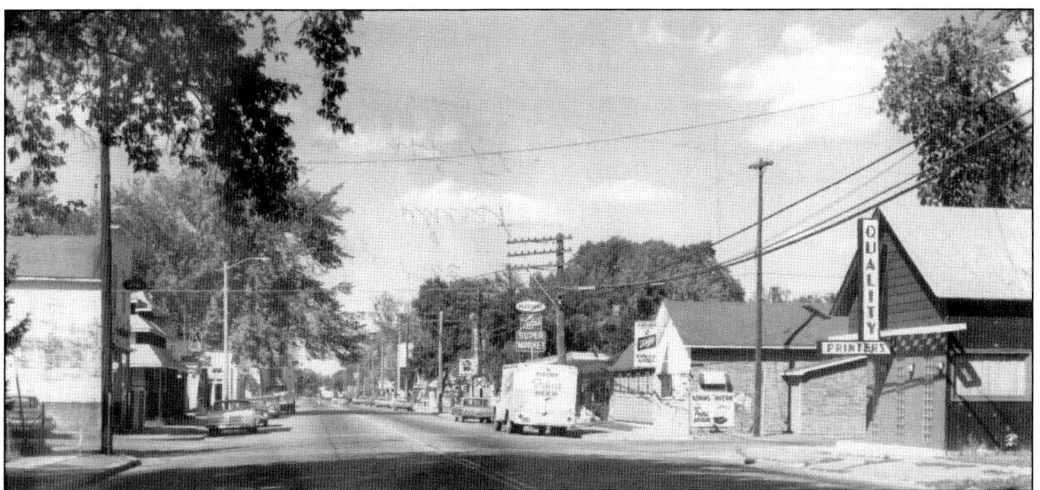

This image looks north on Post Road in 1966 from the intersection with Green Street. On the right, Lila's Supermarket is behind the Point beer truck, and to the right of that is Adam's Tavern. On the left is the Greyhound bus station, which was previously the Pierce grocery store. (*Stevens Point Journal.*)

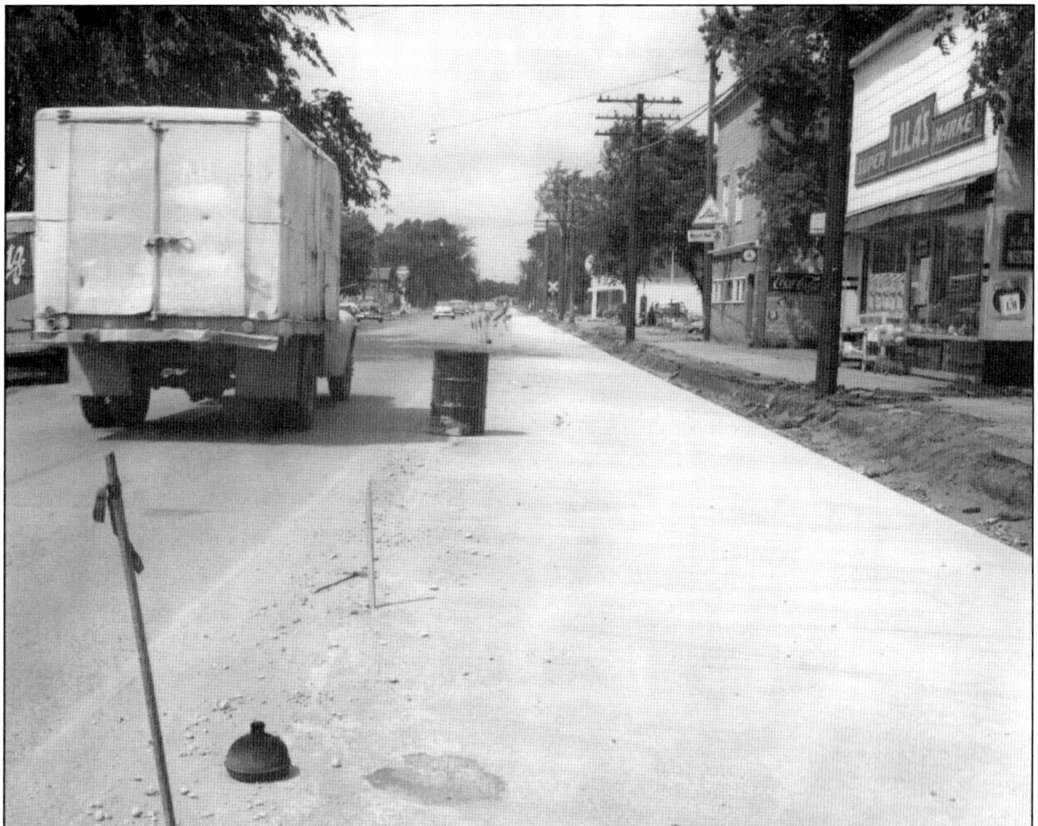

This image is looking north on Post Road/Business 51 as it is being widened in June 1958. The road was widened from McDill Pond to Highway 54 in Plover, and a new curb, gutter, and sewer were added. Lila's Supermarket can be seen on the right. (*Stevens Point Journal.*)

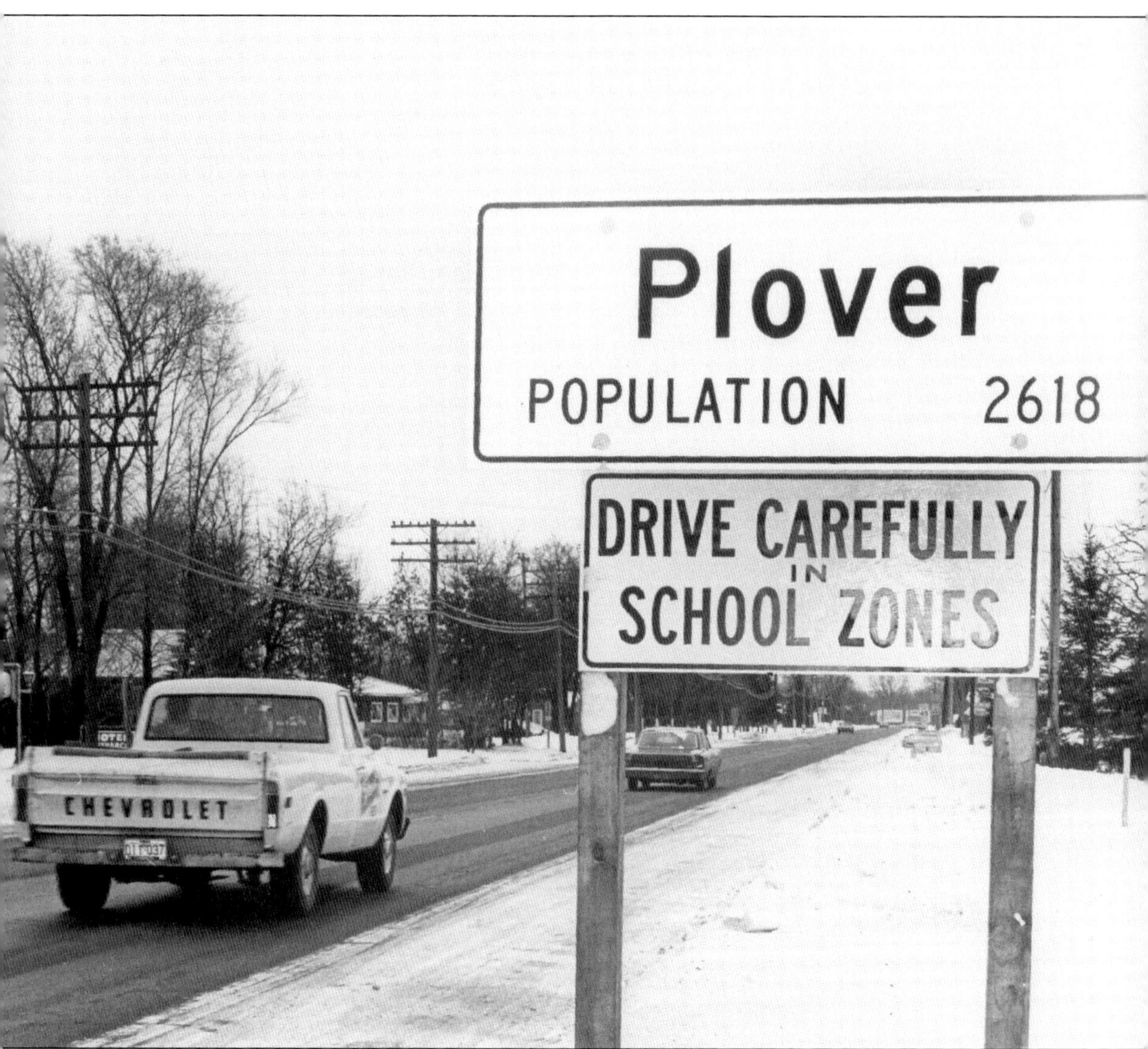

The new village of Plover sign in 1972 identified the village's population at the time of its third incorporation, voted on in September 1971. (*Stevens Point Journal.*)

Two

People and Residences

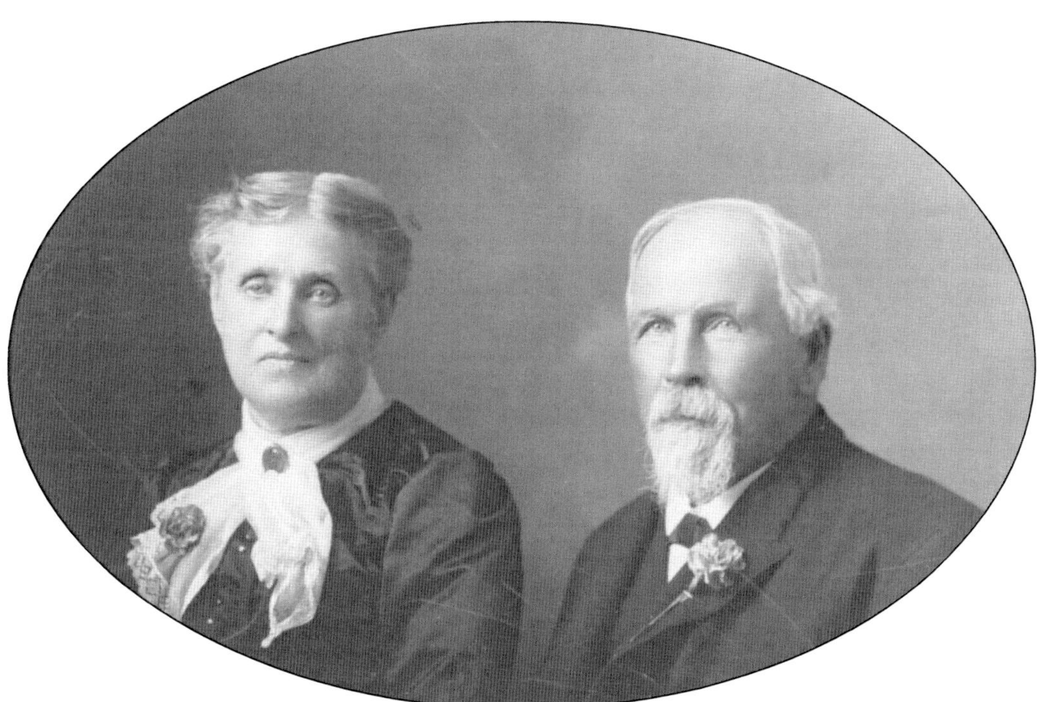

This is a portrait of Plover pioneers Simon Augustus (S.A.) Sherman and his wife, Rachel. Arriving in Plover in 1848, Sherman settled on the north end of the township and had sawmills where the Plover River meets the Wisconsin River. The couple had two sons: Clarence A. and Eugene A. The diaries that S.A. Sherman kept throughout his life are an invaluable historical resource for the settlement and growth of the area. Sherman would later sell his land to George A. Whiting, who built the Whiting-Plover Paper Company.

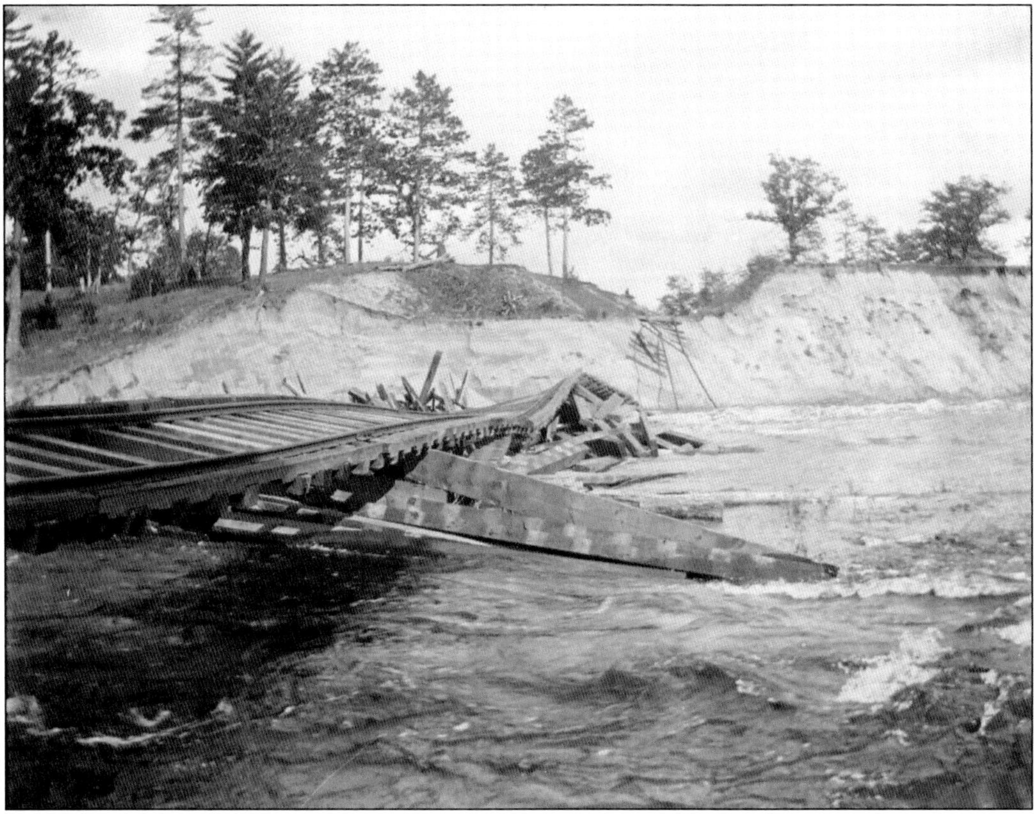

A flood in early October 1900 destroyed the switch track of the Green Bay & Western Railroad. The track passed over the flume between S.A. Sherman's land and the Plover Paper Mill. A large part of the hill in the background was also washed out.

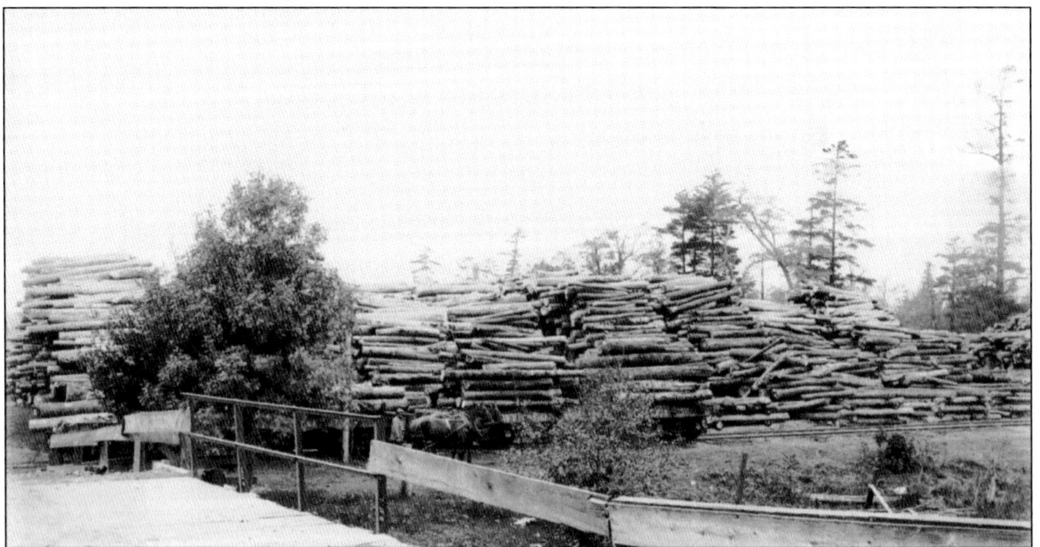

The wood pile of S.A. Sherman in 1904 is being loaded onto Wisconsin Central railcars to be sold elsewhere. Sherman ran sawmills on the Wisconsin and Plover Rivers, assisted by his sons E.A. Sherman and Clarence Sherman from the mid-1850s to the early 1900s.

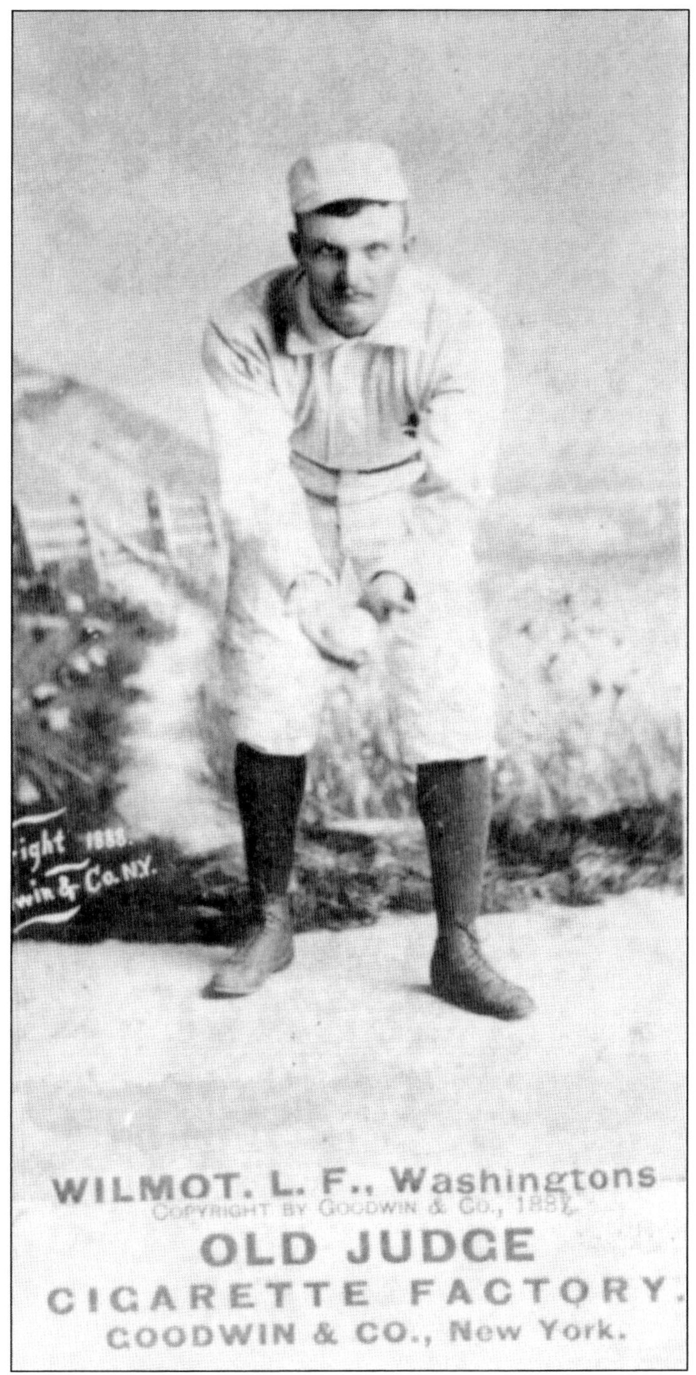

Walt Wilmot was a professional baseball player from 1888 to 1898. He played for the Washington Nationals, Chicago Colts, and the New York Giants. In his career, Wilmot compiled some impressive stats, including leading the league with 19 triples and 139 games played in 1889. In 1890, he tied with two other players for the National League lead in home runs with 13, and in 1891, he became the first player in major league history to be walked six times in one game. (Library of Congress, LC-DIG-bbc-0397f.)

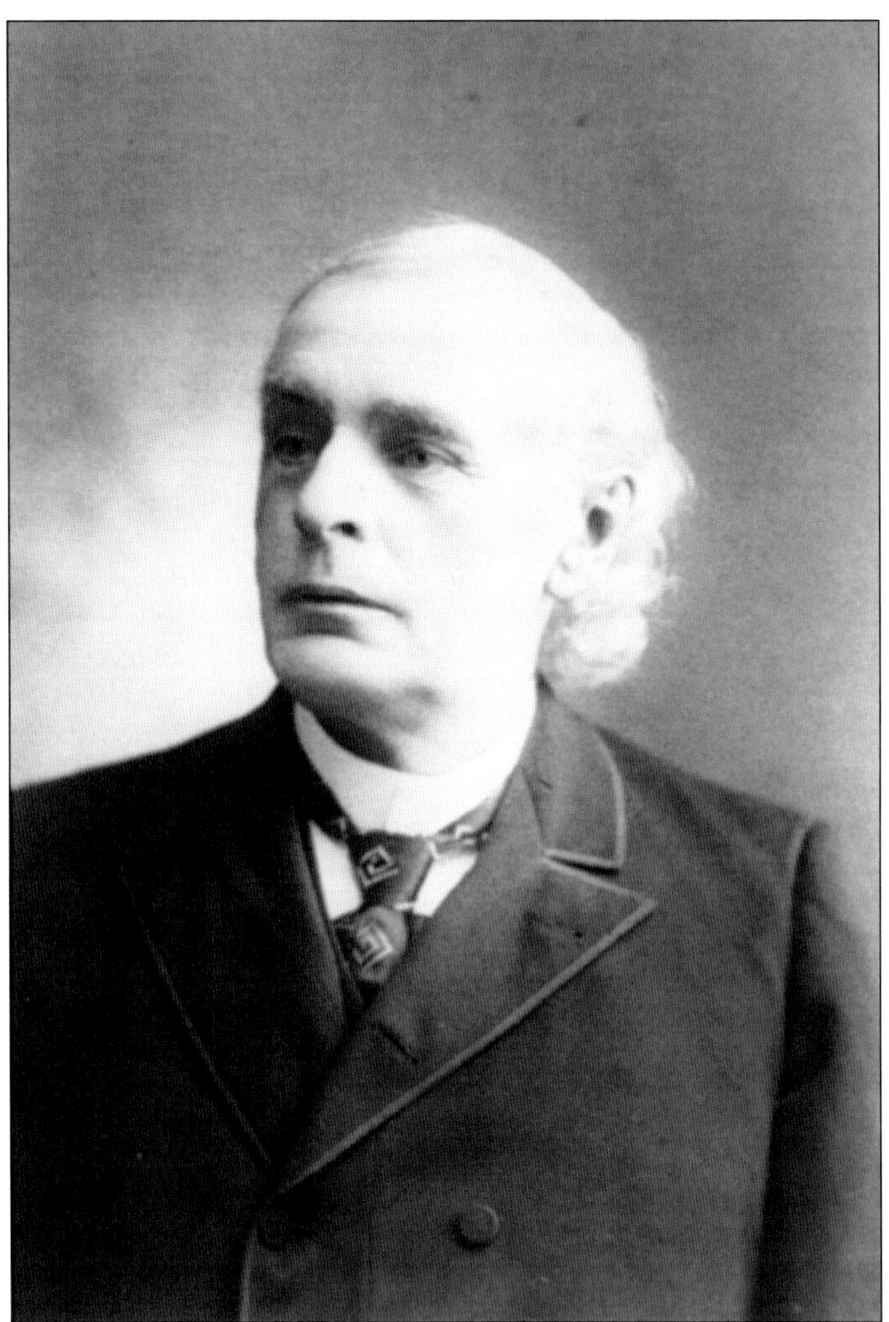

George W. Cate was born in 1823 in Vermont, where he received an education in law. In 1845, he came to Wisconsin and worked in the lumber industry until 1848, when he was drawn to Portage County's new seat in Plover to practice law. He married Levara Serena Brown in 1851 and moved to Stevens Point in 1852. He served in the Wisconsin State Assembly from 1852 to 1853, and in 1854 was elected circuit judge and served four terms of six years each. Cate also served in Congress as the representative of Wisconsin's 8th district from 1875 to 1877. After returning from serving in the House of Representatives, he resumed his law practice in Stevens Point until his death in 1905.

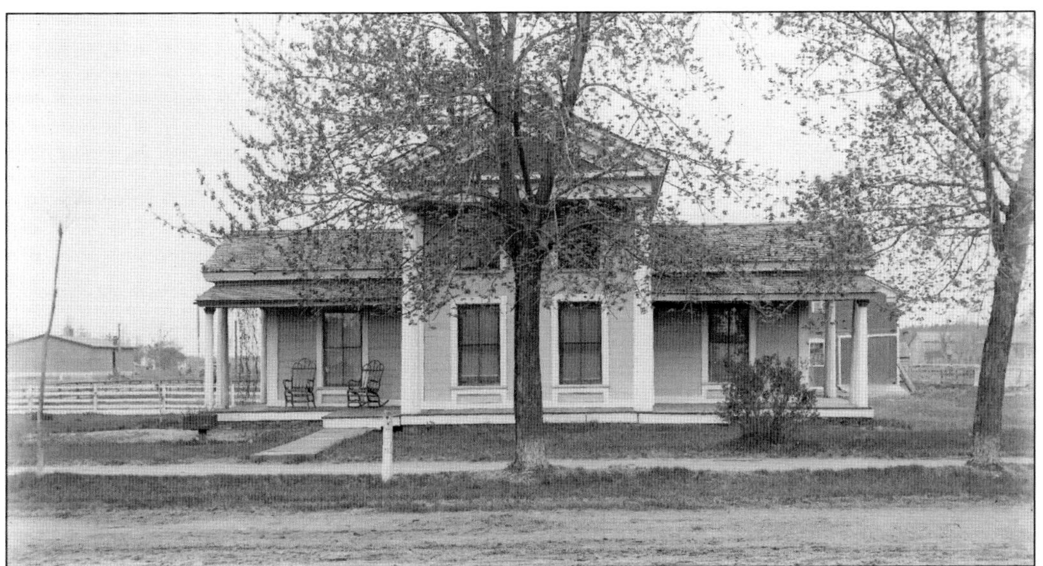

The Cate/Potts house was built by prominent Portage County resident Judge George W. Cate during his short time in Plover. When this photograph was taken, the house was owned by William H. Potts, a Plover liveryman. This house was located on the west side of First Street, just north of the railroad tracks.

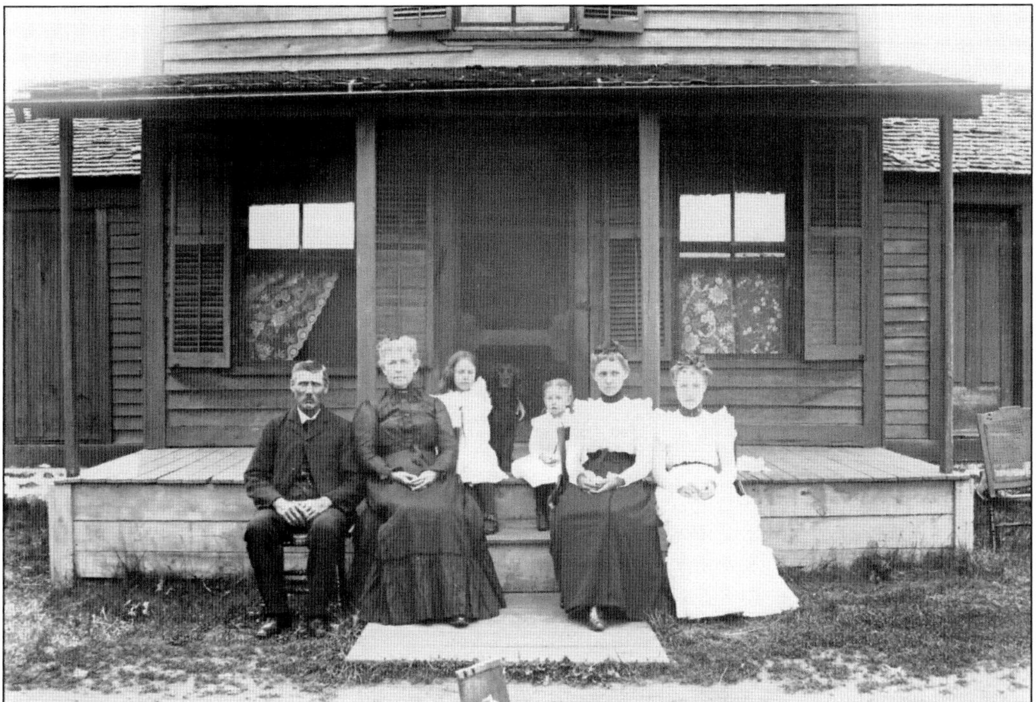

The family of Eugene and Fannie Woodbury sits on the front porch of their house around 1900. The home was located on the west side of First Street, just north of the Potts house near the intersection with Chestnut Street. Eugene was well known in the village, as he worked as a mail carrier on the route between the railroad depot and the post office for 40 years.

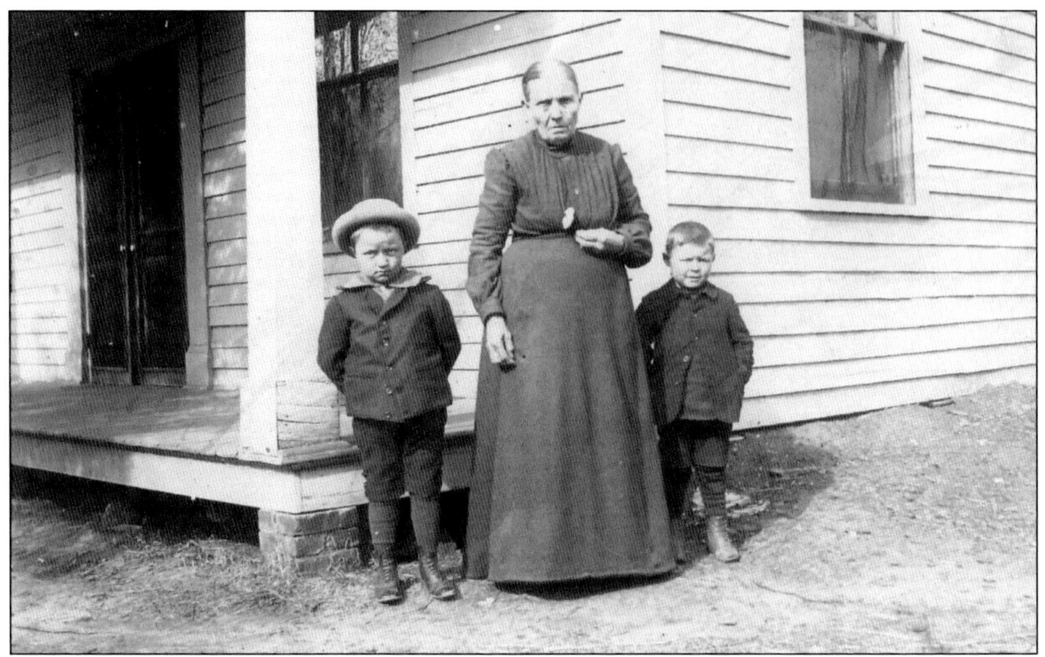

Sarah Barnsdale (center) was born in Bangor, Maine. She married H. Filbrook, with whom she had two children. After his death, she married George Barnsdale on December 2, 1868, in Plover and had one child, Kate. Also pictured are Thad Simonds (left) and George Barnsdale, Sarah's grandson. This picture was taken around 1905 in front of Walter Barnsdale's house.

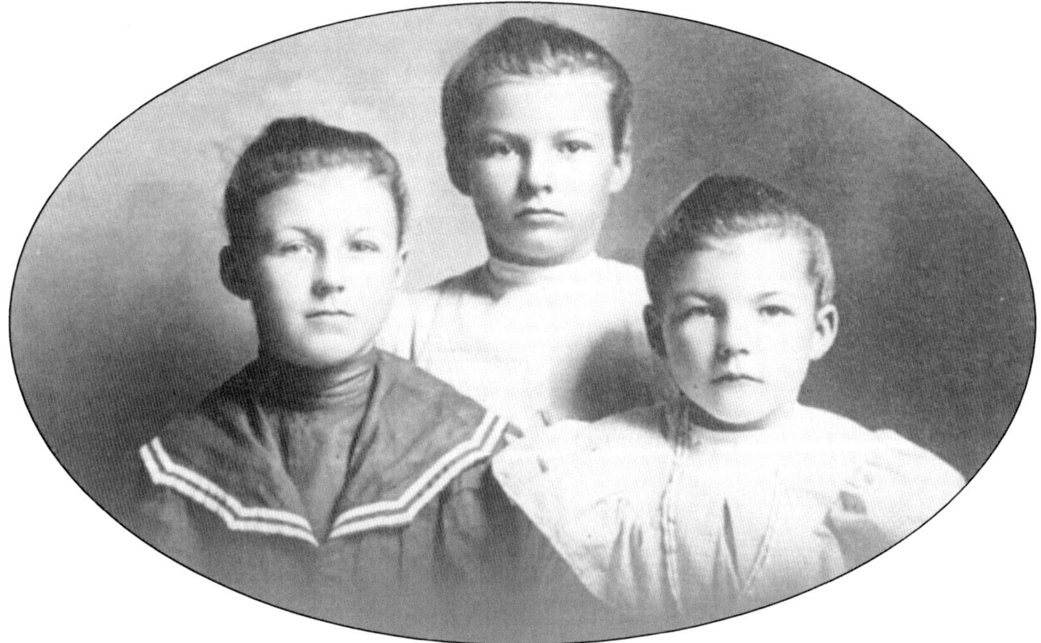

From left to right, Emma, Eva, and Elizabeth Barnsdale were the oldest of the nine children of Walter and Kate Barnsdale. The younger Barnsdale children were George, Francis, Frank, Myra, Walter Jr., and Richard. Eva Barnsdale married Daniel Hetzel, lived in Almond, and worked as treasurer for the Town of Almond.

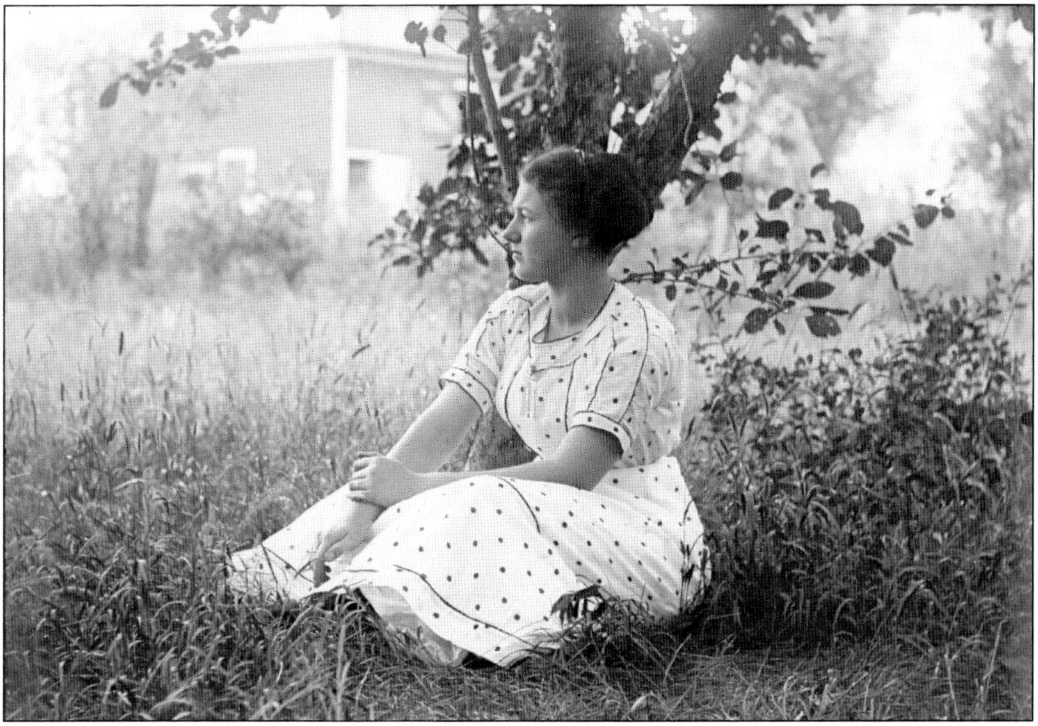

Elizabeth Barnsdale relaxes in the grass under a tree. She married Albert Brown and lived in Plover. In 1926, she shot her lover, Everett Russell, twice at the Green Bay & Western depot in Plover and then committed suicide by swallowing carbolic acid.

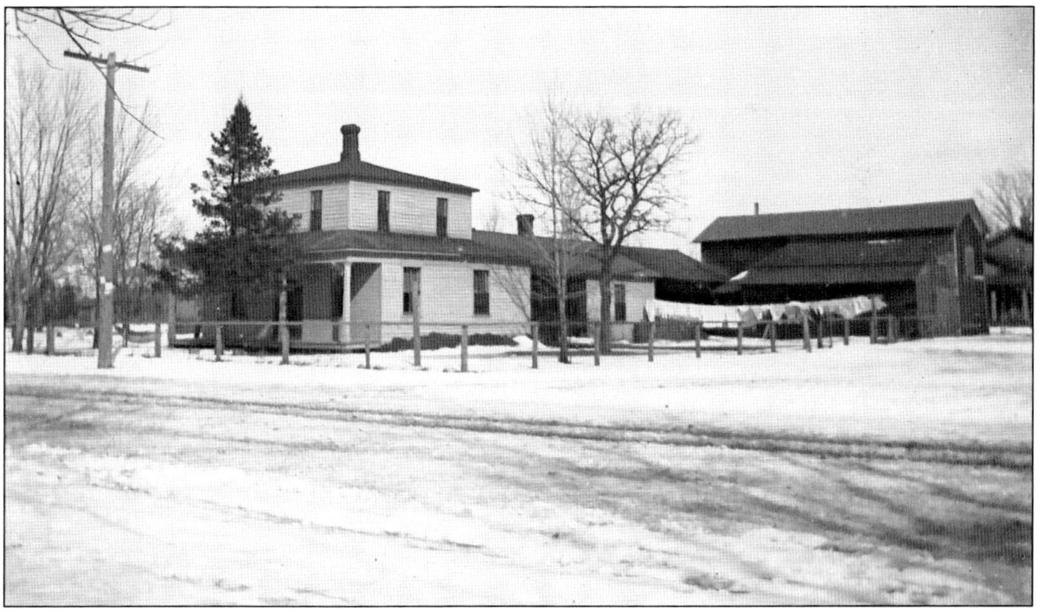

Shown here is the exterior of the Walter and Kate Barnsdale house, located on the northeast corner of First Street (current Post Road) and Elm Street (current Sumac Lane). This home was purchased by the Barnsdale family before 1908, and previous owners included Morton Strope and J.L. Smith. Today, there is a mini mall containing King Kone and a bank on this spot.

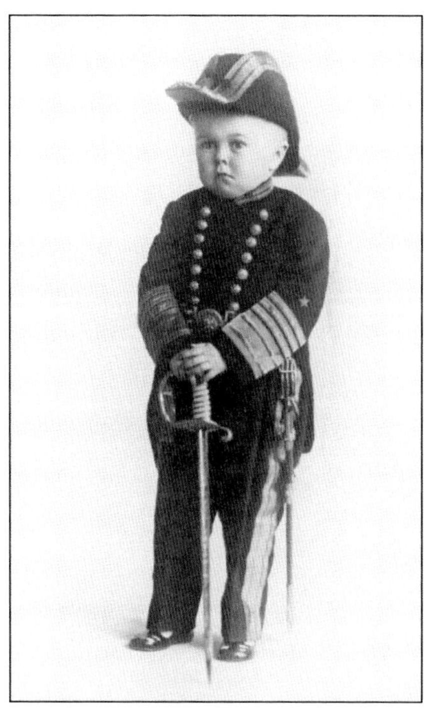

Frank Barnsdale is seen at left dressed as his character Admiral F. Thumb and below at left center. When this promotional photograph was taken, Barnsdale was 24 years old. He was 29 inches tall and weighed 30 pounds. Barnsdale performed in circuses across the country, including the Ringling Bros. and Barnum & Bailey, Hagenbeck-Wallace, and Sells-Floto Circuses. After retiring from performing, Barnsdale worked as postmaster for Plover, bookkeeper for the Plover Farm Cooperative, and Town of Plover clerk from 1965 to 1971.

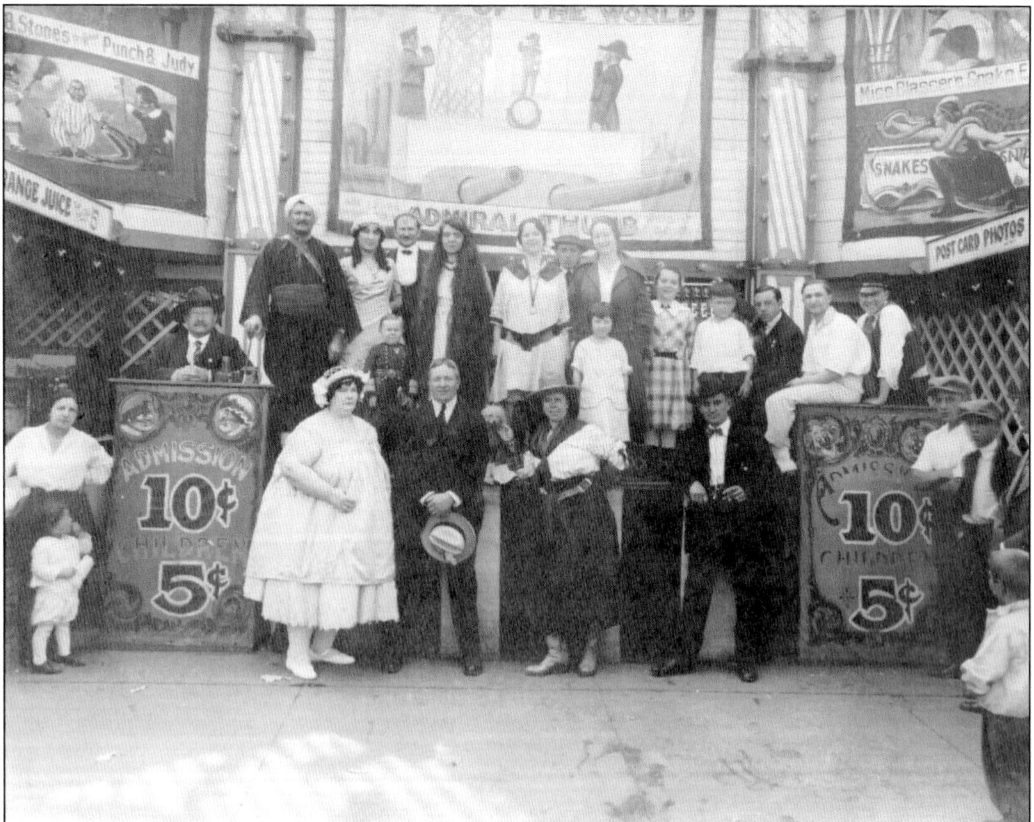

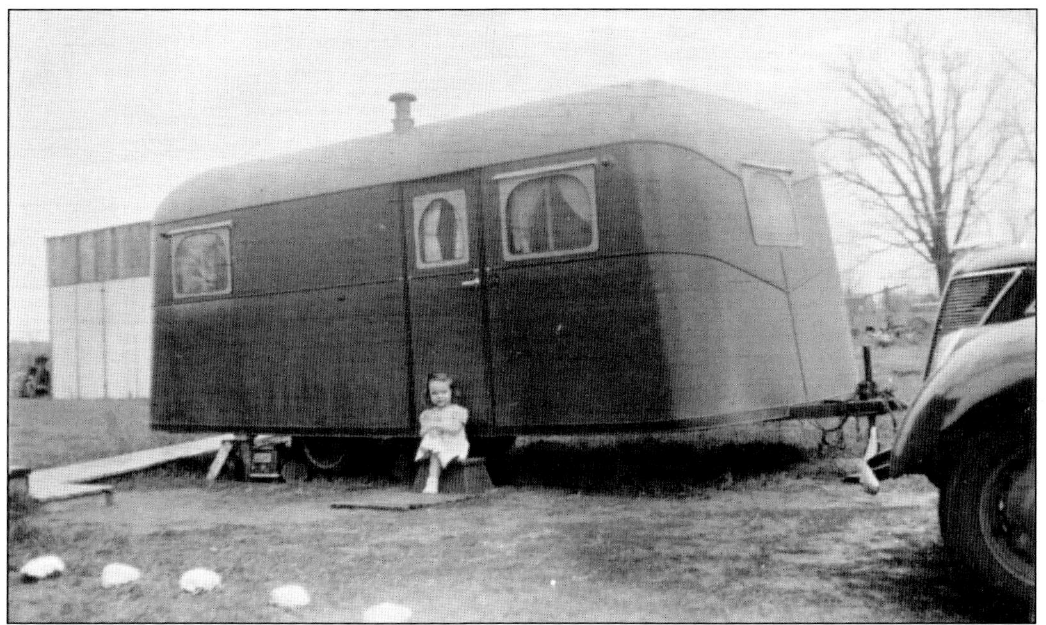

Ruth Engford, three years old, sits in front of the family's circus wagon around 1943. Ruth was the daughter of Harry and Lois Engford, who traveled with their circus, the Engford Family Show. Ruth eventually became an aerialist and performed many daring trapeze acts. She married Frank Clark, and they performed together as Francarro & Estreleta, America's premier aerialists.

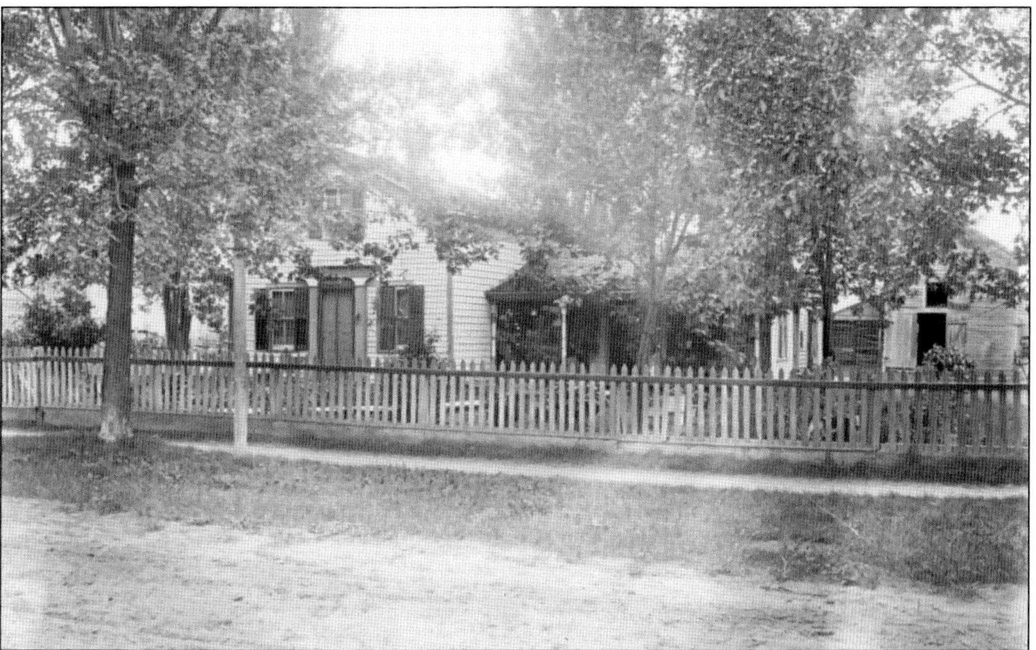

The Engford house, the oldest verified house in Portage County, was built by Miner Strope in 1850, where he lived until his death until 1880. Robert Engford bought the house in 1923 from the Barnsdale family and built a barn/workshop, where he and his family practiced their aerobatic acts. The house was moved to the Portage County Historical Society's Heritage Park on December 7, 2000.

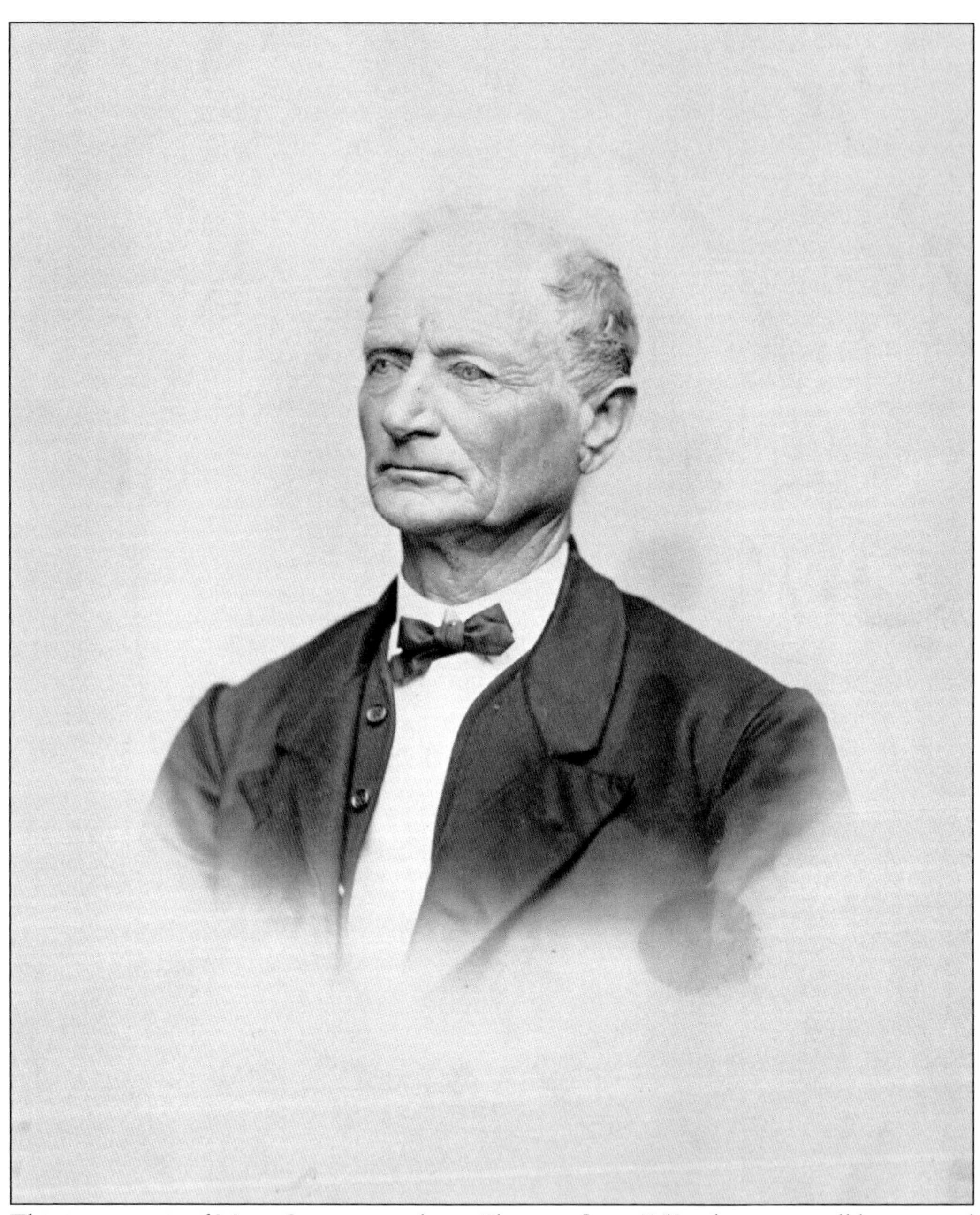

This is a portrait of Miner Strope, a settler in Plover in June 1850, who was a well-known and respected attorney. Born in Luzerne County, Pennsylvania, in 1806, Strope was educated in New York, where he also practiced law from 1831 to 1850. He served as district attorney of Portage and Wood Counties and county judge of Portage County for two terms. He was married twice, first to Mary A. Morton, with whom he had three children. After her death in 1846, he married Ursula Wilmot in 1848 and had three children. He died at the age of 74 in 1880.

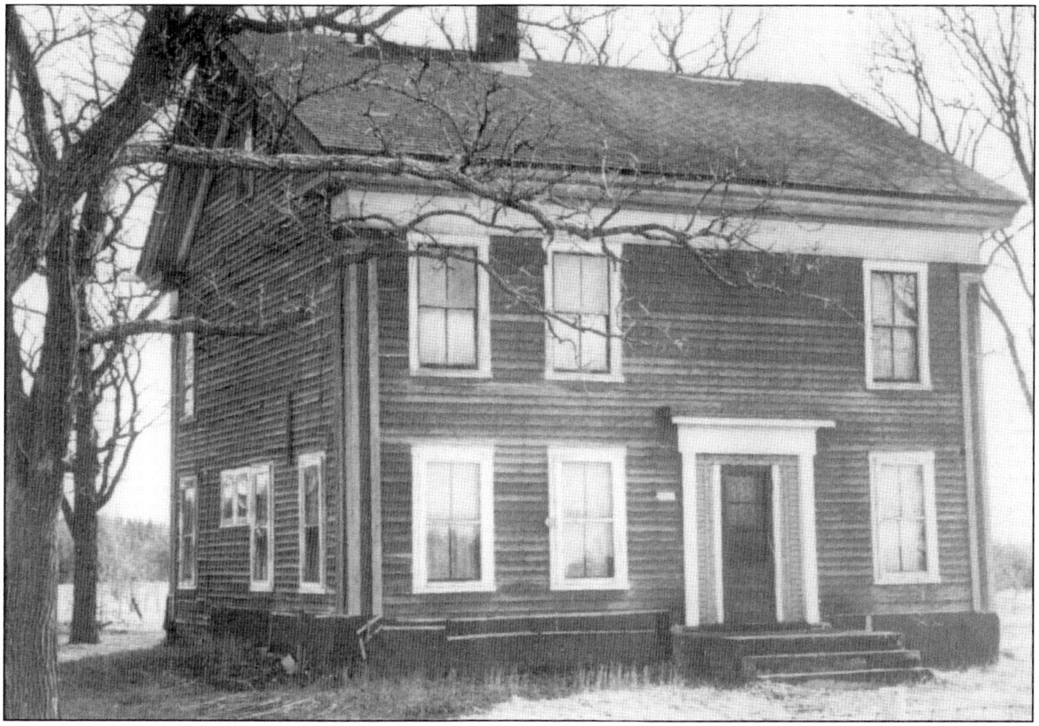

Known as the Franklin-Calkins house, this residence was located east of Plover on the south side of Plover Road, near where Culver's stands today. The house was built by George Washington Franklin around 1855 and later owned by D. Smart and Harry Calkins. The latter farmed the land until 1950 and eventually donated the house to the PCHS. The house was relocated to the historical society's Heritage Park in 1982.

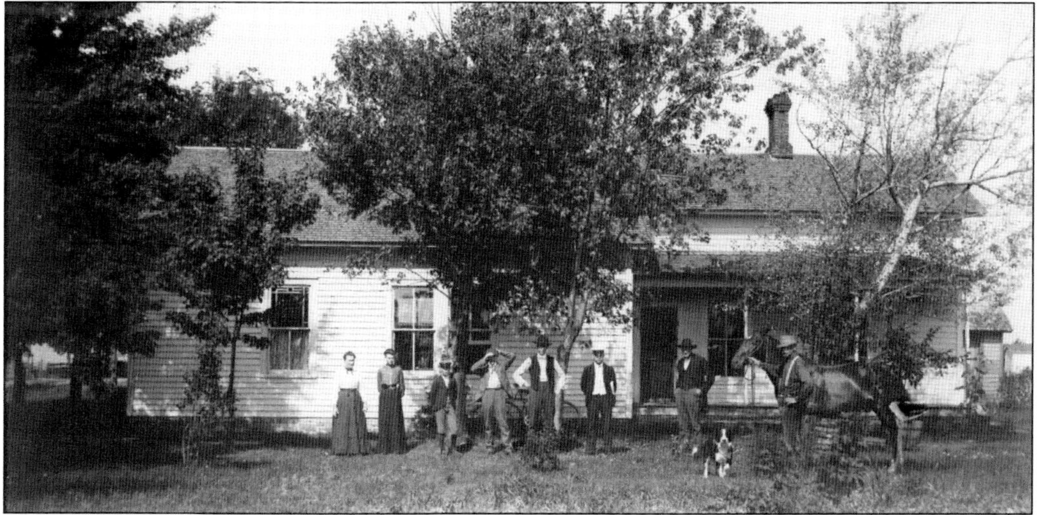

The family of Albertus "Bert" H. Bourn stands outside their home, located on the east side of Wisconsin Street just north of Pine Street. The Bourns moved to Plover from Michigan and lived in Plover for less than 30 years before moving on to Indiana by 1910. Bert had three children—Frank, Nellie, and Fred—and was also the brother of former county clerk, sheriff, and businessman A.E. Bourn.

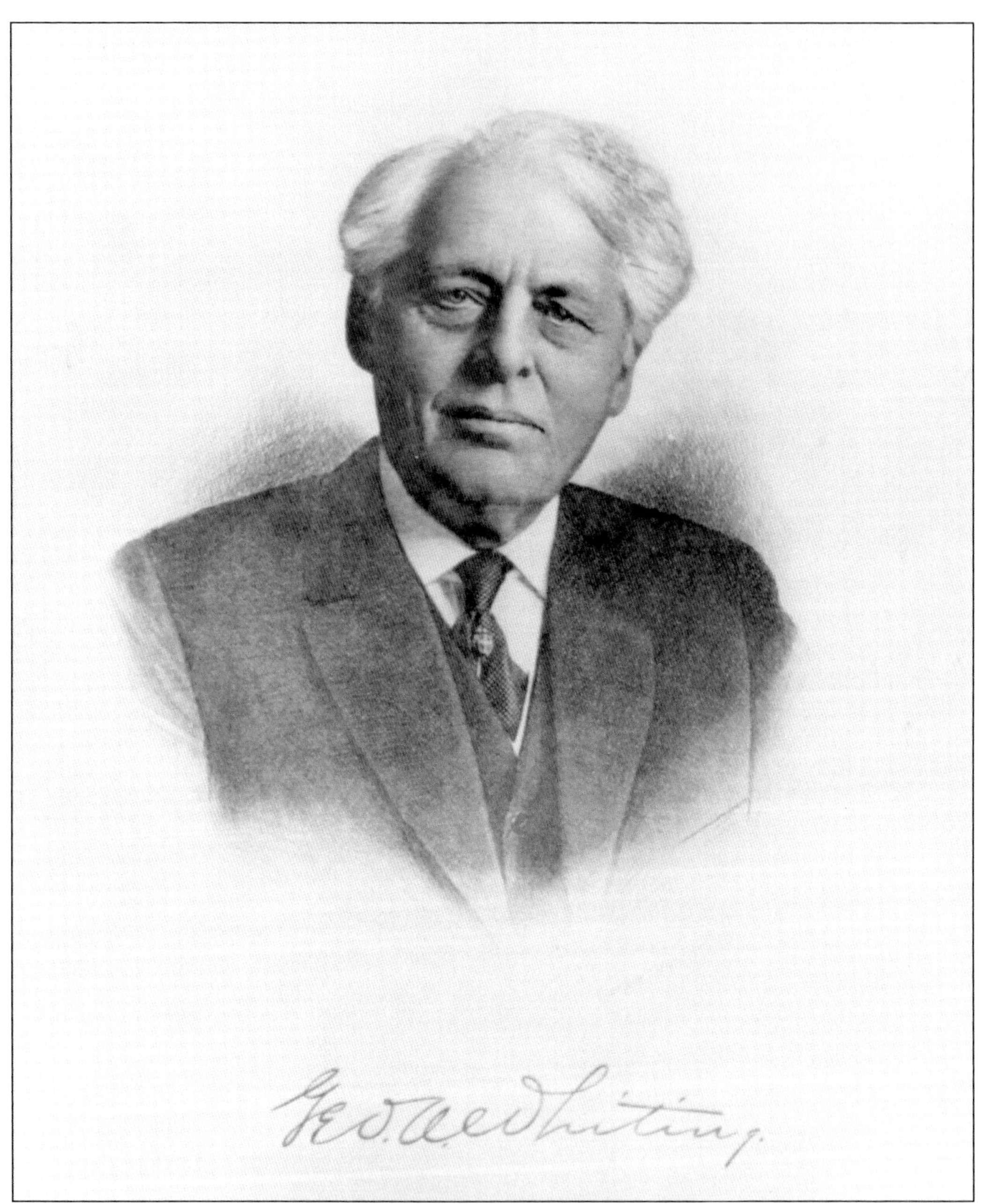

George A. Whiting was born June 6, 1849, in Schoharie County, New York. At the age of five, his family moved to Ripon, Wisconsin, and in 1865, he moved to Neenah where he would reside until his death. Whiting first entered the paper business in 1872 and went on to purchase interest in several more mills between 1874 and 1888. In 1891, he built the Wisconsin River Paper & Pulp Company, and in 1892, he organized the Plover Paper Company. Whiting never lived in or around Plover, but his impact on the town and region has been profound and long lasting.

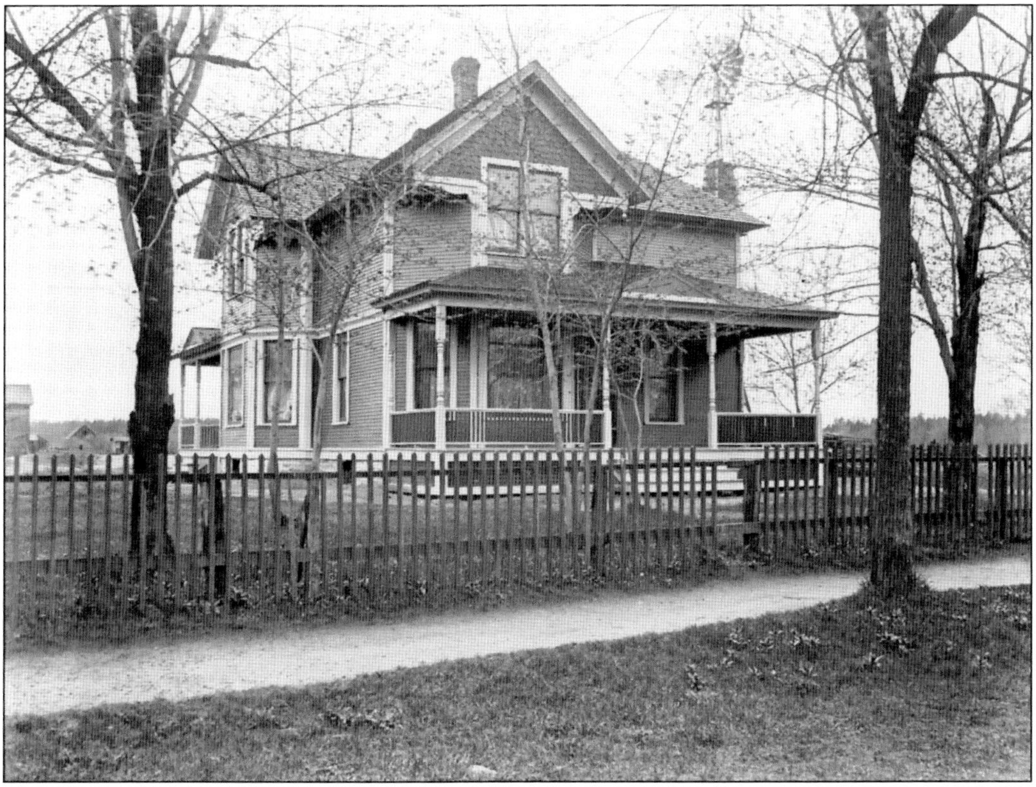

The home of William Carley was built in 1902 and was originally located on First Street. In the 1950s, the house was moved to its current location on Chestnut Street. Carley was a Civil War veteran and a very prominent potato dealer in the area, establishing warehouses at around a dozen points on the Soo Line and Green Bay & Western Railways. It is also rumored that he shipped the first carload of potatoes ever sent out of Portage County.

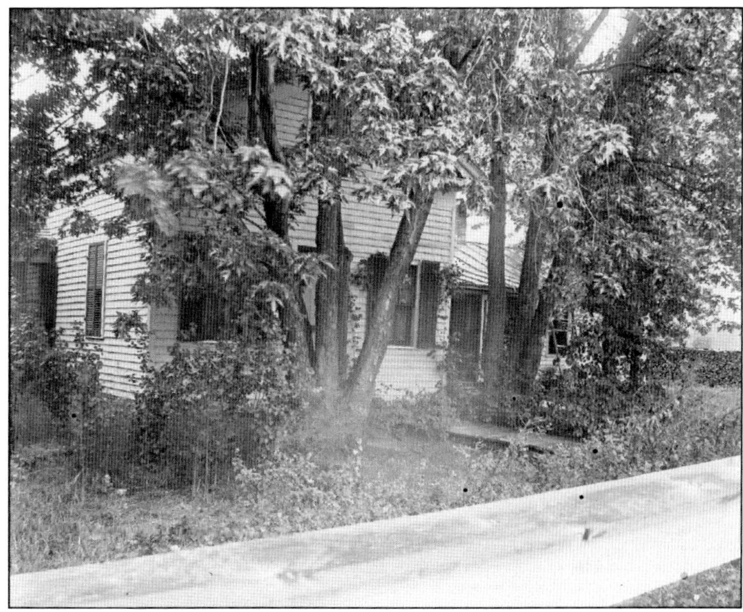

The residence of Silas D. Clark was located on the north side of the village. Clark, after several failed attempts, enlisted in the Union army even though he was underage. He moved to Plover in 1871 and married Clara Luce on February 19, 1876. He had several professions, including farming, lumbering, and owner of a sorghum mill and hardware business. He was a very civic-minded individual and active in the community.

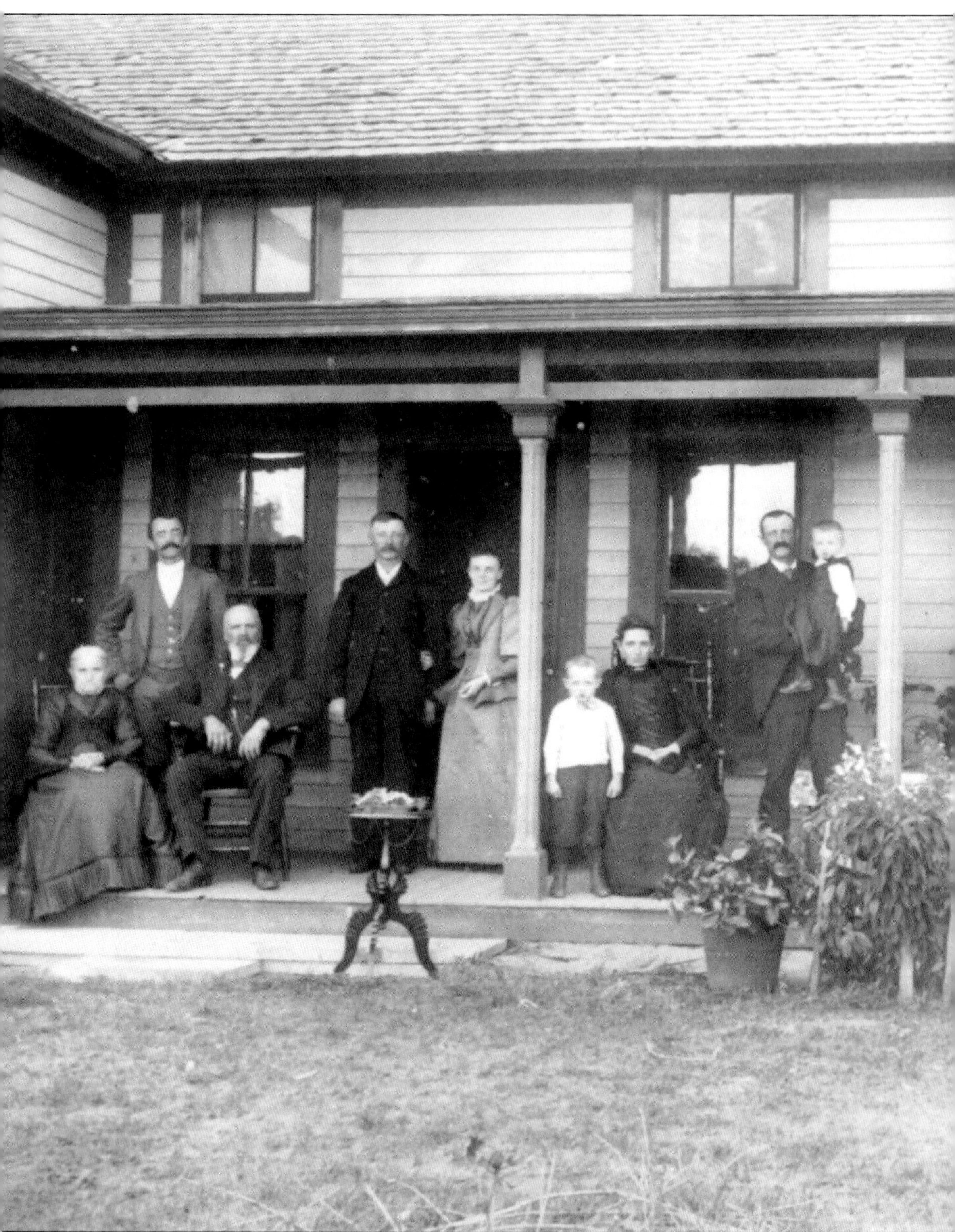

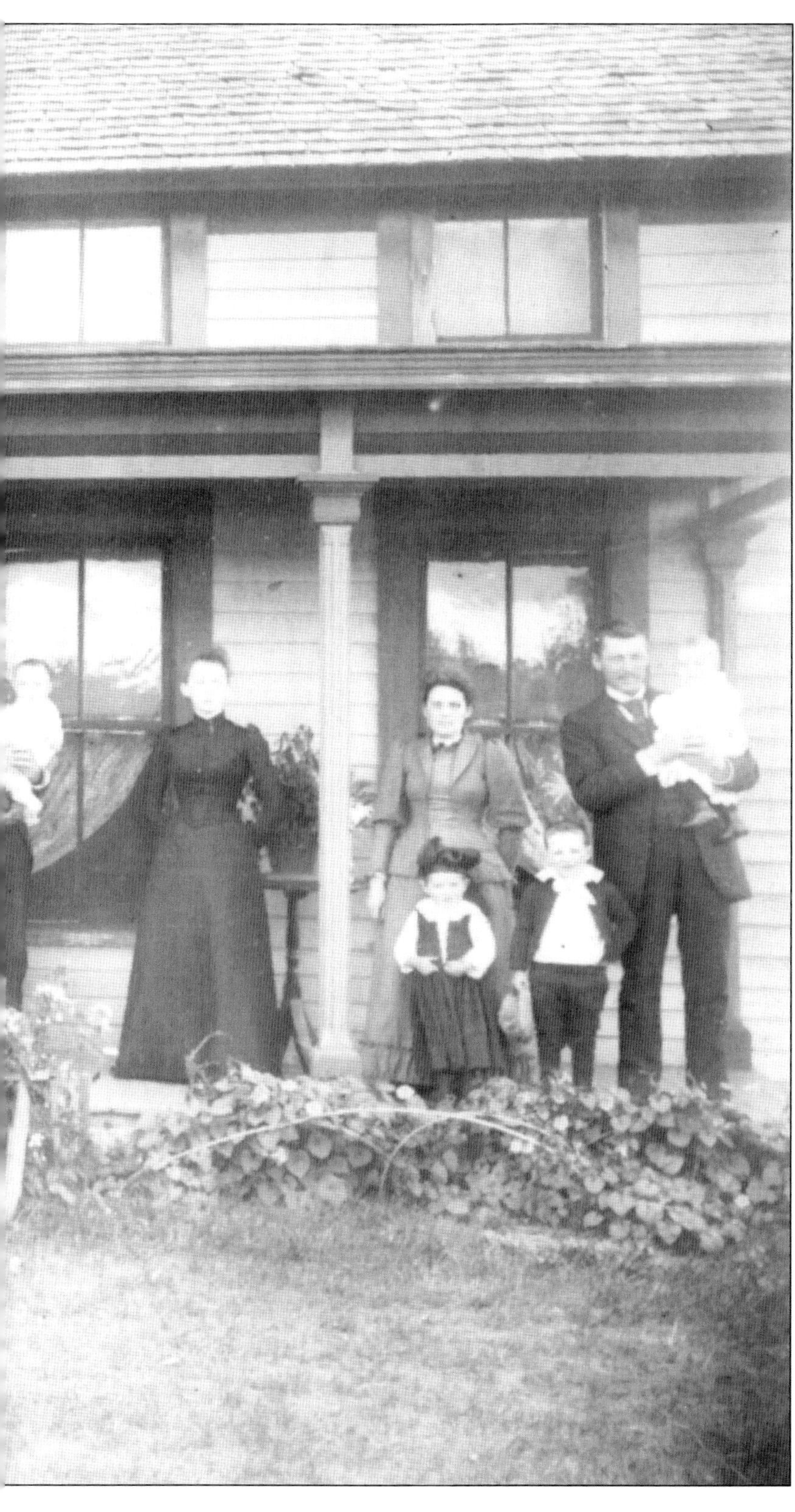

The Eckels and Warner families gather after the wedding of Charles Eckels and Sarah Warner on September 3, 1891. From left to right are Nancy Warner, Frank Warner, Amasa Warner, Charles Eckels (groom), Sarah Warner (bride), Clint Warner, Mary Warner, Walter Warner, Fred Warner, Laird Warner, Sadie Warner, Myra Young, Harry Young, Hume Young, Stanley Young, and Myrle Young. This was taken in front of the Warner house, located near Stage Road east of Coopers Corners (corner of Post and Porter Roads). Amasa Warner came to the town of Plover in 1857. Charles Eckels was a farmer.

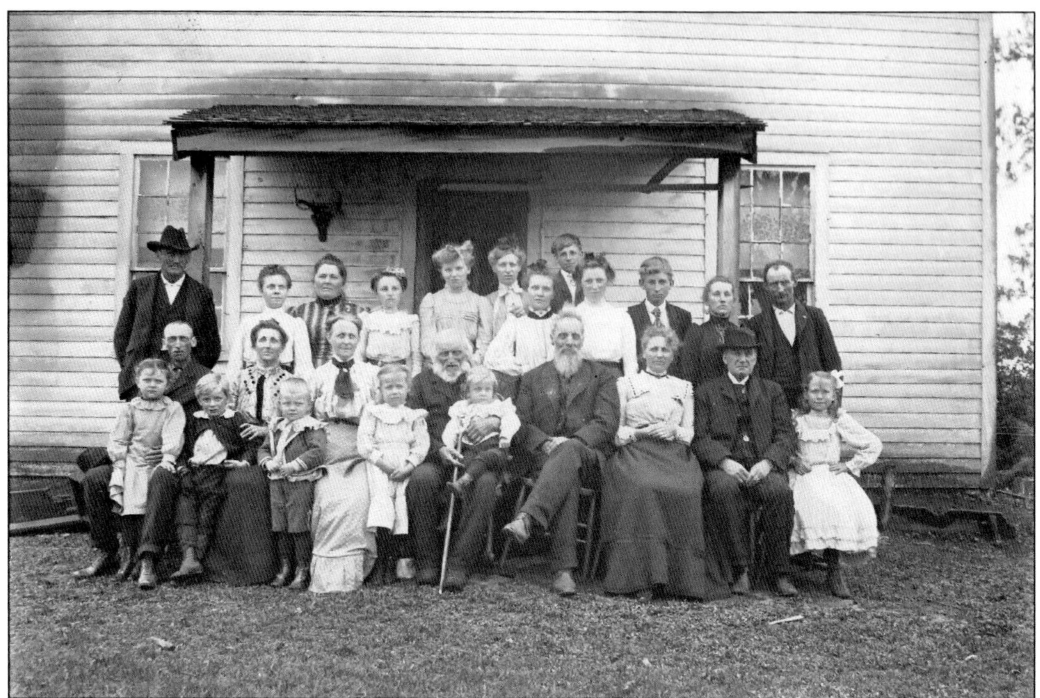

The George Sterling family stands in front of their farmstead just east of the village in 1903. The house was located on what is now the south side of County Highway B, directly across from where the Del Monte plant now stands. Sterling (center, holding child) was known to be one of the oldest residents of Portage County upon his death in 1907. At the time of this photograph, he was 89 years old.

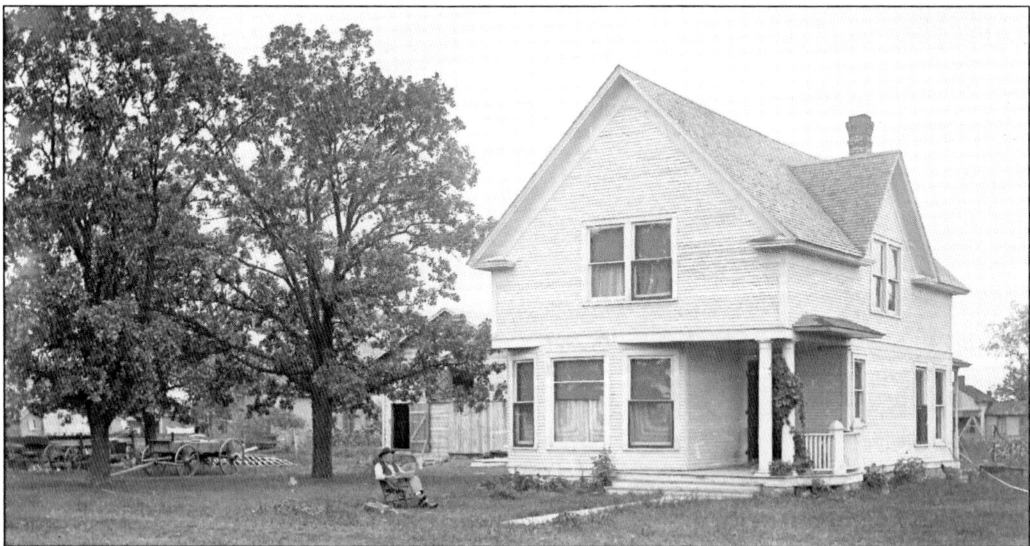

Wilmot Pierce is seated in front of the Weinholt house. Wilmot was born in 1877 to Marcus F. and Eva Pierce and was the older brother of Frank and Lawrence. He worked as bookkeeper for his father and later moved to the Chippewa Falls and Stanley areas, where he worked as a druggist before returning to Stevens Point, where he was employed as an accountant. Wilmot married Marion Maxfield in 1904.

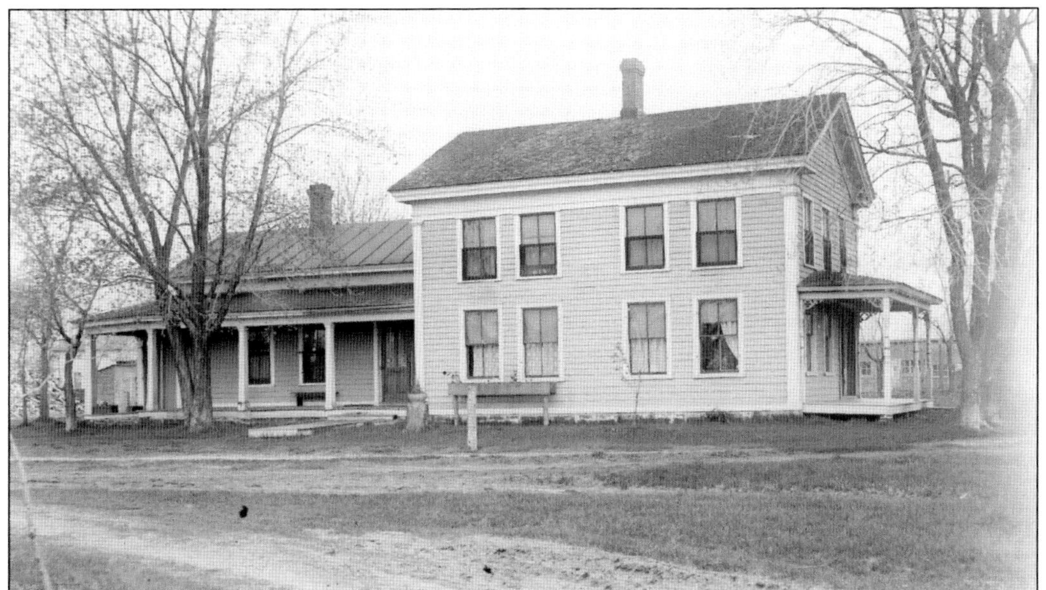

This house, which no longer stands, was located on the northwest corner of Wisconsin and Elm Streets (current Sumac Lane). The house was once owned by Lewis Cass Beach, whose widow sold to Dr. Lindores in 1908. Dr. Lindores lived there until 1910, when William J. Calkins bought the house, living there with his wife, Julia, and daughter Hazel until 1919.

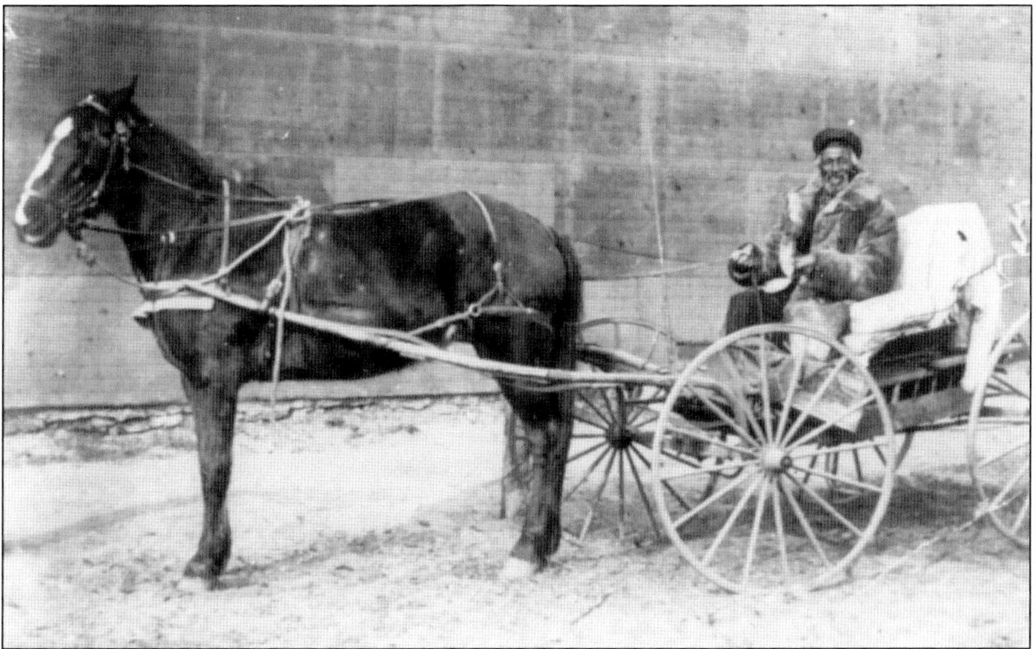

Dennis Peebles, one of the few African Americans residing in Portage County during the early 1900s, passes by the south side of the Pierce store. He was born in Vermont, was a Civil War veteran, and lived in Menasha before coming to Plover. Peebles worked and lived at the Charles Parkhill farm in the town of Plover and is remembered by those who knew him as a man of great character. Peebles had two daughters—Mrs. Lark and Mrs. McCray—neither of which settled in Plover.

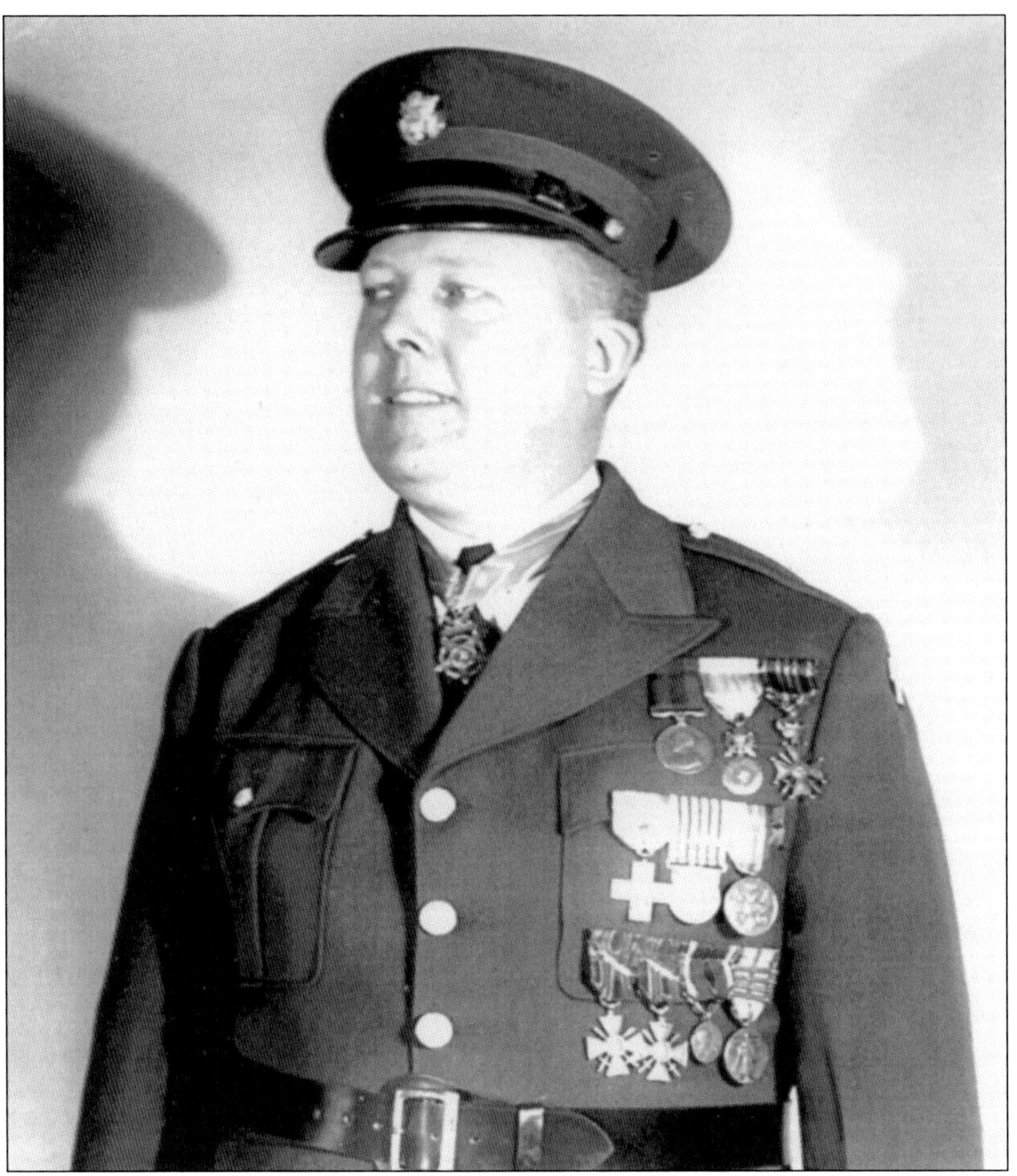

Portage County's only Medal of Honor winner, Clayton Slack, was born at Meehan Station in the town of Plover on February 23, 1896. Slack joined the US Army in September 1917 and was a private in Company D, 124th Machine Gun Battalion, 33rd Division during World War I. He won the Medal of Honor for single-handedly clearing out a German machine gun nest resulting in 10 prisoners and the capture of two machine guns on October 8, 1918, in the Meuse-Argonne offensive.

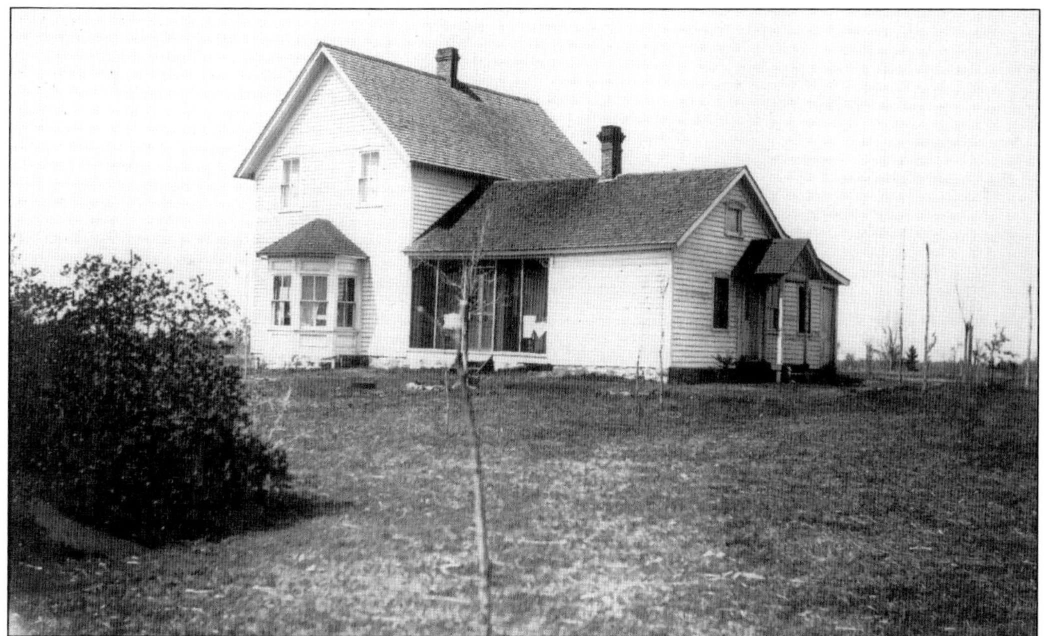

The home of Ransler and Ada Parks of Meehan, shown here around 1878, was located in Meehan north of Grand Rapids Road/Highway 54 at the north end of current Hayes Avenue. Ransler was born in New York and came to Wisconsin at the age of four. After marrying Ada Clussman in 1879, he moved from Linwood to this farmhouse. Ransler also served as supervisor of the Town of Plover and served the school district. (Ryan Berrend.)

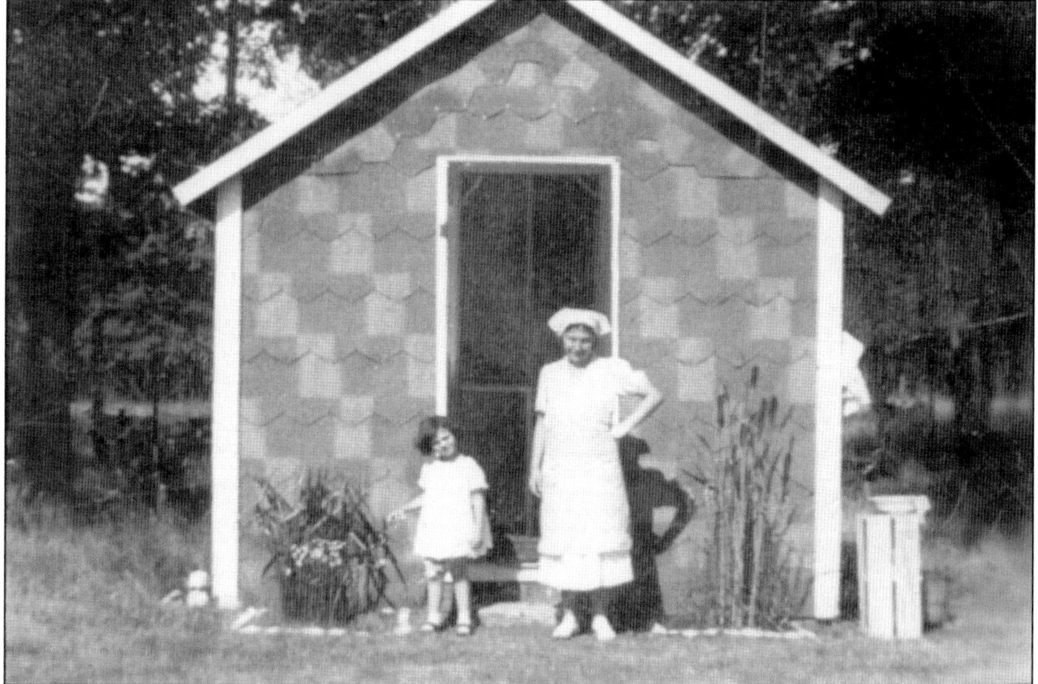

Jean and Bertha Fox stand in front of a cabin at Love Creek Resort in Meehan. The resort was located at the end of Pierce Avenue and was run by Charles Clussman. (Wayne and Ryan Berrend.)

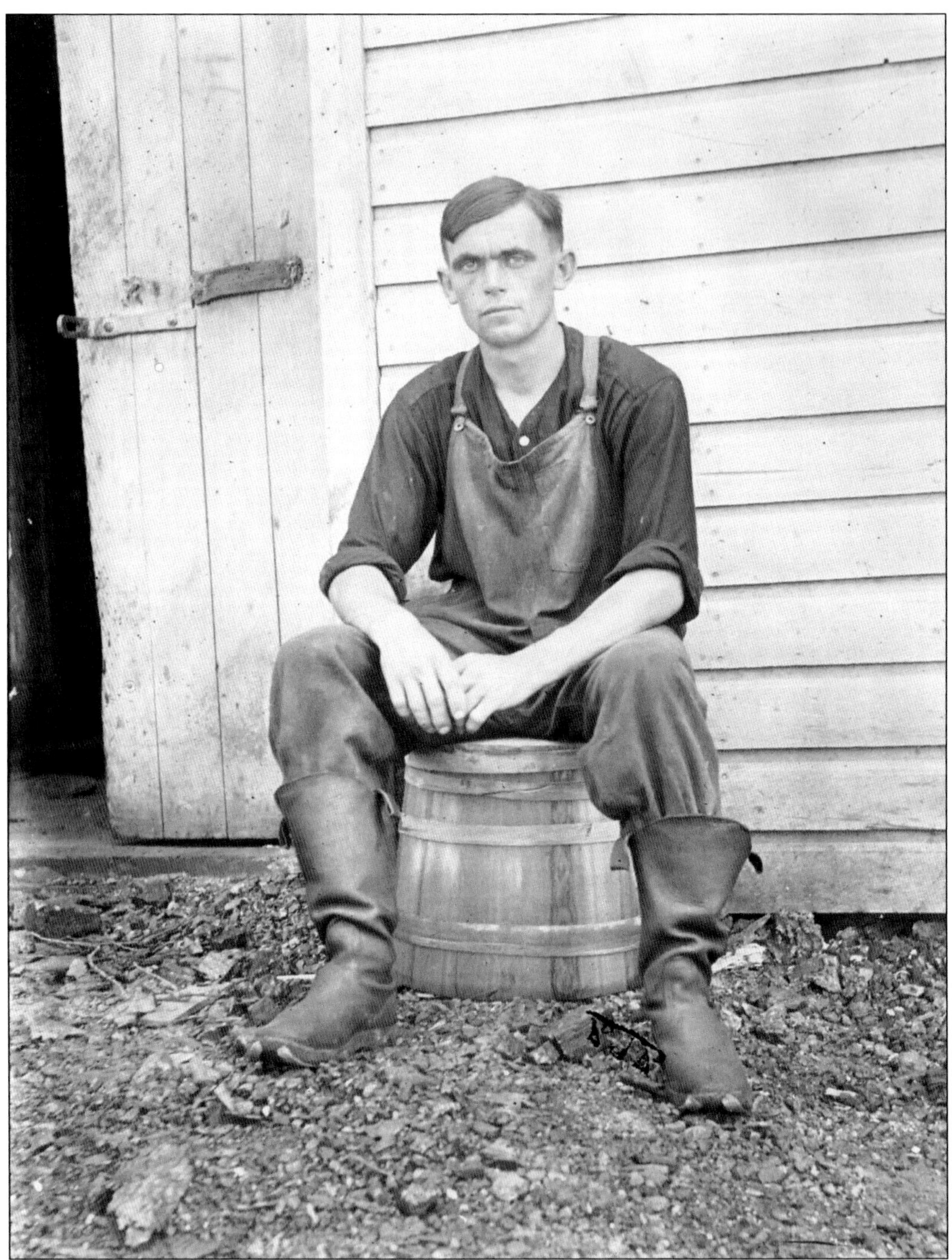

Morris Rasmussen takes a break from making butter at the Plover Creamery. Rasmussen was the butter maker at the Buena Vista Creamery before purchasing the Plover Creamery in the early 1900s. He later sold the creamery to a stock company organized among the farmers in the area in January 1909.

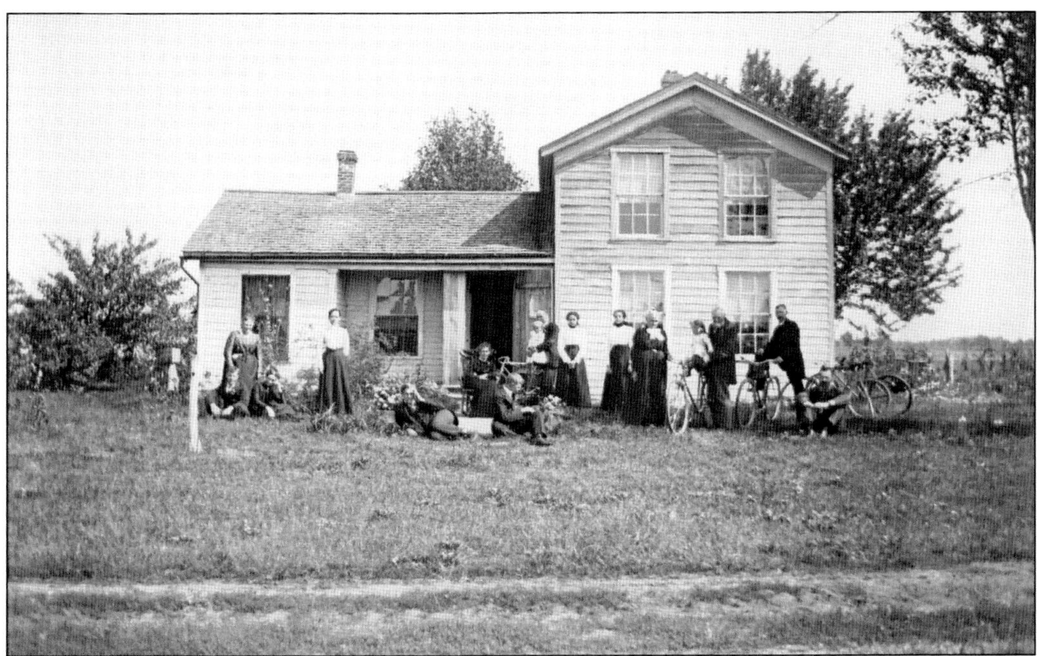

The home of Jane Russell and her husband, George, located on the northeast corner of Washington and Elm Streets (current Sumac Lane), still stands today. Jane's first husband, Elias Marlatt, died in 1865 in the Civil War, and she later married George Russell. The Marlatt family is likely pictured here, as George had no children.

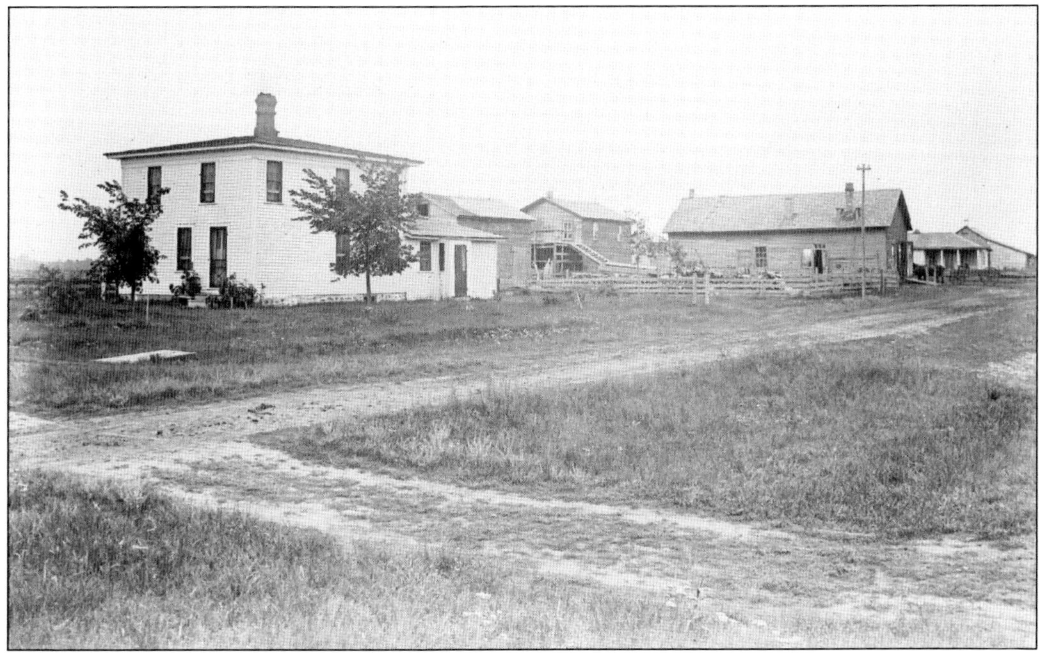

The home of Henry A. Marlatt, located on the southeast corner of Wisconsin and South Streets, was demolished in 2015. Marlatt was a blacksmith, and his shop can be seen at the rear of the property on Union Street (current Plover Road). The family moved from Plover around 1920 to Waterloo, Iowa, and then to West Allis, Wisconsin, where Henry passed away.

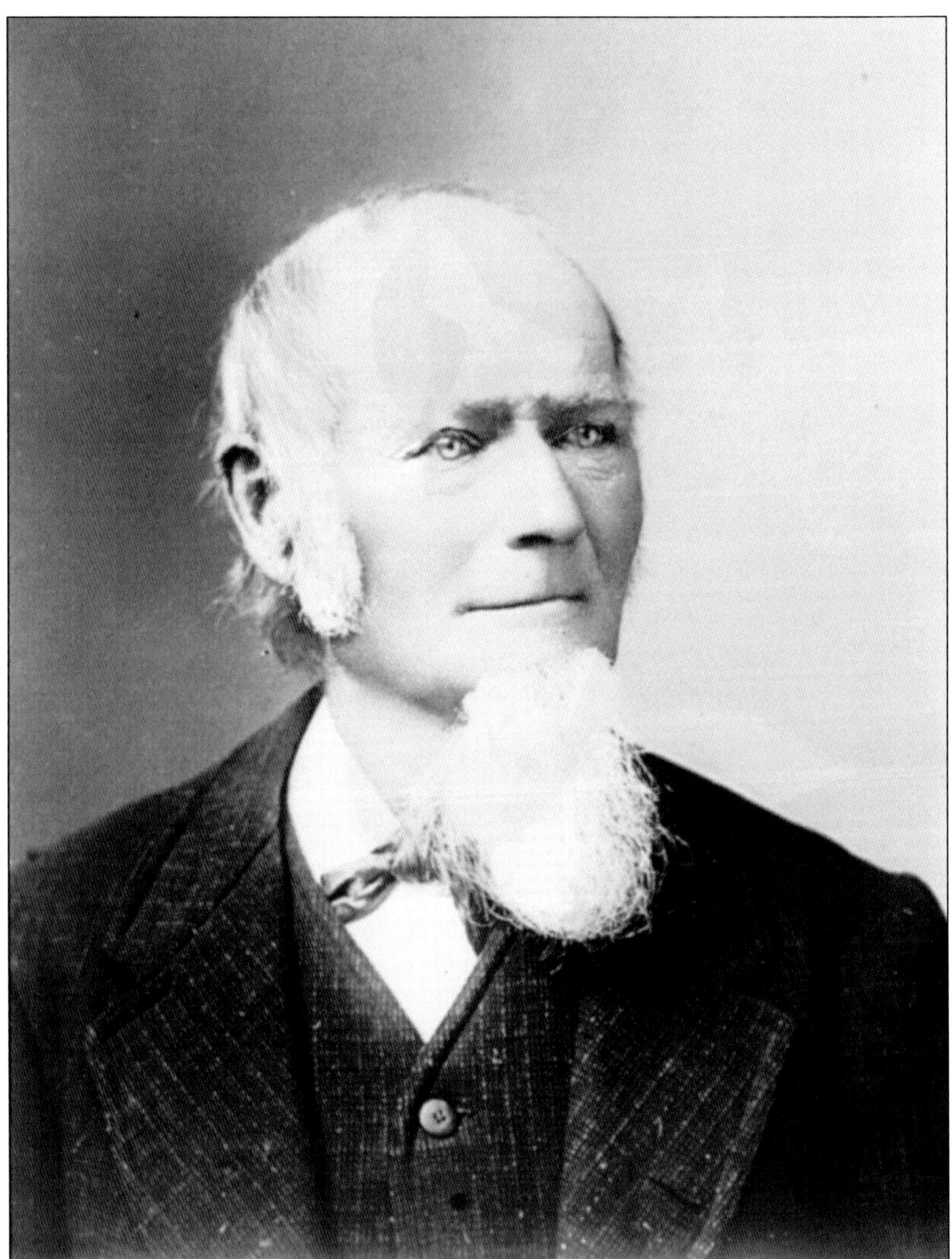

This is a portrait of George Warner, who was born in Canada in 1814, moved to Portage County in 1871, and lived in Plover with his son Horace "Hod" N. Warner for his final 22 years. Affectionately known as "Uncle George" around town, he was known to be very active and full of life well into his 80s. George had three daughters and two sons: Flora Bigelow Duchene, Martha Powers, Mary Dolloff, George Warner, and Horace N. Warner. George's son Horace was proprietor of the Warner Hotel.

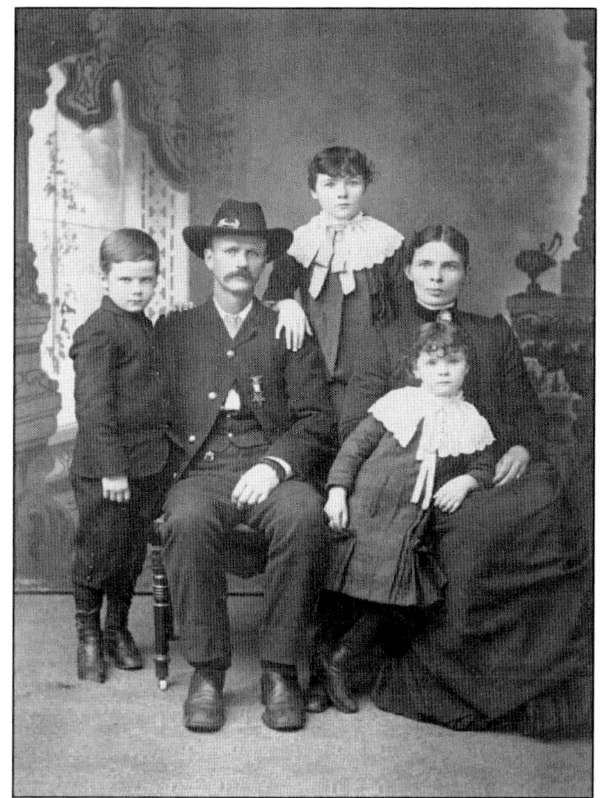

The family of James A. Bremmer is seen here, likely in the mid-1880s. From left to right are Charles, James, Edith, Elizabeth, and Emma (seated). Emma M. (McMillan) Bremmer was born and raised in the town of Stockton. James served as Plover town treasurer, constable, and deputy sheriff; he was also on the school board and was the first postmaster of the village of Arnott. In 1887, the family moved to Stevens Point, where James was the first buyer and shipper of potatoes in the city.

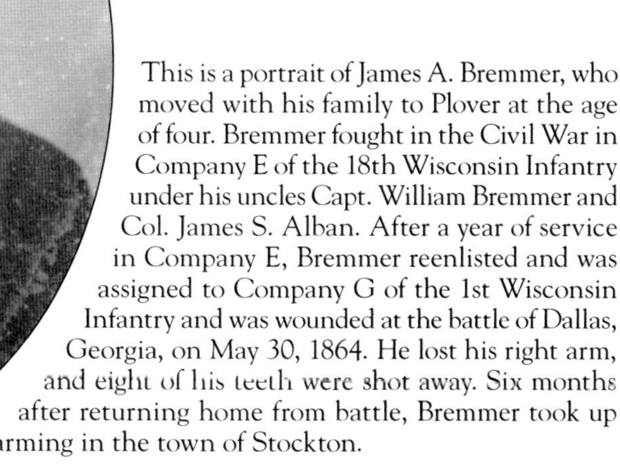

This is a portrait of James A. Bremmer, who moved with his family to Plover at the age of four. Bremmer fought in the Civil War in Company E of the 18th Wisconsin Infantry under his uncles Capt. William Bremmer and Col. James S. Alban. After a year of service in Company E, Bremmer reenlisted and was assigned to Company G of the 1st Wisconsin Infantry and was wounded at the battle of Dallas, Georgia, on May 30, 1864. He lost his right arm, and eight of his teeth were shot away. Six months after returning home from battle, Bremmer took up farming in the town of Stockton.

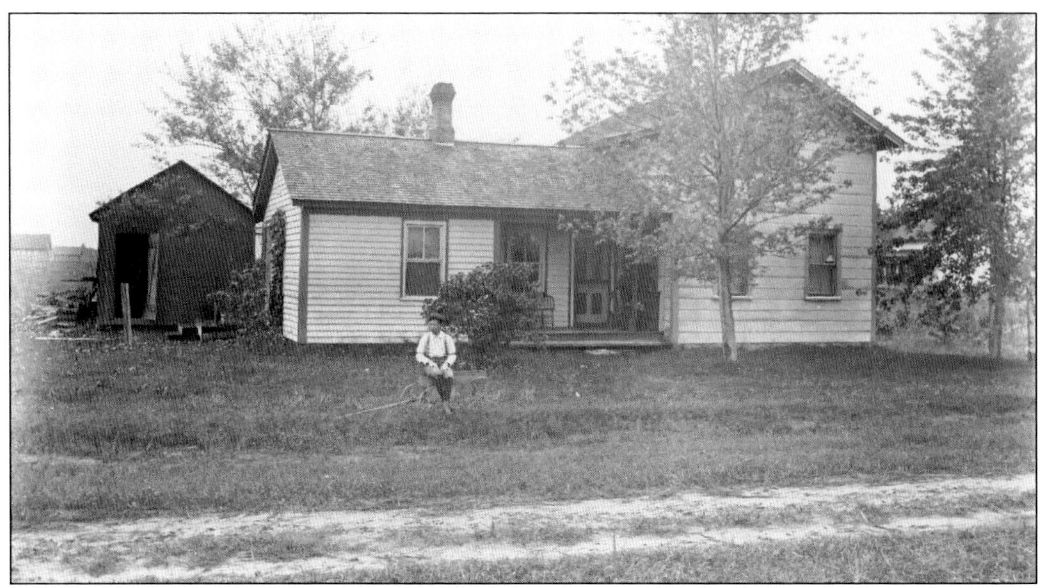

A boy sits in a wagon in front of the Frank Halladay house, which was built in 1878. The house is still standing on the south side of Willow Street just west of Second Street (current Earhart Avenue). Frank was married to Isabelle and they had a son, Frank Jr.

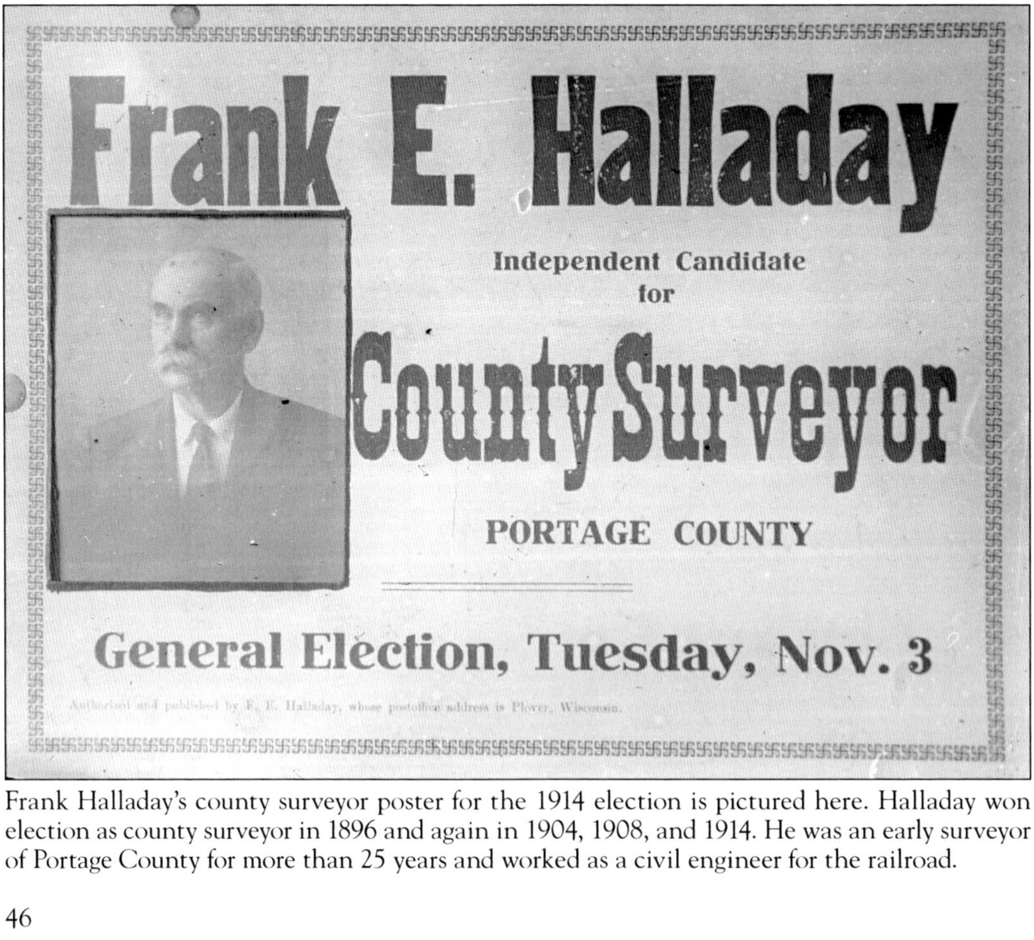

Frank E. Halladay

Independent Candidate
for

County Surveyor

PORTAGE COUNTY

General Election, Tuesday, Nov. 3

Authorized and published by F. E. Halladay, whose postoffice address is Plover, Wisconsin.

Frank Halladay's county surveyor poster for the 1914 election is pictured here. Halladay won election as county surveyor in 1896 and again in 1904, 1908, and 1914. He was an early surveyor of Portage County for more than 25 years and worked as a civil engineer for the railroad.

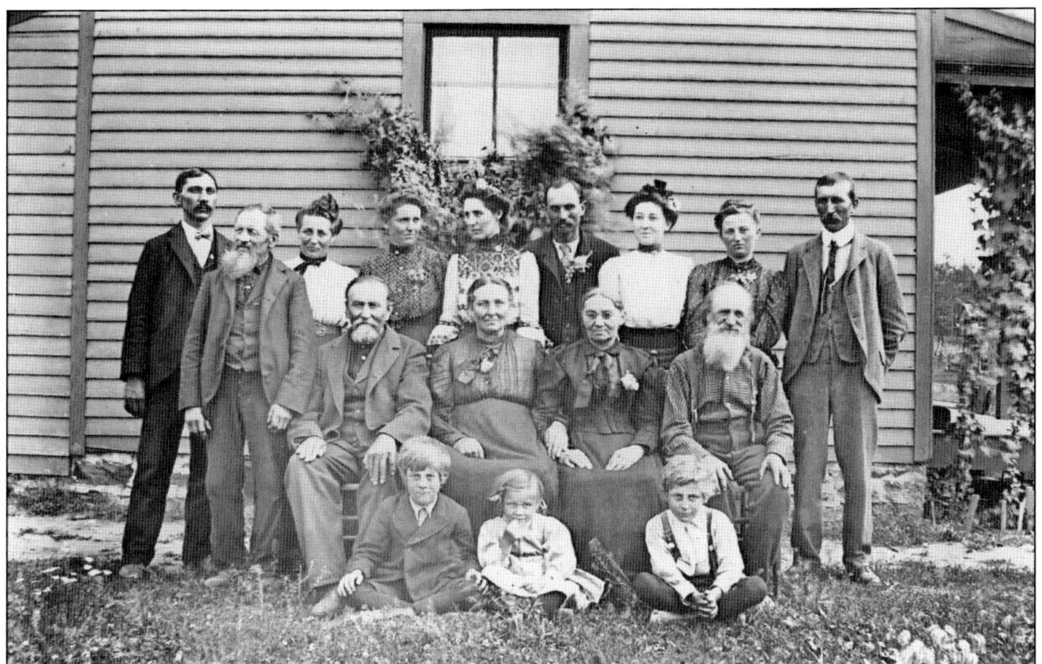

It is unclear if this photograph of the family of Jacob and Eva Schwartz was taken at Jacob Schwartz's home in the village of Plover or at his son John's farm, located east of the Town of Plover. Schwartz was a German immigrant and lived in Buffalo County before moving to the Plover area. Upon his death in 1912, he was survived by 10 children.

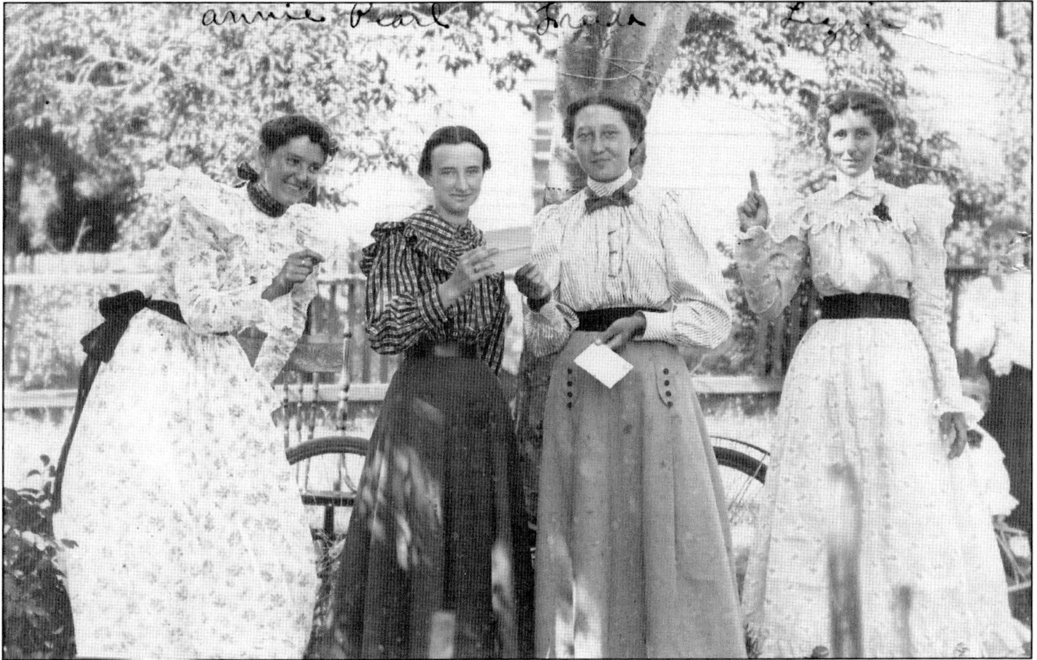

Four Plover ladies pose for a photograph; from left to right are Anna Schwartz Zimmer, Pearl Carley Bourn, Frieda Schwartz Cram, and Lizzie Schwartz Carley. The three Schwartz ladies were daughters of Jacob Schwartz.

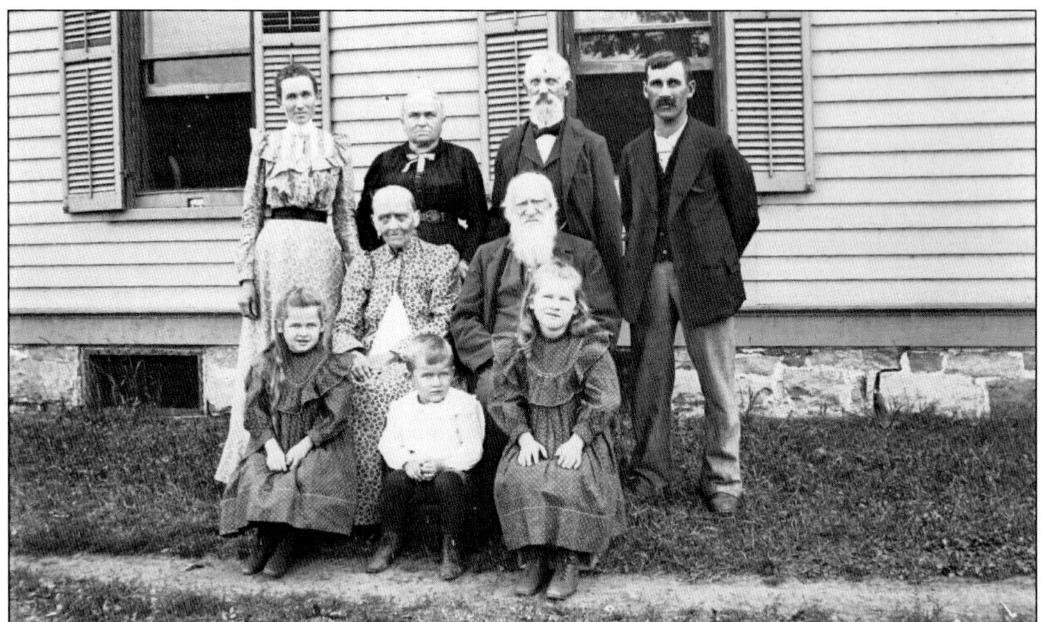

The family of Almon Maxfield is pictured in front of their house, which is now known as the Morgan House. Maxfield originally bought land surrounding what would be the location of Morrill School and developed a farm. In 1886, he moved to the village of Plover, where he opened a general store, which he operated until his retirement in 1900. He purchased the house in 1895, and it stayed in the family until 1956, when Julian Maxfield sold to the Wallins family.

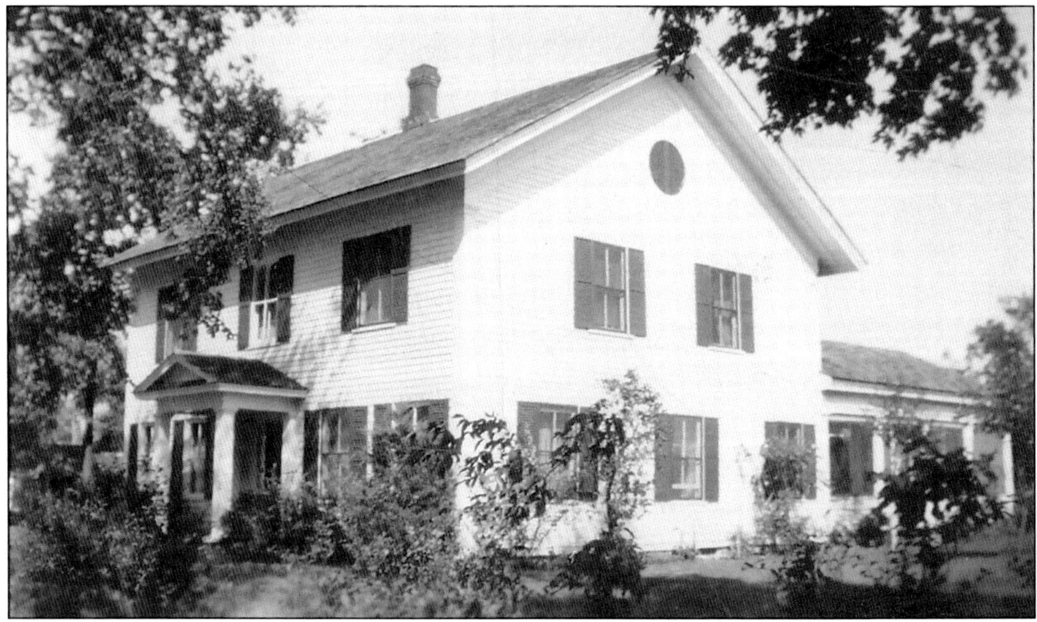

Originally built as a one-story house in 1850 for Dr. John Morrison, this house is located on the southeast corner of South Drive and Post Road. A second story was added in 1876. Some of the past owners include E.A. Sherman, James W. Pierce, and James's son Leo Pierce. Since 1982, it has been operated as a restaurant under the names Sherman House Restaurant, the Cottage, and Cottage Cafe. This photograph is from the mid-1940s, when it was owned by Otto Hilmer.

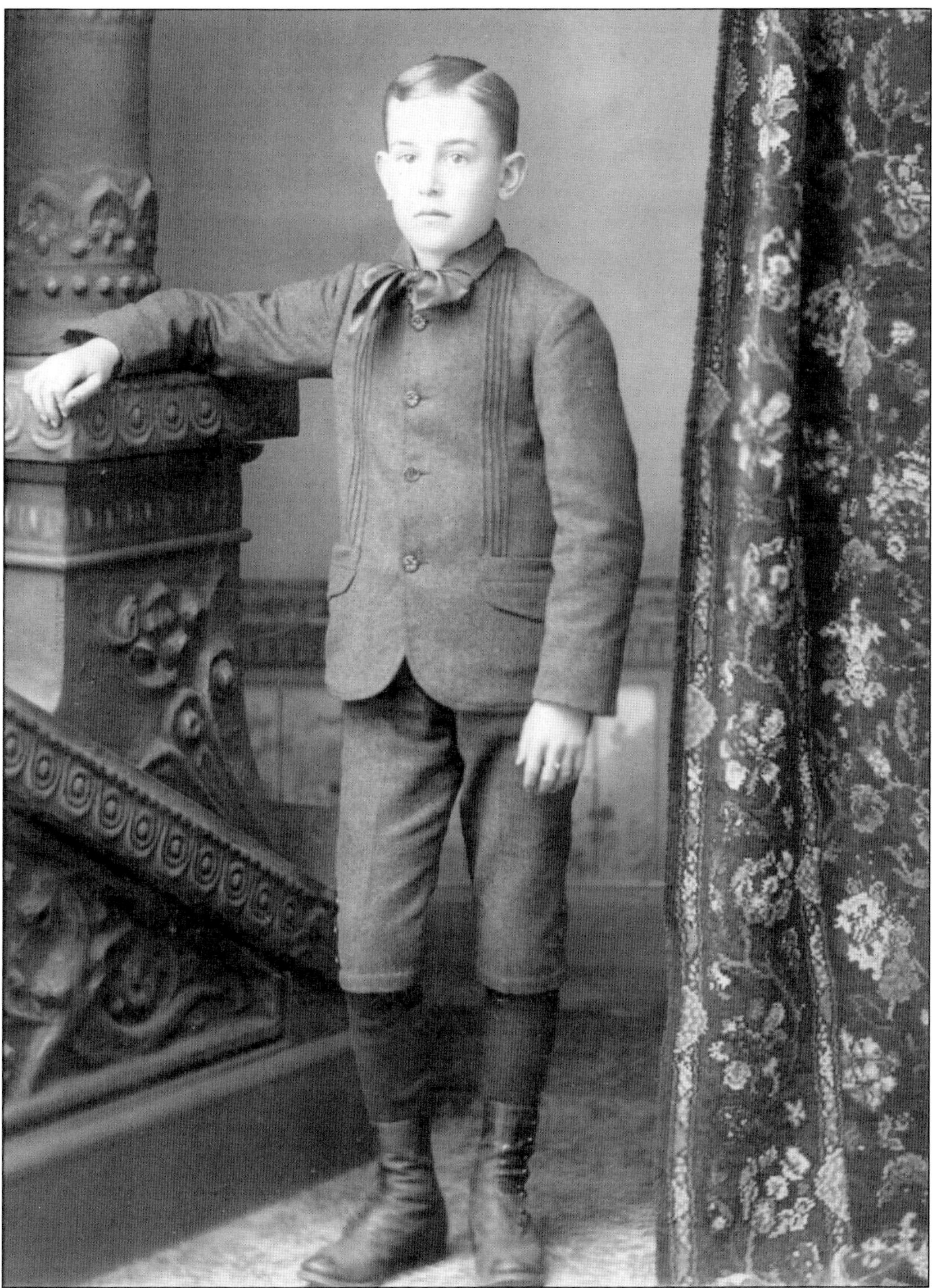

This is a portrait of Marcus F. and Eva Pierce's son Frank Pierce as a boy. Frank was the middle child to brothers Wilmot (older) and Lawrence (younger). He was also the nephew of James W. Pierce, the owner of Pierce's grocery store. Frank married Bertha Churchill and moved to Medford, where he worked as a merchant.

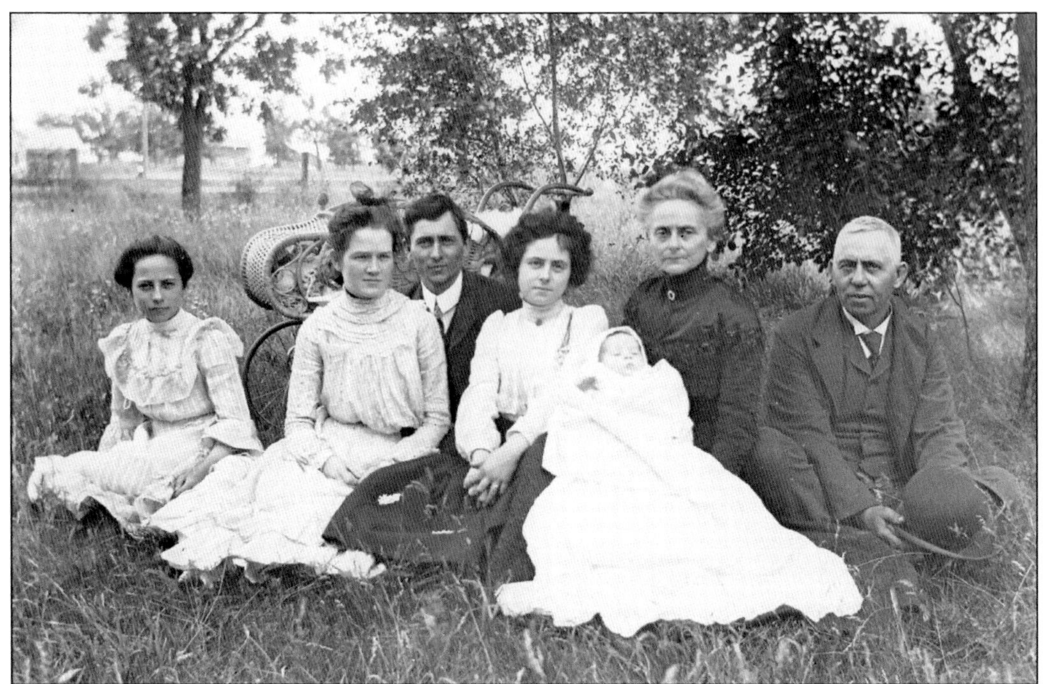

The Bahner family relaxes in the grass in July 1903. From left to right are Etta, Mary, Kellogg, Jessie, Margaret (infant), Mary, and Felix. Felix worked over 20 years as a salesman for the Gross & Jacobs Company hardware store, a tinsmith, and a conductor of bands in Amherst and Plover.

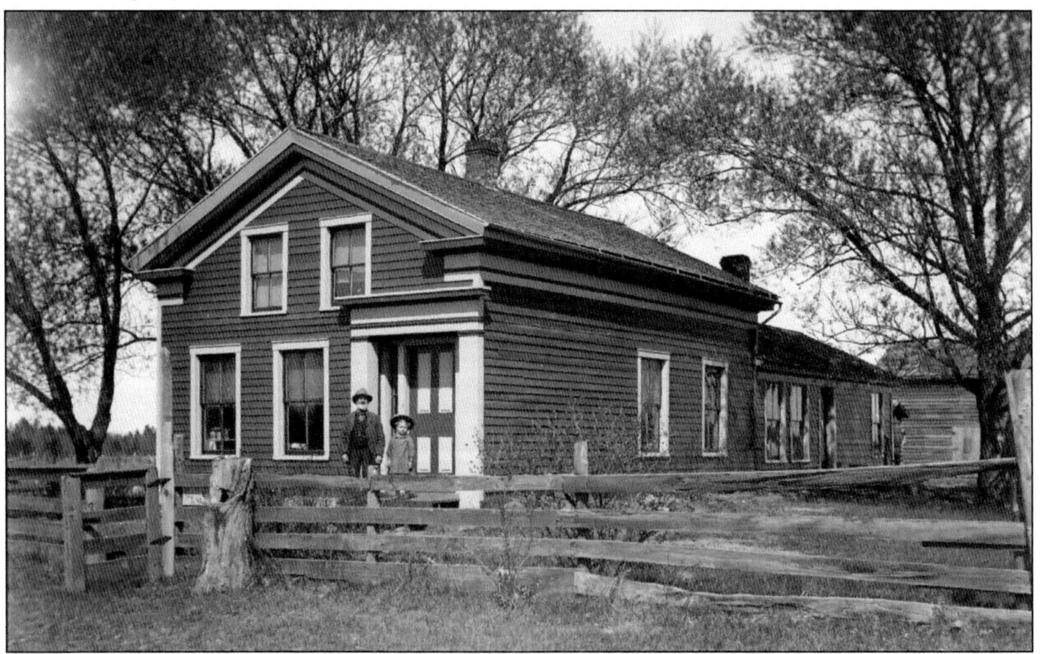

George Washington Altenburg stands in front of his house in 1904. The home was located on today's Highway 54, just northwest of the intersection with Isherwood Road. Altenburg was a farmer and lived in Plover for 60 years. He was 80 when this photograph was taken. He married twice—first to Anna and later to Sarah—and had four children: Edward, Elizabeth, Katie, and Anna.

Three

Daily Life

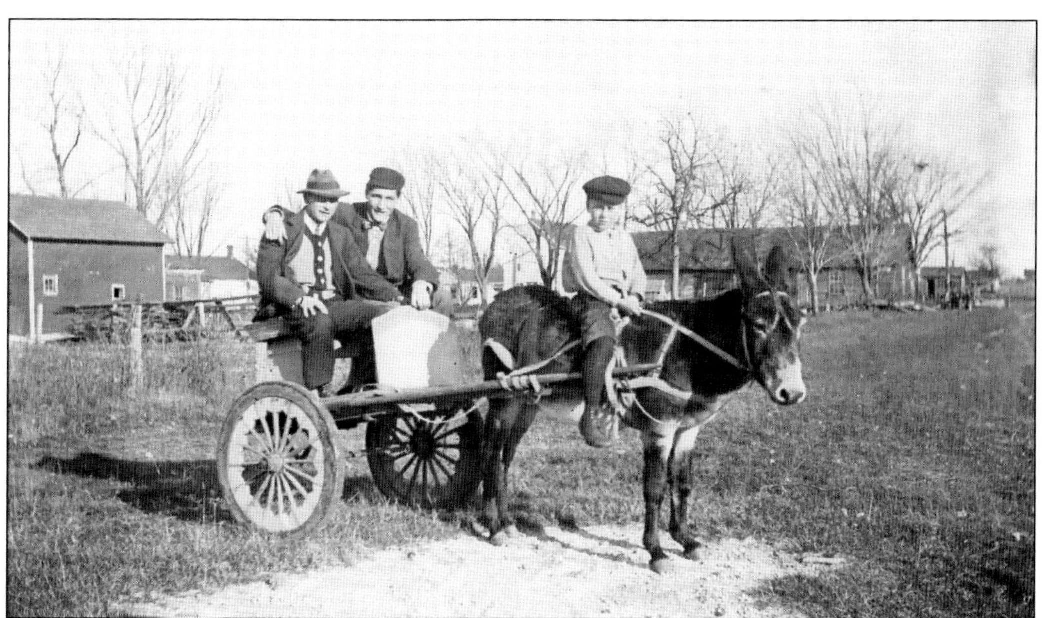

From left to right, Martin "Tune" Booth and Leo Pierce enjoy a casual ride in a cart pulled by a donkey ridden by an unidentified Krueger child around 1910. This form of transportation was common in the area during this time before automobiles became affordable and readily available.

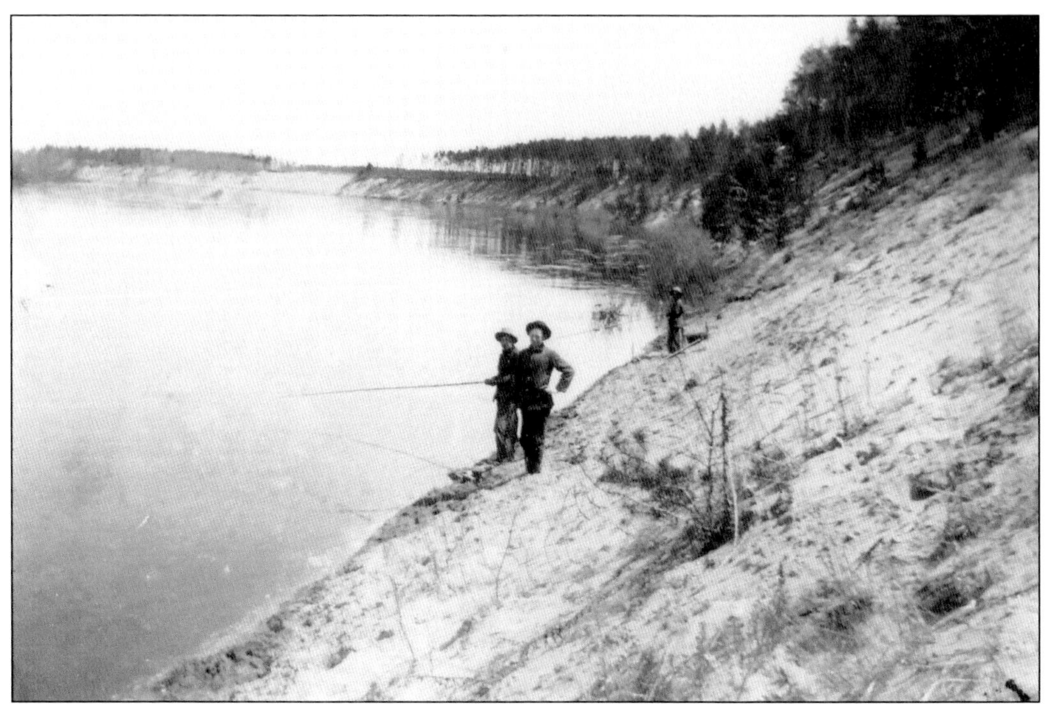

Three unidentified men fish on the Yellow Banks of the Wisconsin River at Plover.

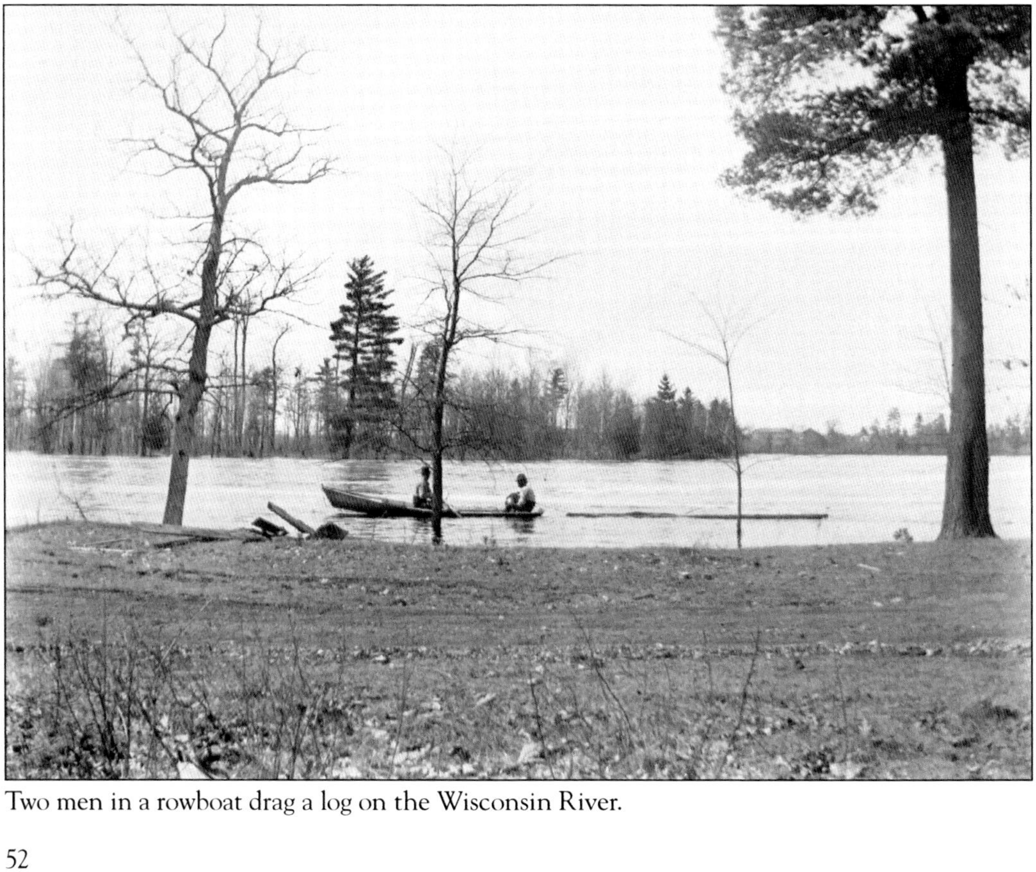

Two men in a rowboat drag a log on the Wisconsin River.

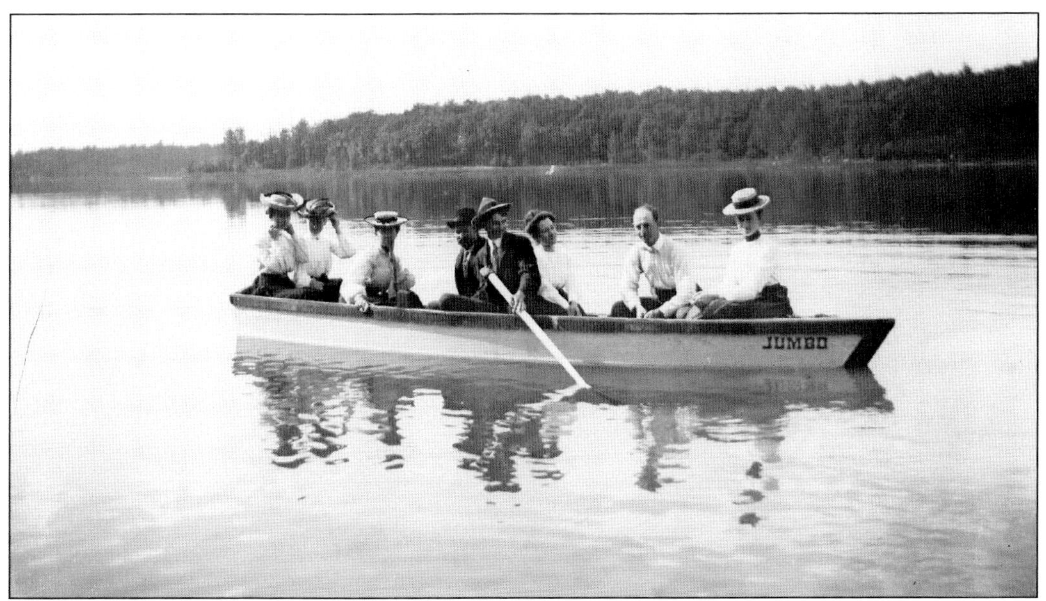

A group of Ploverites take to their rowboat to enjoy a relaxing day on the Wisconsin River.

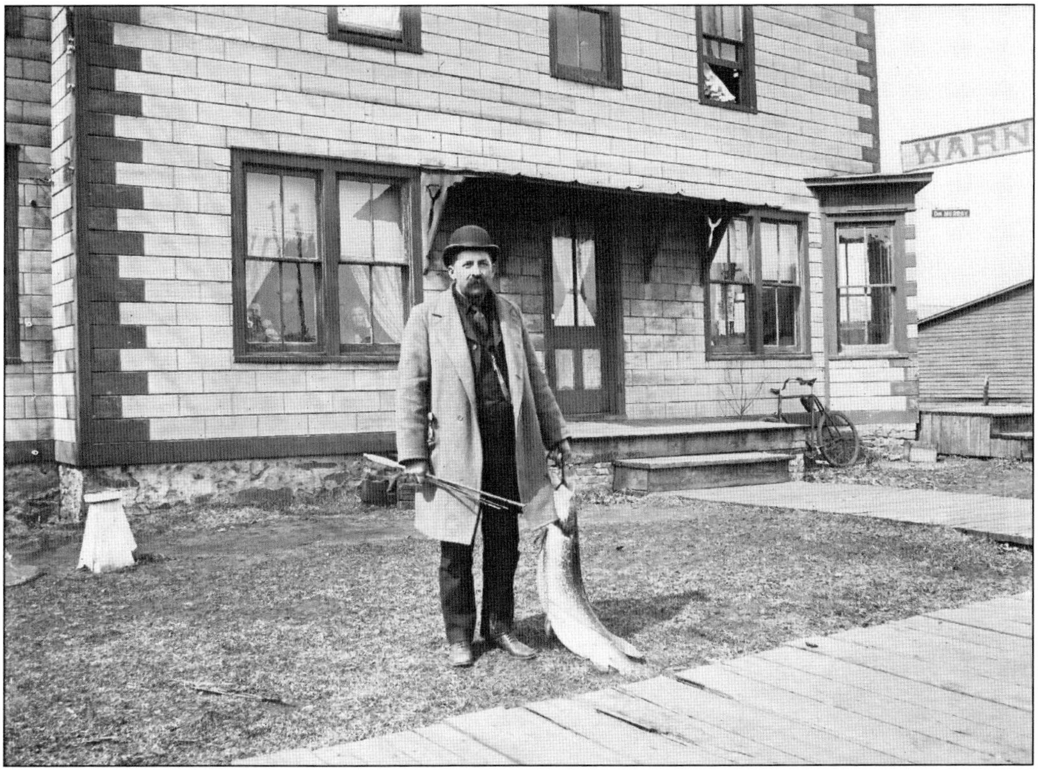

A man stops in front of the Warner House hotel to pose with his catch. The small sign on the corner of the Warner House identifies that Dr. David Murray saw patients in the hotel. In 1903, Dr. Murray found himself embroiled in a murder trial when Jennie Harroun (whom he was allegedly having an affair with) was accused of poisoning her husband Walter Harroun, a crime for which she was ultimately acquitted.

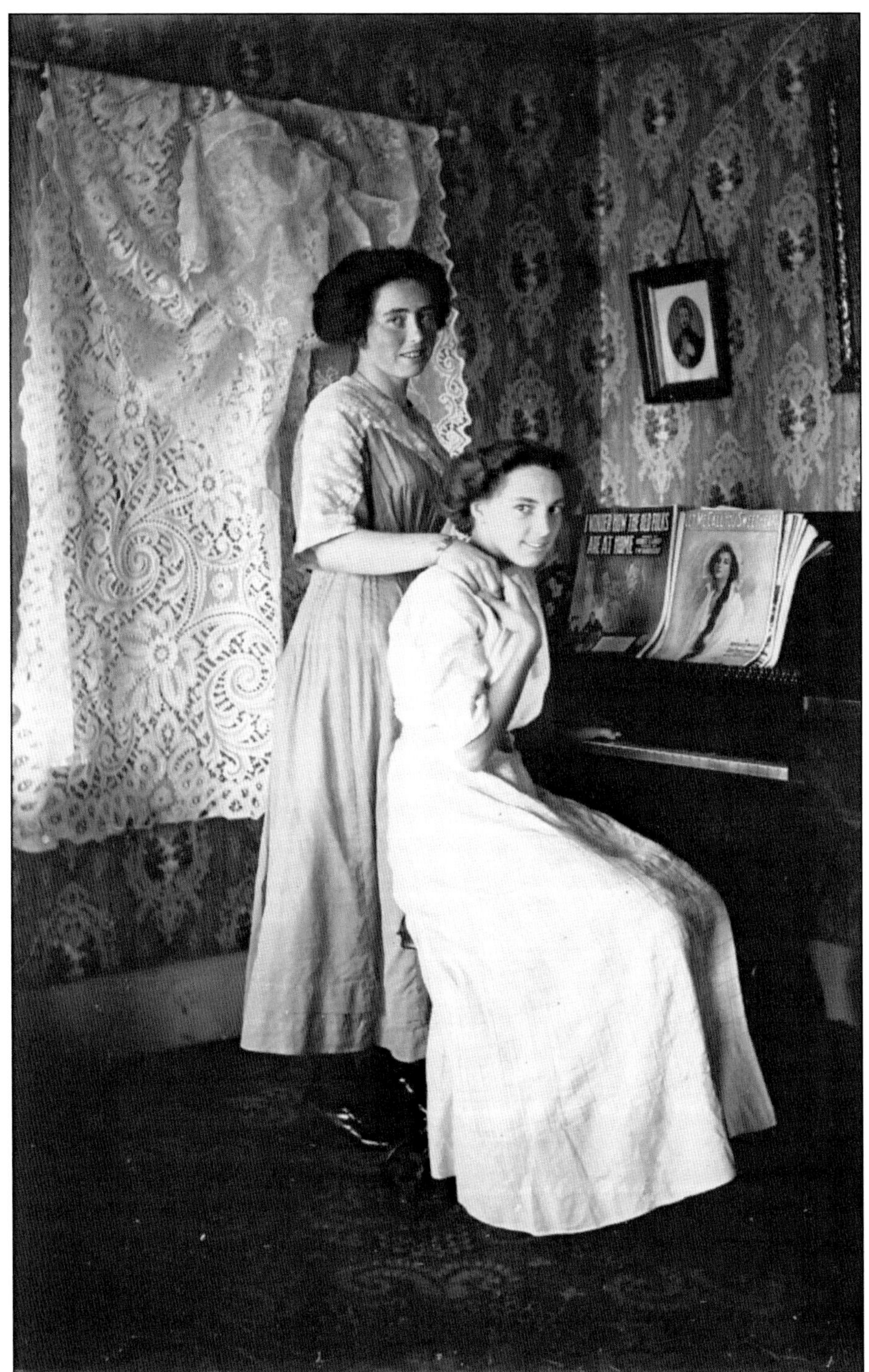

Mabel Altenburg (standing) and Isla Warner pose in front of the piano in the parlor of the Warner home in 1910. Warner was a school teacher at Plover grade school before moving to Shiocton to teach, and later married Jeffry Miller. Soon after this photograph was taken, Altenburg married Carl Raymond and moved to Pardeeville.

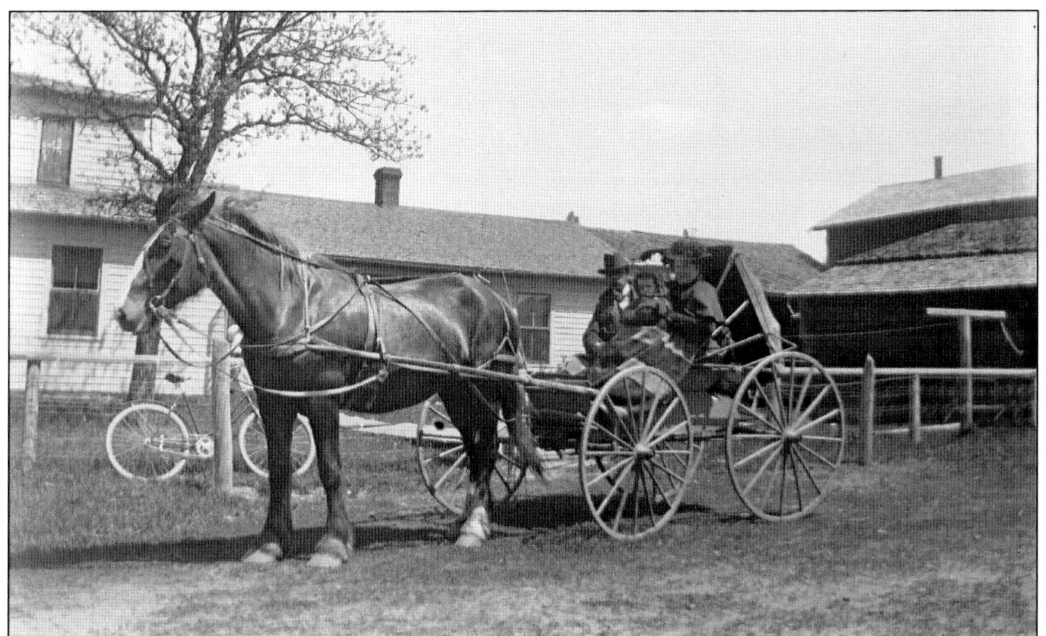

Horace Lombard of Lanark passes by the Walter Barnsdale house on Elm Street (current Sumac Lane) with his mother-in-law Sarah Young and daughter Ione. Horace was married to Belle Young, and Sarah was married to Simon Young, a pioneer of the Plover area who had worked in lumber and also at the McDill mill for 14 years.

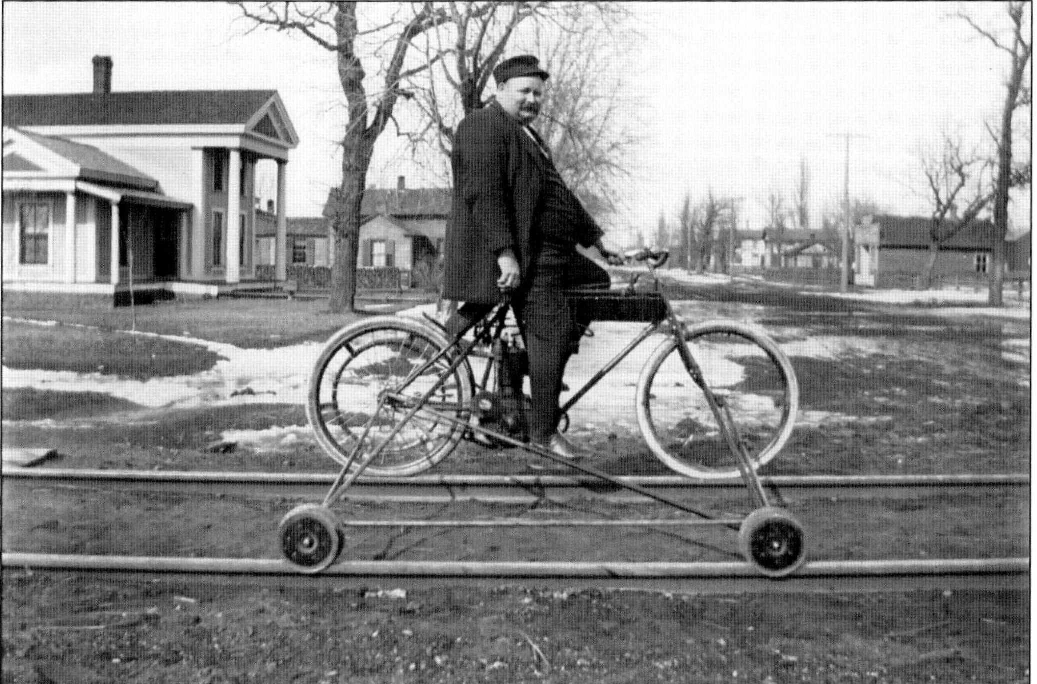

Frank Singley poses on a railroad motorcycle contraption that was likely a creation of Walter Barnsdale. He is shown here headed toward First Street passing by the Cate/Potts house. Singley owned Singley's Saloon, which was located on today's Post Road.

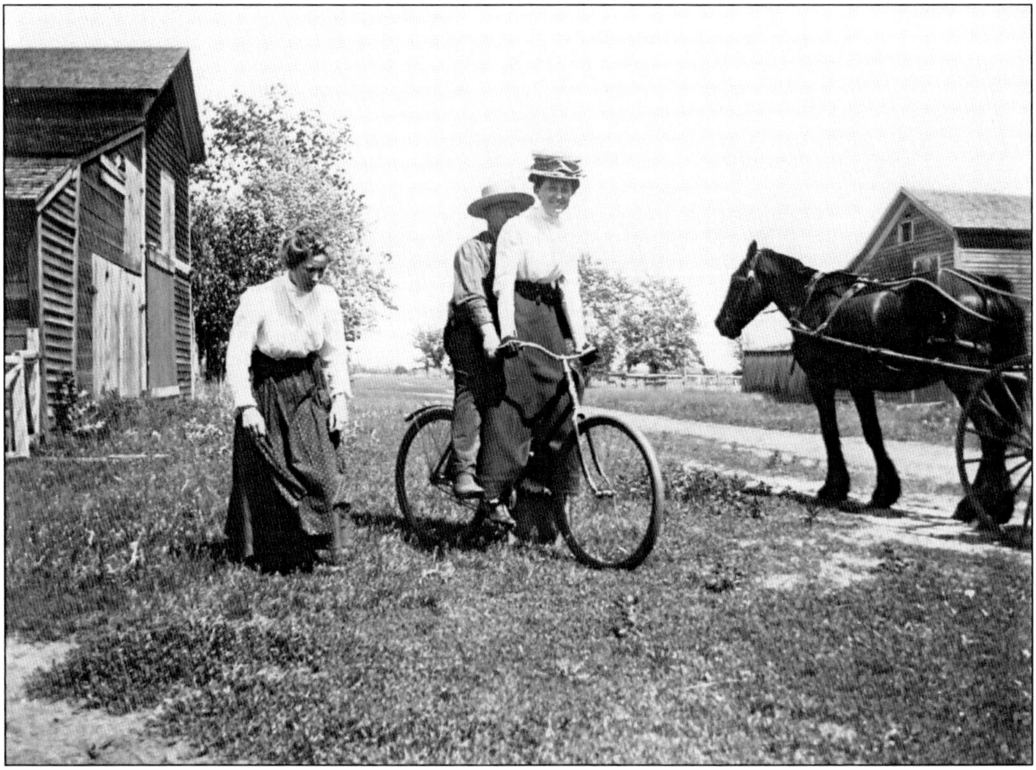

Kate Barnsdale and a young man only identified as Fred try riding a bicycle together as an unidentified woman stands nearby. Kate was the wife of Walter Barnsdale, photographer and early movie creator and presenter. She also served as Plover postmaster from 1925 to 1942.

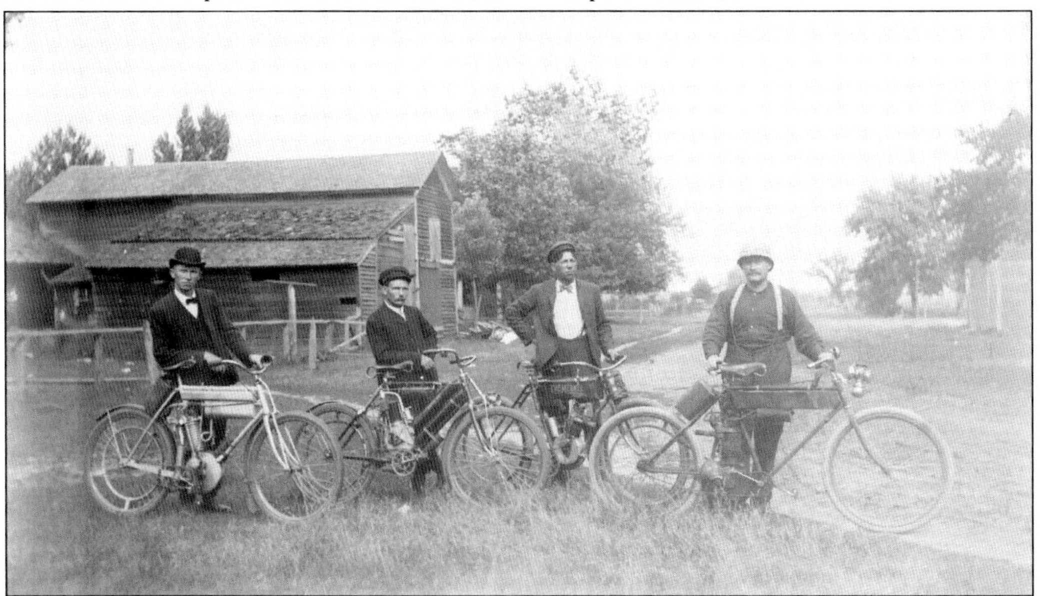

Four men show off their motorcycles; the second from right is identified as "The Merkel." This photograph was presumably taken before the Flying Merkel began production in 1910. The Merkel company was based in Milwaukee during this time.

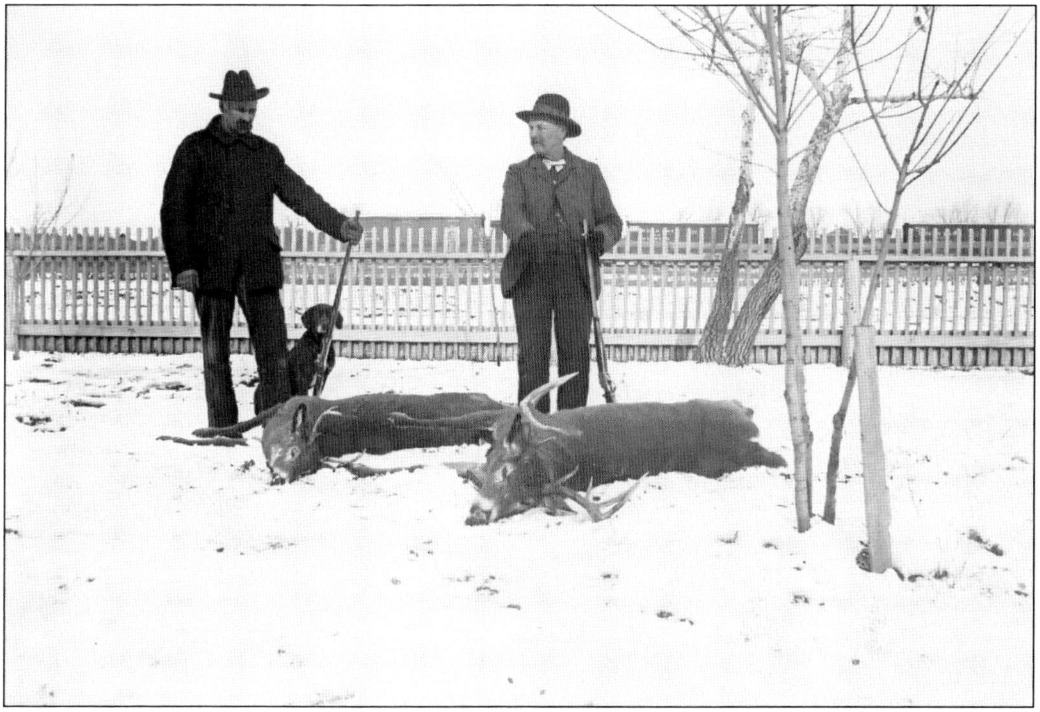

Two Plover men pose with their trophies. In the background are cars for the Green Bay & Western Railroad, indicating this photograph was taken on the north end of the village.

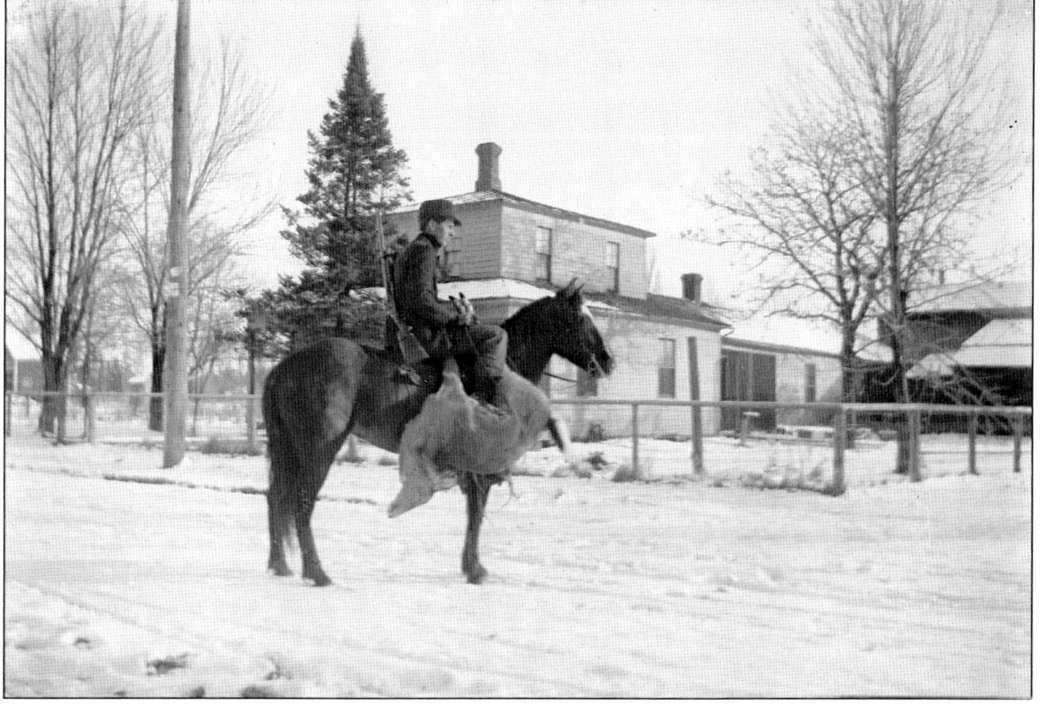

An unidentified man brings home his trophy from the hunt. He is passing in front of the Walter Barnsdale house on First Street on the north end of the village.

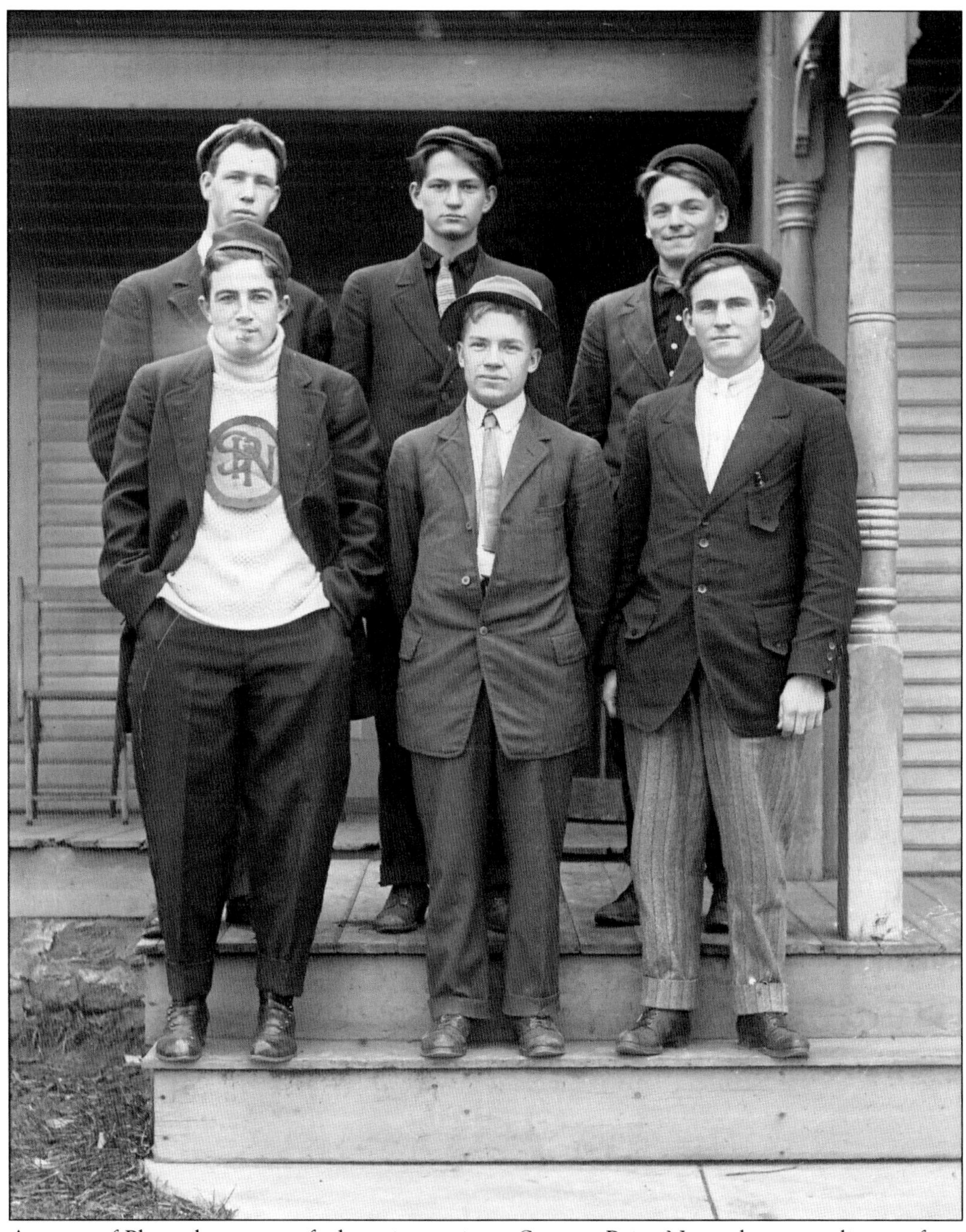

A group of Plover boys, one of whom is wearing a Stevens Point Normal sweater, line up for a photograph. Paul Pierce is on the left in the second row. Many Plover residents attended the Plover grade school until the eighth or ninth grade, then attended Stevens Point High School, and continued their education at the Stevens Point Normal School.

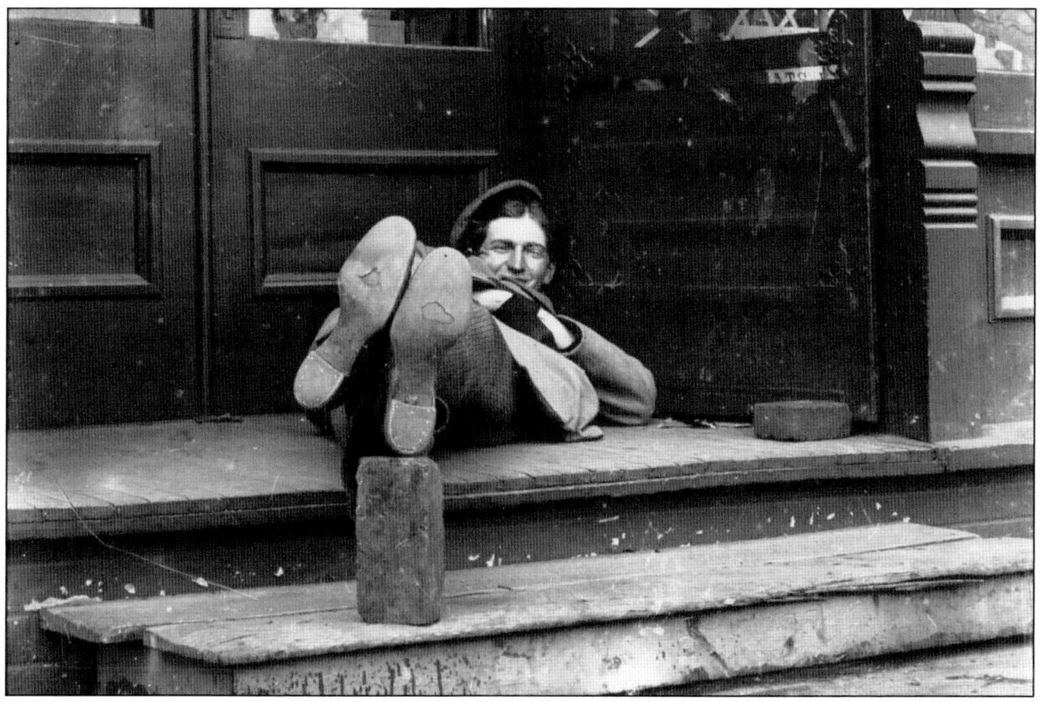

One of James W. Pierce's sons relaxes in the entryway of the Pierce grocery store.

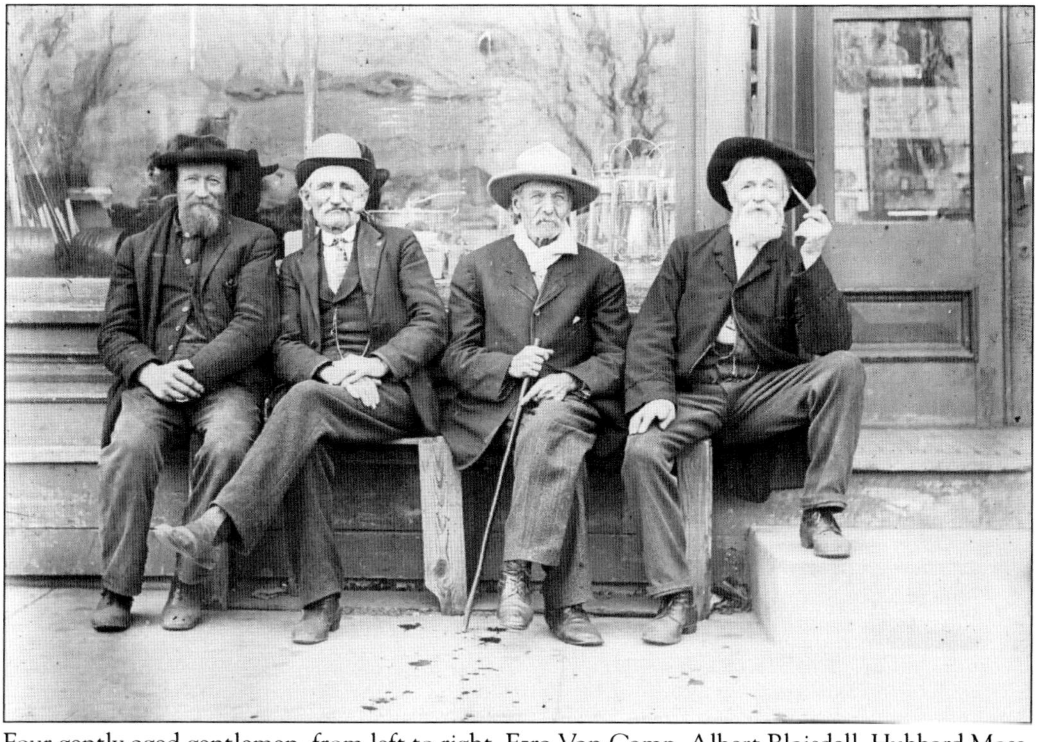

Four gently aged gentlemen, from left to right, Ezra Van Camp, Albert Blaisdell, Hubbard Moss, and George Wilmot, relax outside a store on First Street in the village of Plover.

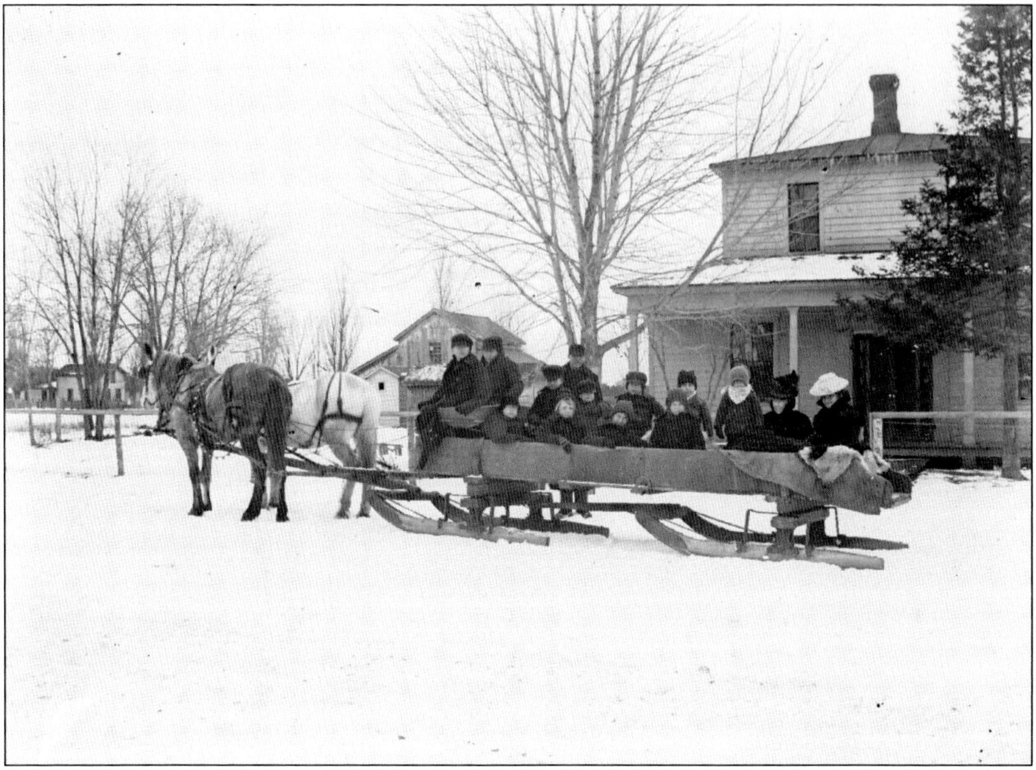

A group of winter revelers piled into a two-horse open sleigh pass in front of the Walter Barnsdale house on First Street.

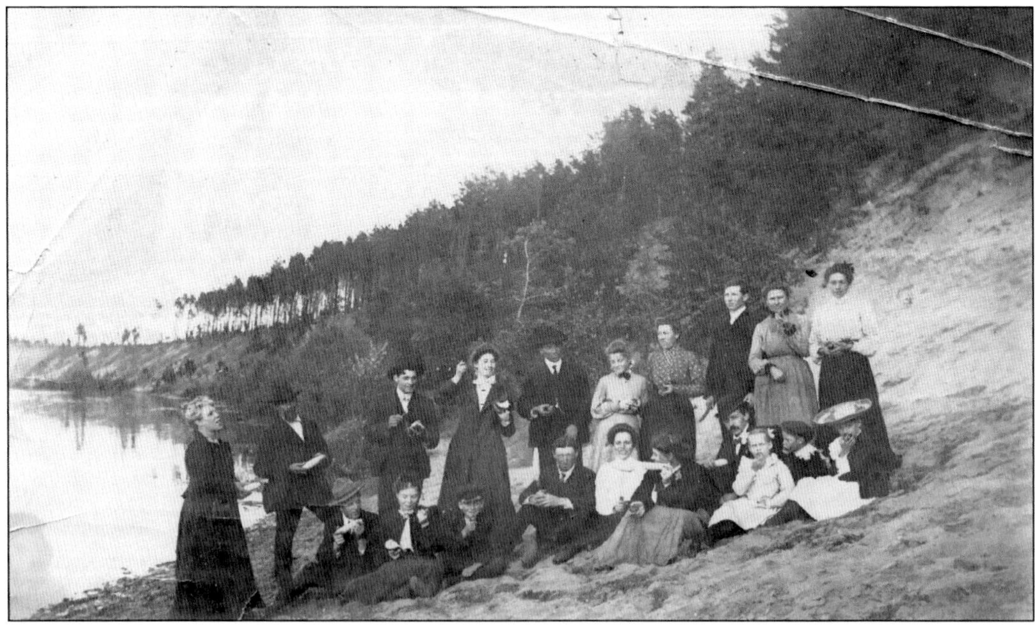

A group gathers on the Yellow Banks of the Wisconsin River. The river was not only used for commerce and travel, but also recreation. Ploverites often used the river and its banks for various activities, including boating, fishing, and picnicking.

Four

Where a Community Comes Together

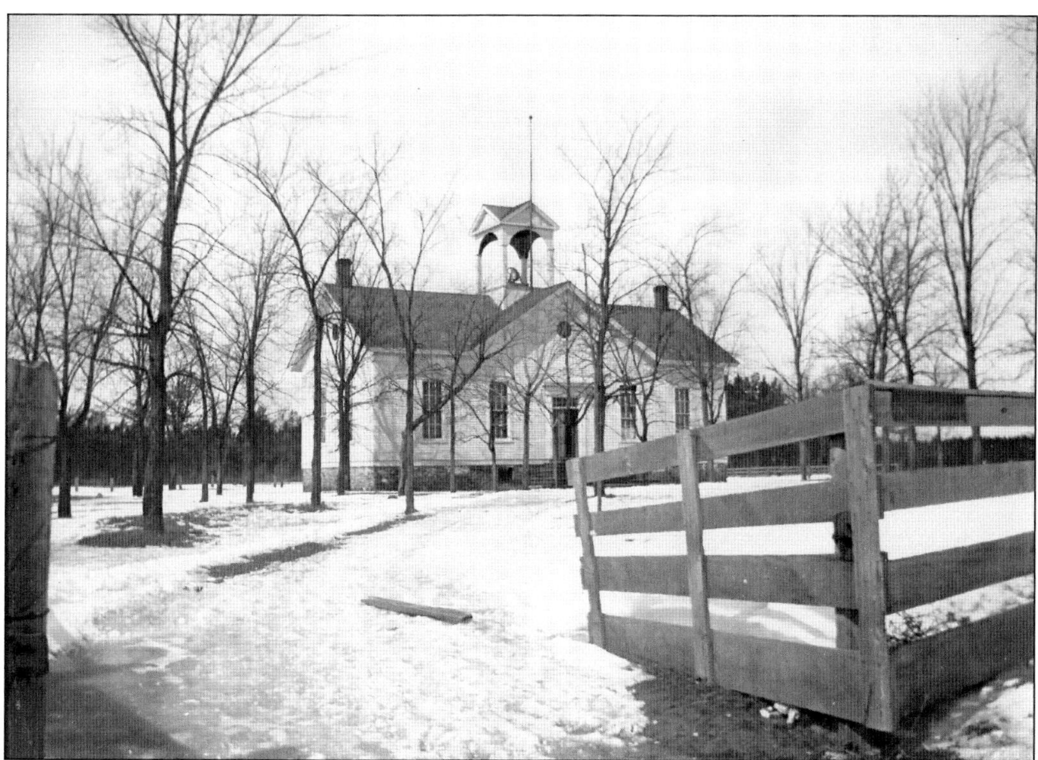

The Plover grade school was built in July 1876 after the prior schoolhouse was destroyed by fire in January 1875. The school pictured stood on the west side of the current Post Road just north of the intersection with River Drive. The school consisted of two rooms, the primary and higher departments, and an addition was put on in 1904. It became known as Roosevelt School in the early 1920s. Construction on the new Roosevelt School at Wisconsin Avenue, School Drive, and Roosevelt Drive started in 1956, and classes began in fall 1957. It is still used today.

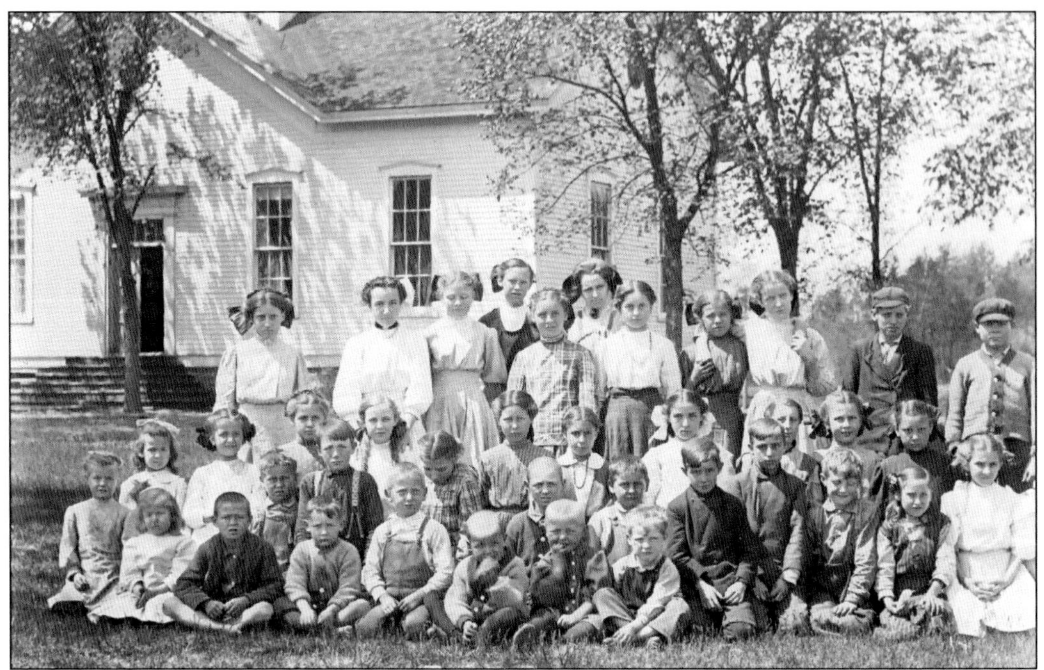

Students stand in front of the Plover grade school around 1910, including children from the following local Barnsdale, Bremmer, Carpenter, Cram, Dakins, Krueger, Newby, Rogers, Shannon, Skinner, and Zinda families. Students from the grade school could continue their education at the high school in Stevens Point.

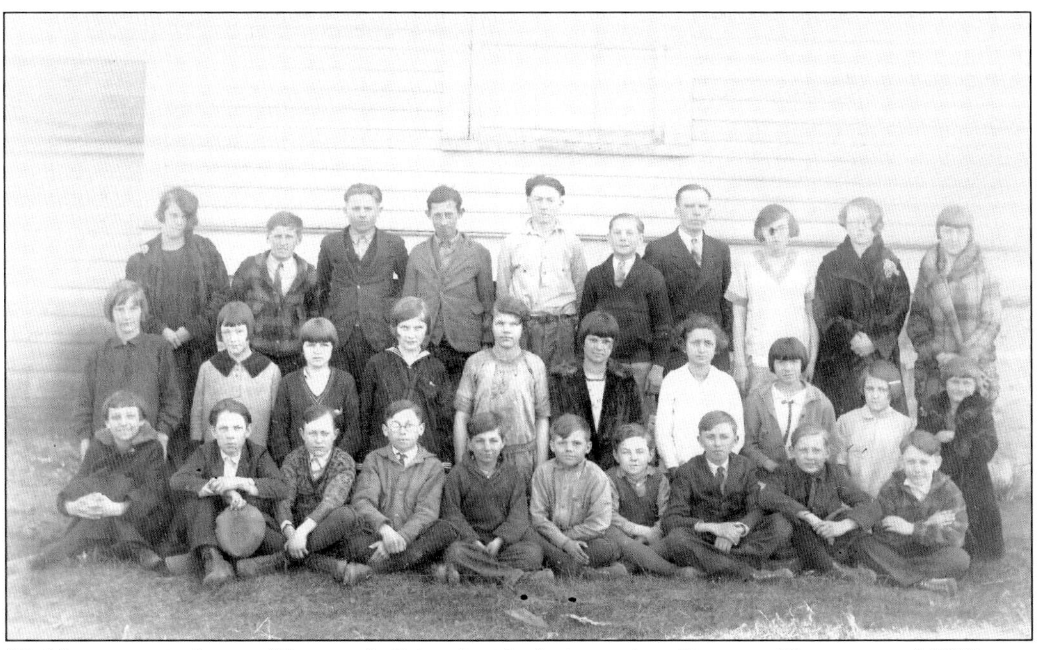

Children pose in front of Roosevelt School with their teacher Gustave Olson around 1930.

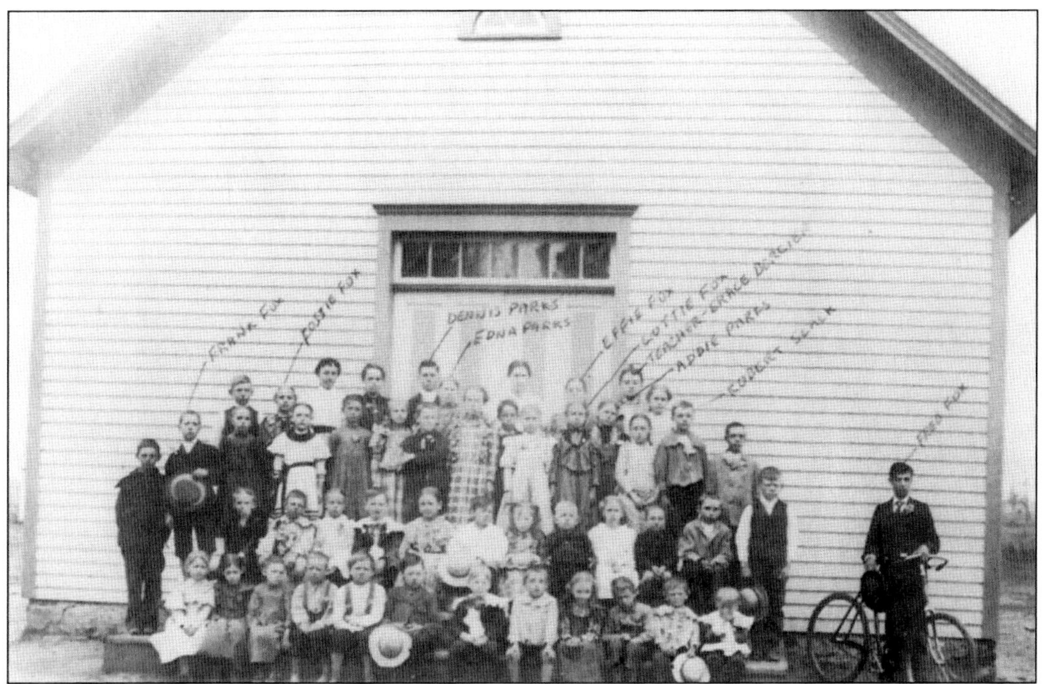

The Meehan schoolhouse was located on Meehan Drive. These students stand in front of the original schoolhouse that was destroyed by a cyclone. Those identified include Frank Fox, Fossie Fox, Dennis Parks, Edna Parks, Effie Fox, Lottie Fox, teacher Grace Borgier, Addie Parks, Robert Slack, and Fred Fox. (Meehan Church.)

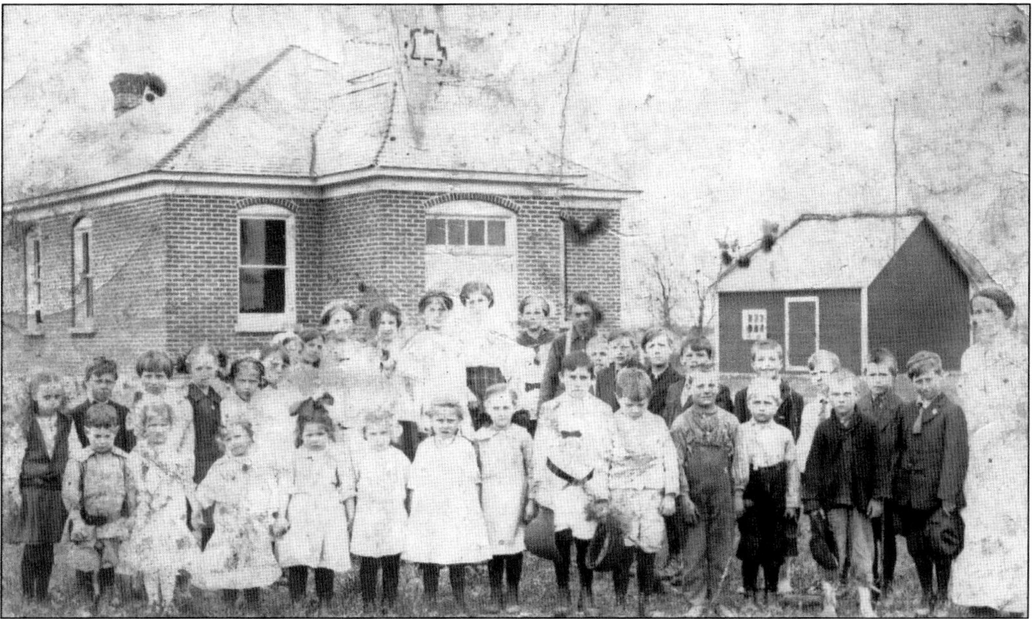

This group is lined up in front of the Meehan schoolhouse in 1918. The Meehan schoolhouse was built when the original wood structure was destroyed by a cyclone on November 25, 1908. This schoolhouse was built by F.M. Playman and completed in June 1909. The school is still standing and located on Meehan Drive, just south of Highway 54.

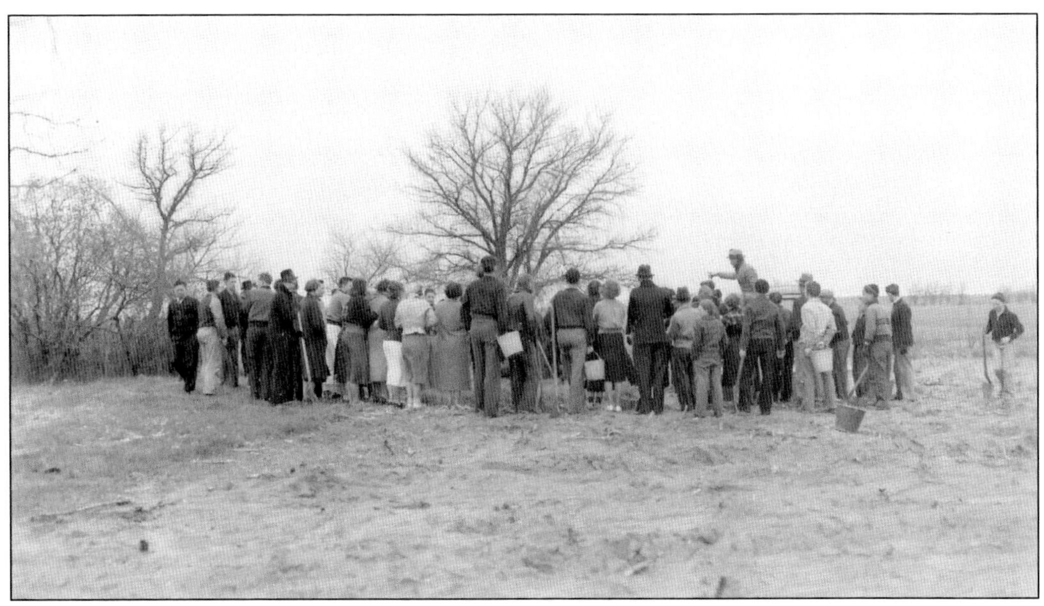

This picture was taken during a tree planting at Boston School Forest in April 1938 with Portage County agent Harrison R. Noble speaking. The Boston School Forest began with 80 acres donated by Harry D. Boston in 1937. The forest was to be divided for use between the Central State Teachers College, the Stevens Point School, and Town of Plover schools Roosevelt, Maine, and Isherwood.

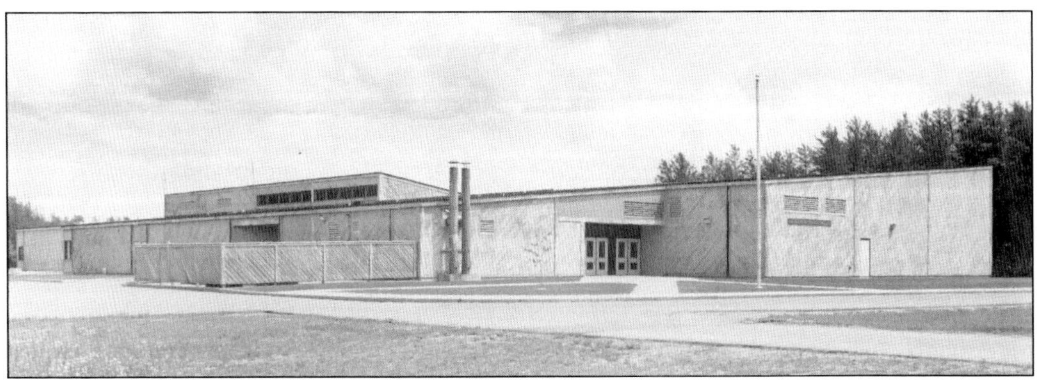

The Plover-Whiting Elementary School officially broke ground on September 13, 1973, and was dedicated on November 23, 1975. The school was designed with an open concept to foster flexibility and individualized learning. A group of women from the Plover area fought hard to get this new elementary school built. (*Stevens Point Journal.*)

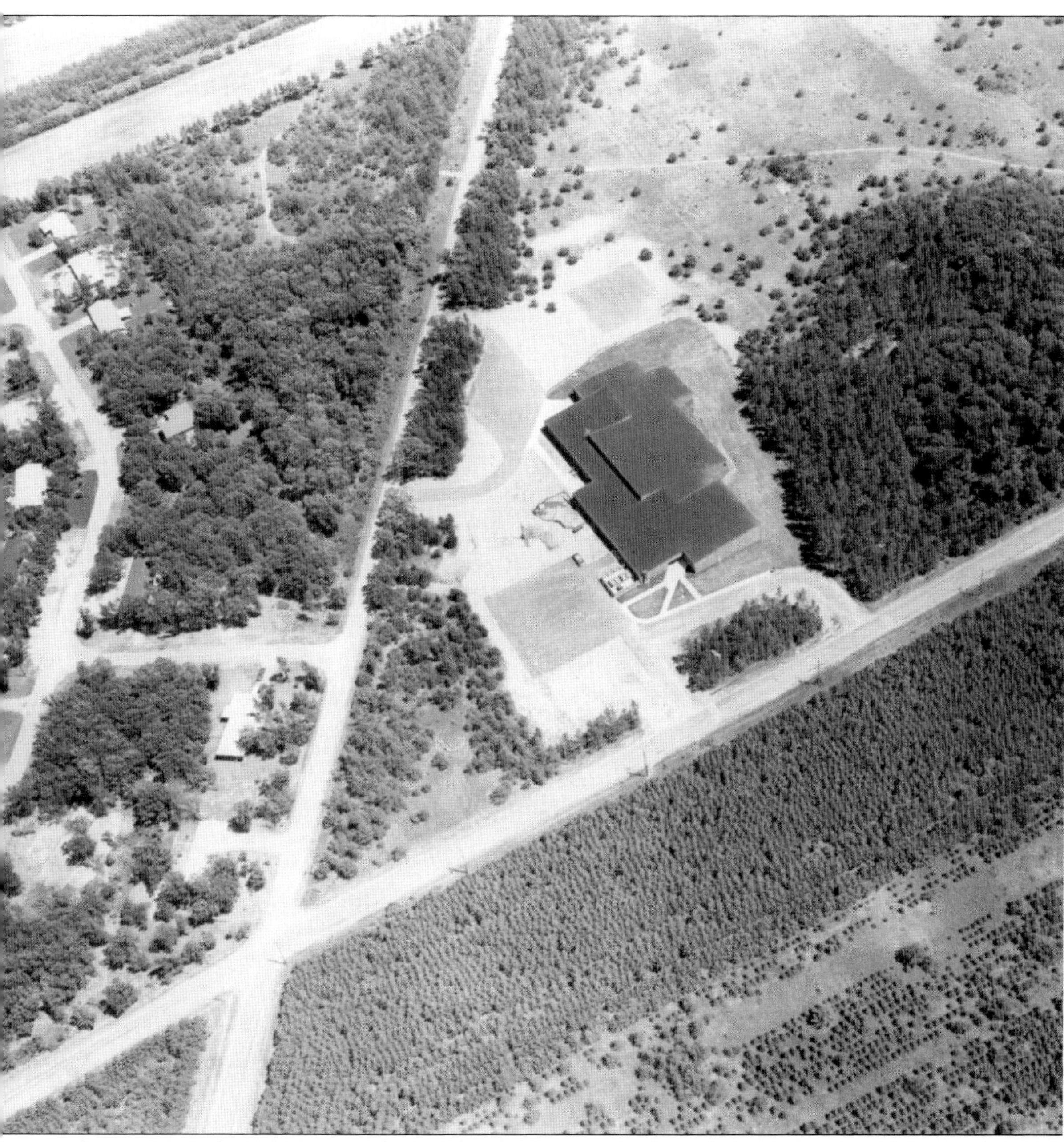

In this c. 1975 aerial view looking southeast is the Plover-Whiting Elementary School at the intersection of Hoover Avenue and Airline Road. This new school was built to alleviate overcrowding.

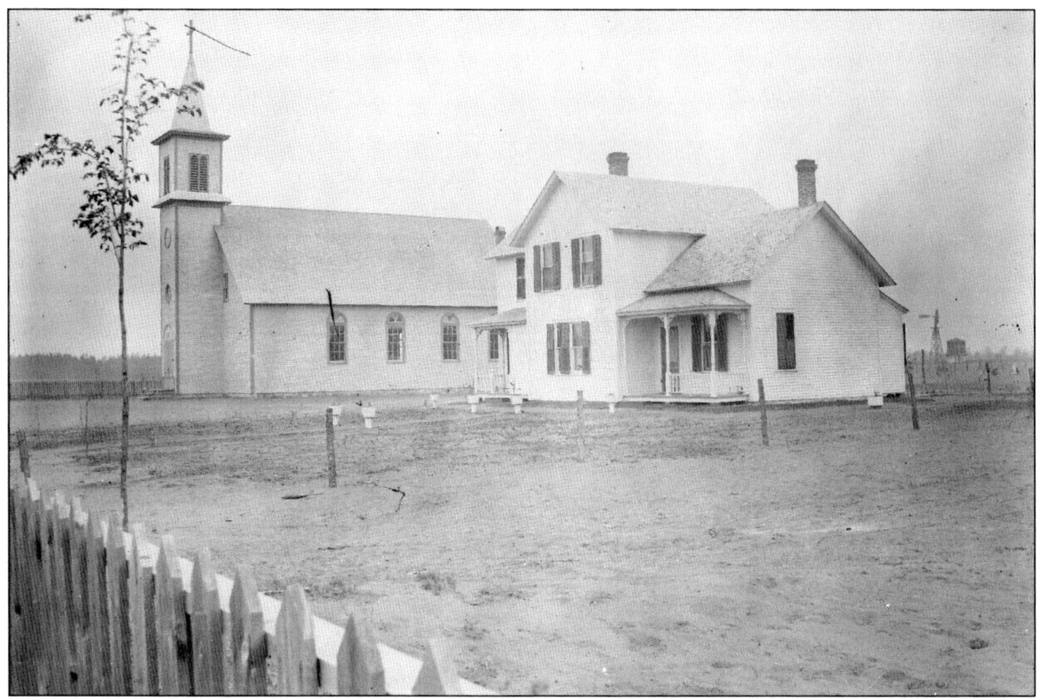

Bishop Sebastian Messmer of the Green Bay Diocese gave permission to 60 families to start a Catholic parish in Plover on October 12, 1896. The church was named after the Polish saint Blessed Bronislava, selected to honor the Polish heritage of a large majority of the parishioners. On the left is the first St. Bronislava Catholic Church building, erected in 1897, and to the right is the rectory, which was built in 1900. This original wooden church structure was struck by lightning and destroyed by fire on August 8, 1910.

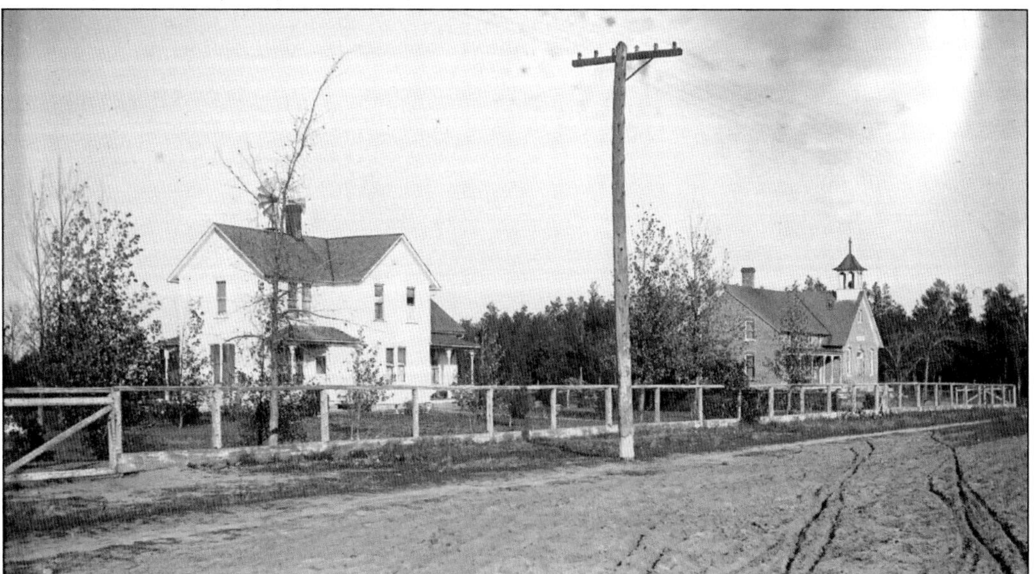

On the left is St. Bronislava rectory, which was built in 1900 and replaced in 1958 with a ranch-style home. To the right is the old St. Bronislava School built in 1908, which burned in 1936. Both of these buildings were located on Highway 54 west of the village.

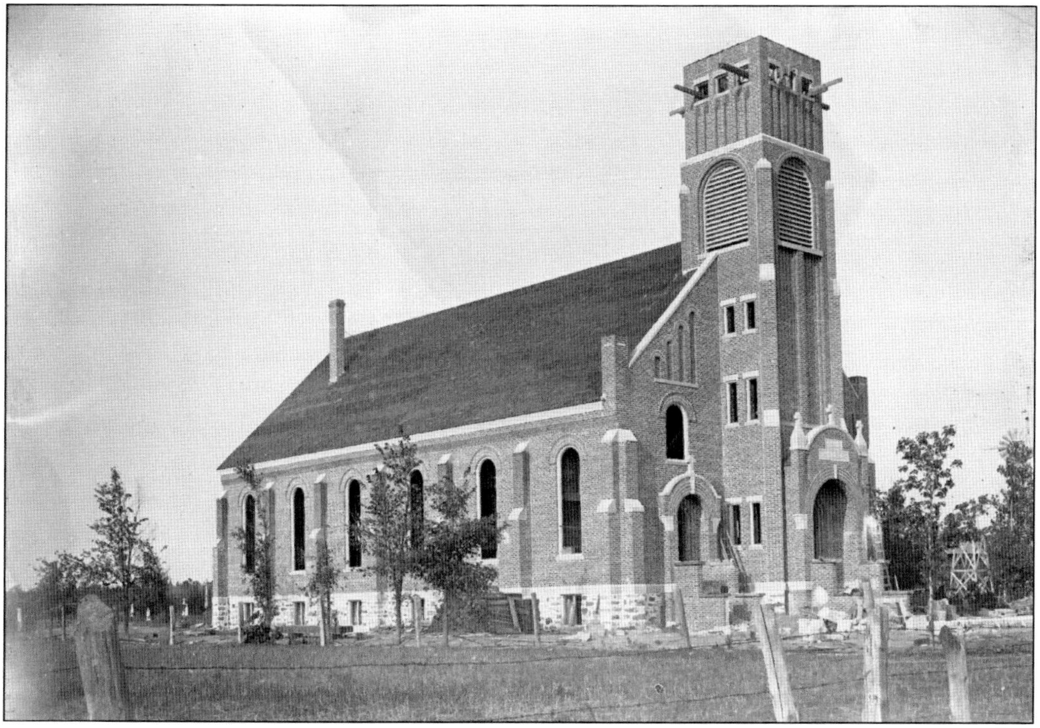

This 1911 photograph of St. Bronislava Catholic Church was taken during construction. The new brick church was built by Kramp & Ceman of Berlin with a bid of $8,250, and the plans were drawn by Frank Spalenka of Stevens Point. This building was dedicated on November 20, 1911, and used until the current church was dedicated on April 28, 1991.

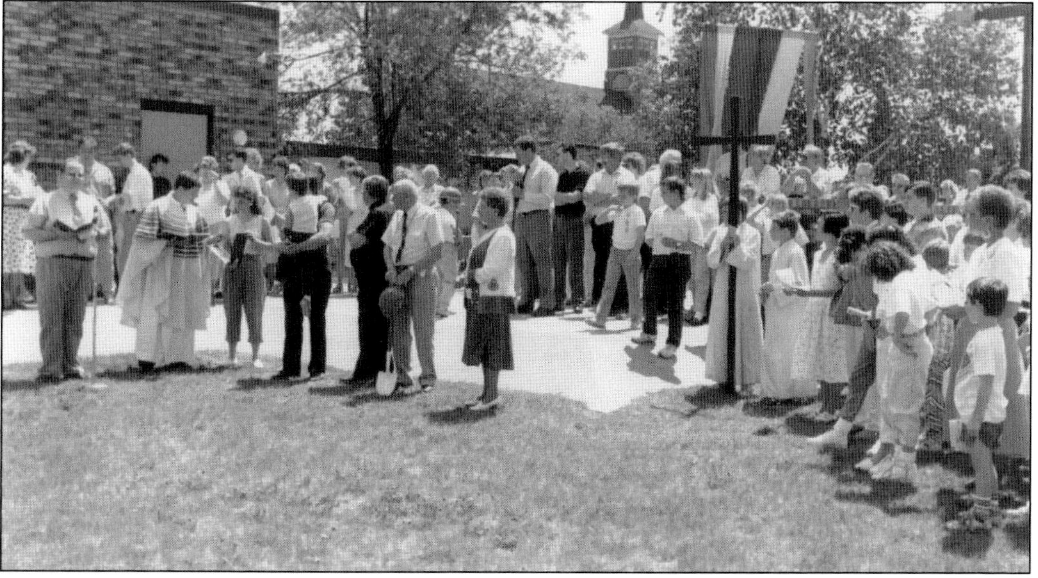

The ground breaking for the new St. Bronislava church is shown here on June 21, 1990. The church was completed and dedicated on April 28, 1991. The priest on the left is Fr. James Logan. (*Stevens Point Journal.*)

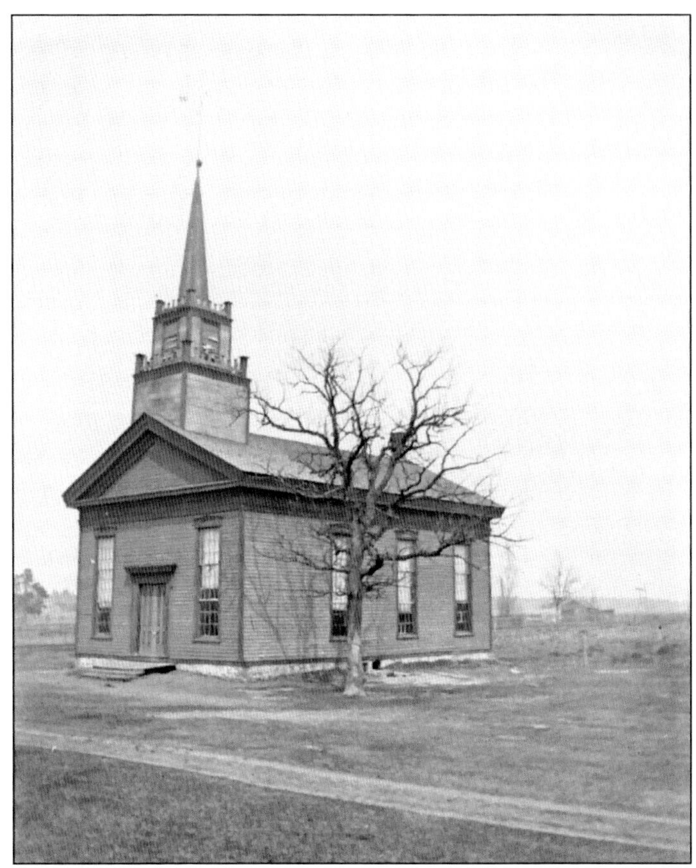

The Plover Methodist Episcopal Church, seen with its steeple still intact, was located south of the railroad tracks on Main Street (now Madison Avenue). The church was originally built by the Presbyterians in 1858 and used until the late 1880s, when their numbers began to dwindle. It was bought by the Methodists in 1887 and used until 1964.

The Portage County Historical Society purchased the Plover Methodist Episcopal Church in 1977, and it was listed in the National Register of Historic Places on March 27, 1980. Currently, the church is used for museum displays in the Portage County Historical Society's Heritage Park.

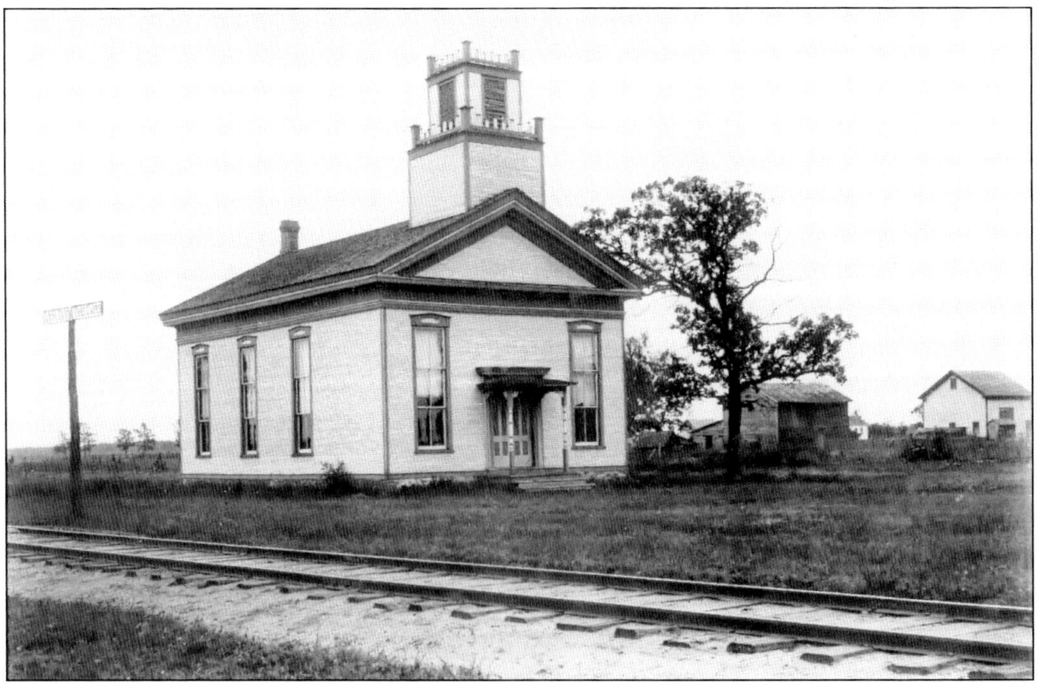

Rev. Herbert Lane was pastor at the Plover Methodist Episcopal Church from 1911 to 1912 and then transferred to Iola. Reverend Lane's first appointment after seminary in England was pastor at Plover and Buena Vista, and it is said that his English mannerisms made him quite conspicuous around town.

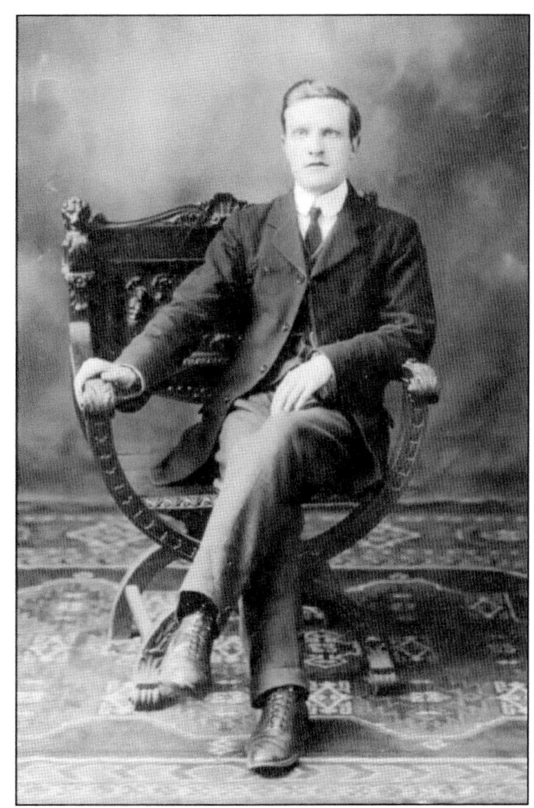

The Plover Methodist Episcopal Church choir gathers in the front room of Leo Pierce's house for a party in 1934. From left to right are (first row) Leo Pierce and Merle Rupp; (second row) Marion Calkins, Lillian Mansavage, Dorothy Calkins, Lois Espenscheid, Florence Engford, and Eva Pierce; (third row) Jane Pierce, Bernice Cartmill, Evelyn Dakins, George Cartmill Jr., Gustave Olson, Cecelia Olson, George Gilman, Ruth Yorton, unidentified, Lois McCormick, Jack Maxfield, Hazel Thierback, Minnie Cliff (minister), Donald Calkins, Irma Wiese, Harold Knutson, and Harry Engford.

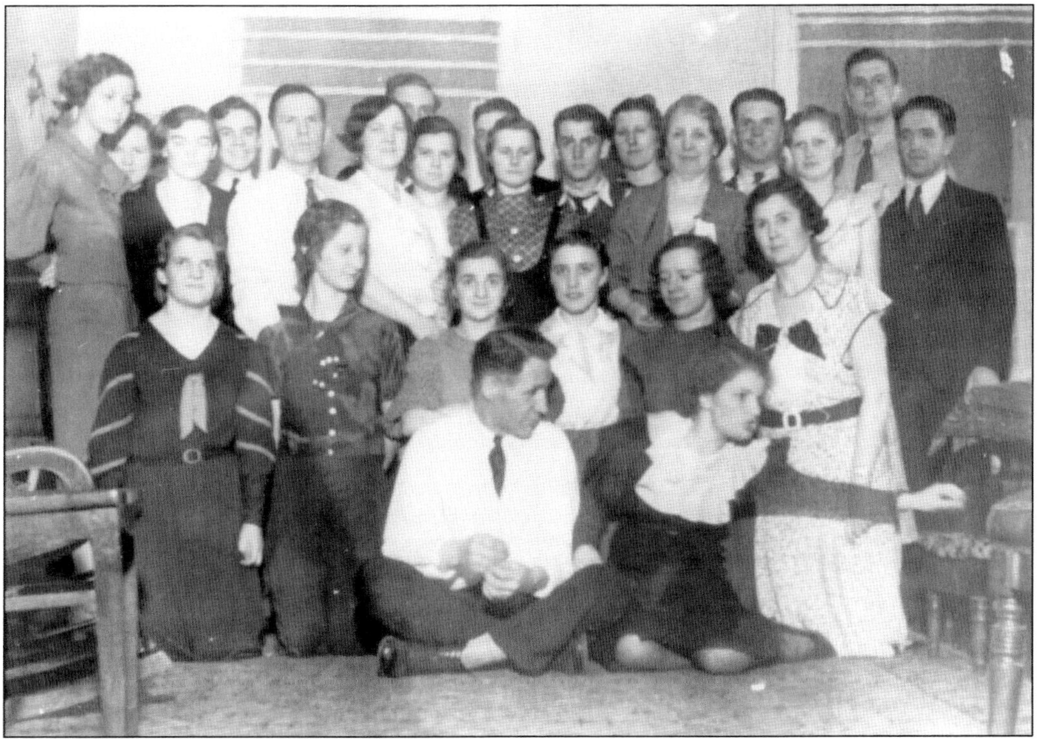

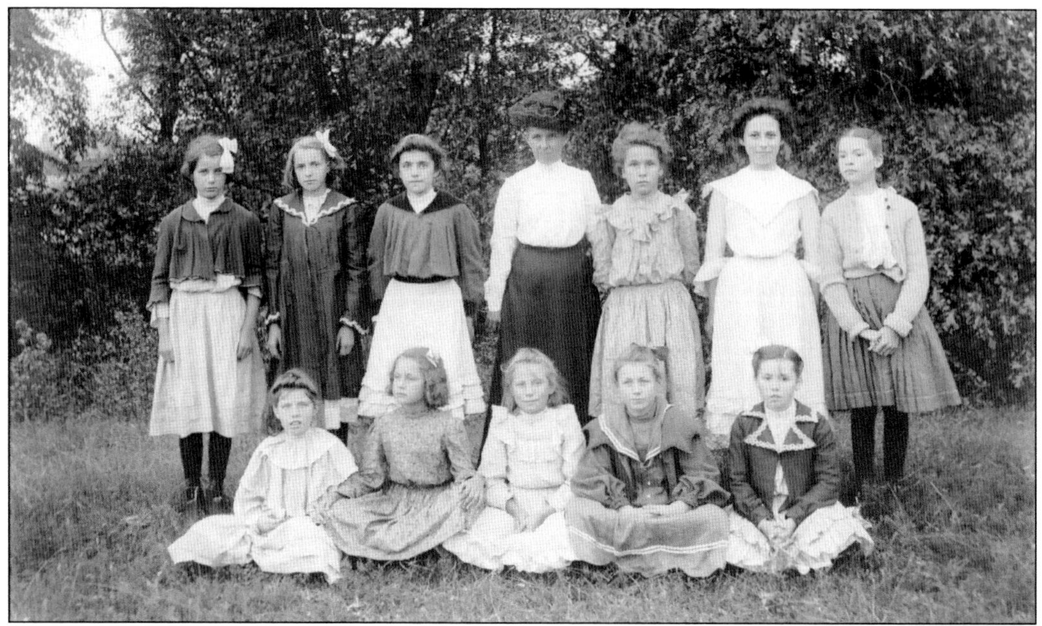

Mayme Skinner's Plover Methodist Episcopal Church Sunday school class picnic in Springville is shown here on August 9, 1904. From left to right are (first row) Bea Donovan, Eva Gee, Effie Sterling, Elizabeth Barnsdale, and Mabel Altenburg; (second row) Bernice Pierce, Isla Warner, Frances Donovan, Skinner, Halley Clendenning, Etta Bahner, and Eva Blaisdell.

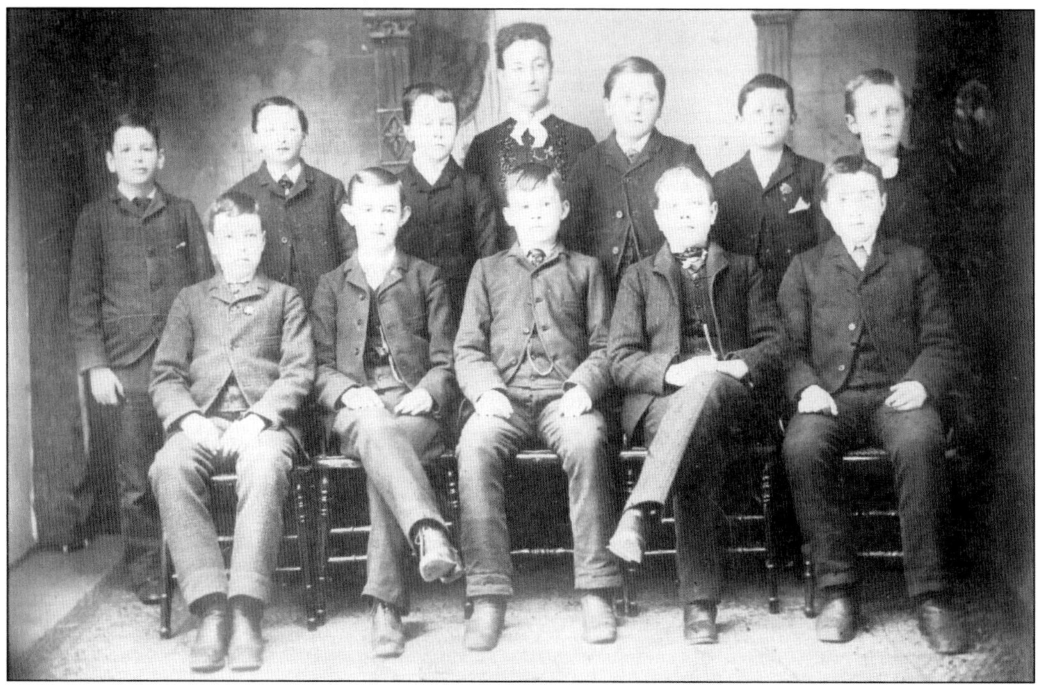

A Sunday school class of the Plover Methodist Episcopal Church poses for a photograph. From left to right are (first row) Paul ?, Wilmot Pierce, Charles Bremmer, Frank Bean, and Elmer Dickerman; (second row) Wallin Verzy, Olaf ?, Maurice Halladay, teacher Eva Pierce, Joe Baker, Kellogg Bahner, and George Packard.

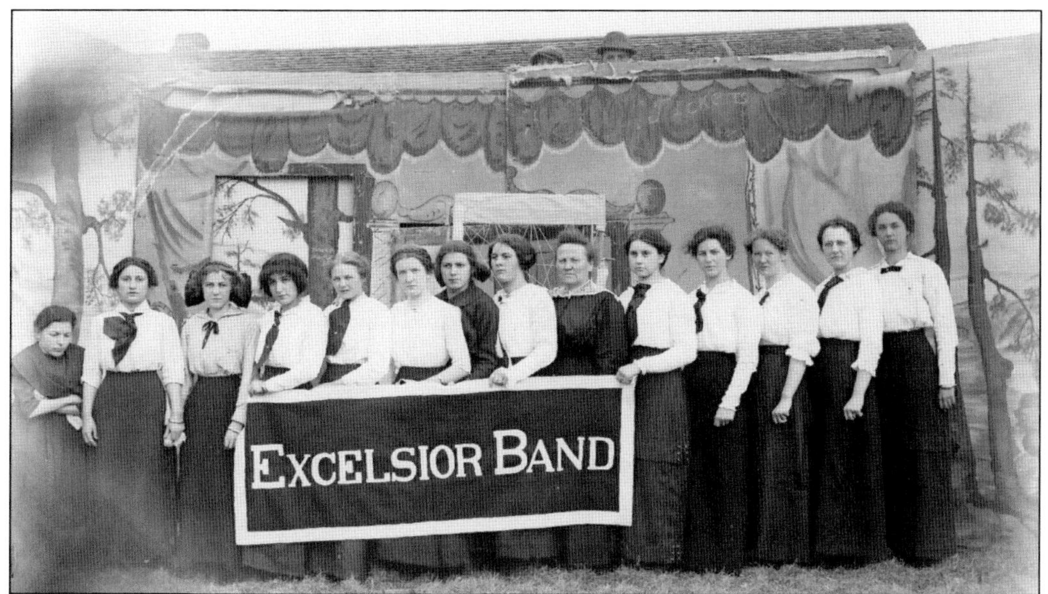

The Excelsior Band was an organization of the Plover Methodist Episcopal Church made up of Florence Parker's advanced Sunday school class of young ladies. The group put on plays, hosted lecture courses, and organized social gatherings. The officers in 1914 were Bernice Pierce, president; Hazel Calkins, vice president; Irene Newby, secretary; Frances Barnsdale, treasurer; and Eva Gee, press correspondent.

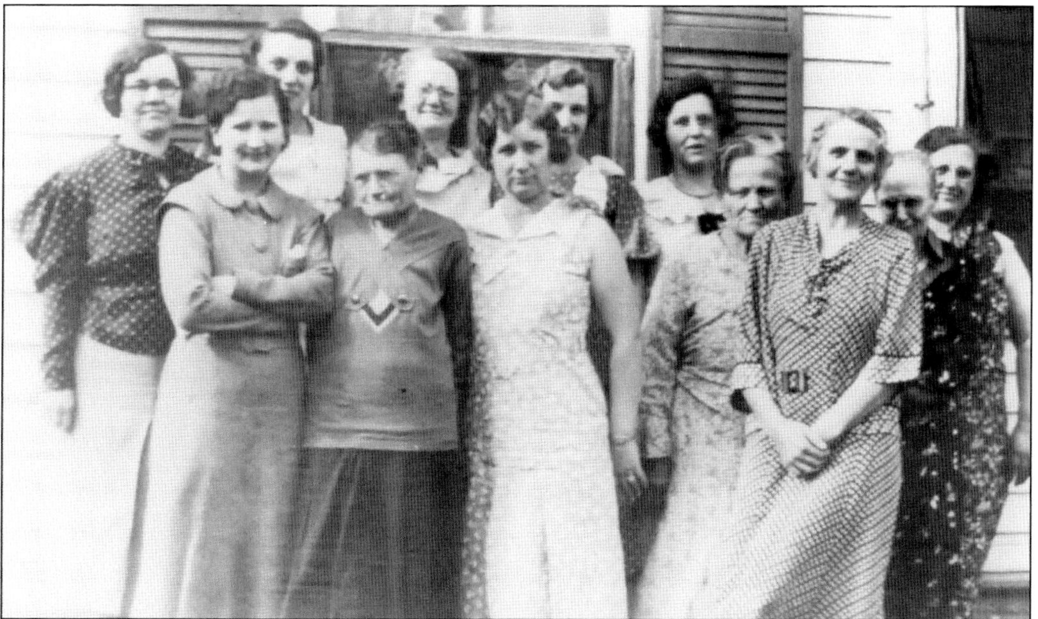

The Busy Stitcher's Club poses for a photograph in front of the Maxfield garage (known as the Morgan House) in 1933. This social organization made the upkeep of the Plover Cemetery central to their purpose. They planted flowers, cleared unwanted growth, planned for the purchase of a new fence, and organized fundraisers for their endeavors. The Plover Cemetery was an integral part of the town, with the Decoration Day commemorations being held there, attracting many visitors and past residents from far away. The group later changed its name to the Plover Women's Club.

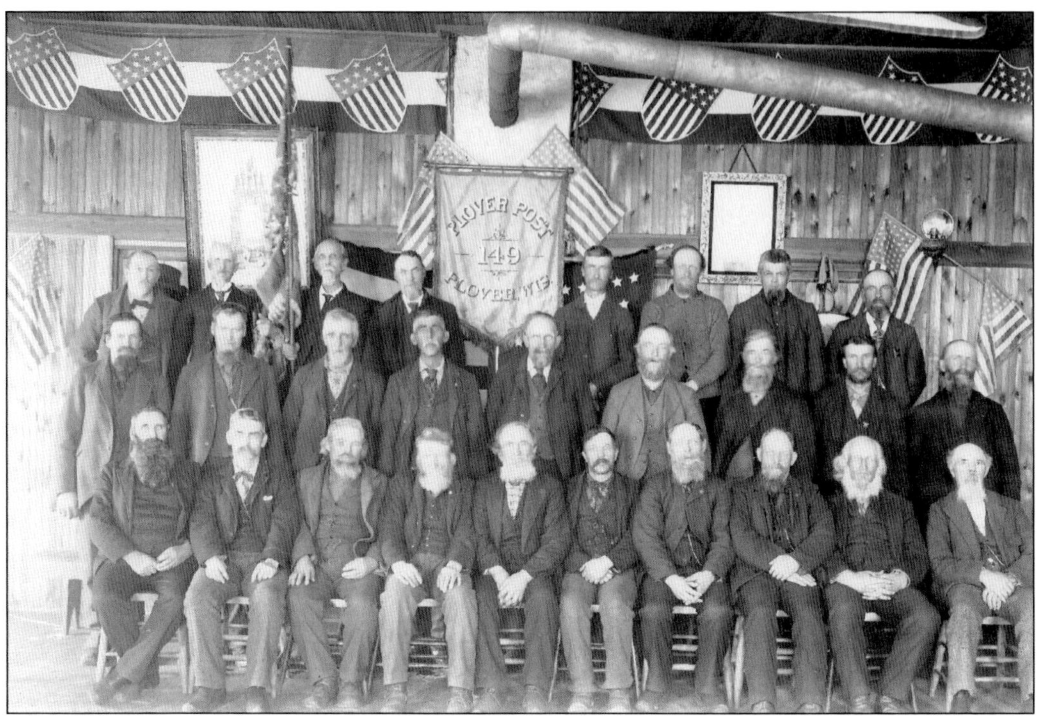

Members of the Grand Army of the Republic Plover Post 149 sit for a photograph. From left to right are (first row) N.C. Parsons, LeRoy Shannon, Walter Parsons, ? Bailey, ? Stover, Billy Crofoot, Fon Crofoot, ? Eagleburger, ? Foss, and ? Crary; (second row) Volney Topping, William Hurlbut, H. Sherman, William White, B.F. Parker, John McGowan, A.M. Blaisdell, unidentified, and Silas D. Clark; (third row) William Shepard, James A. Bremmer, H.G. Ingersoll, H. Webster, Walter Whittaker, Hubbard Moss, Henry Johnson, and Schuyler Whittaker.

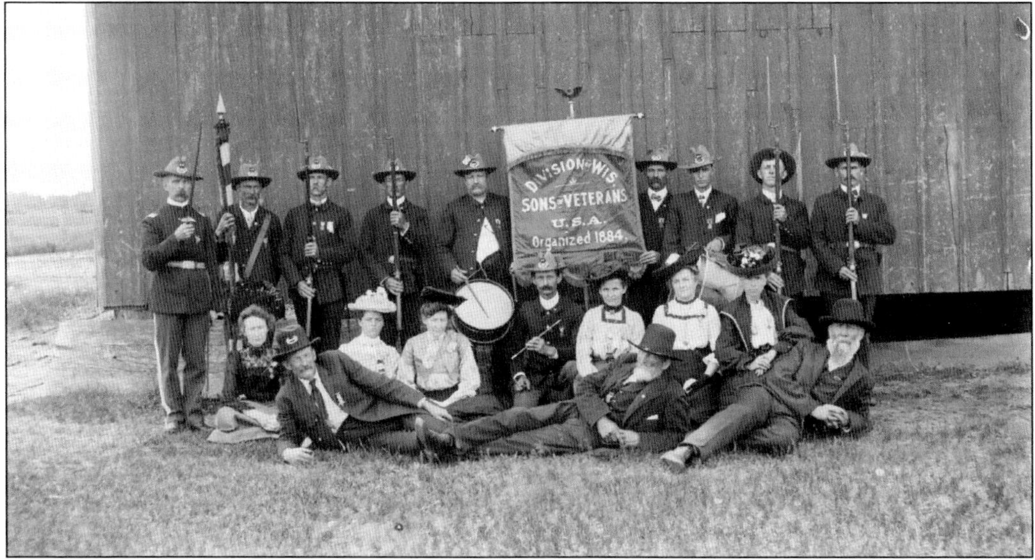

The Portage County Sons of Veterans gather for an event in Plover in June 1904. Plover's camp was known as A.J. Welton Camp 83 of the Sons of Veterans before it merged with the Stevens Point camp. The Sons of Veterans was under the umbrella of the Grand Army of the Republic.

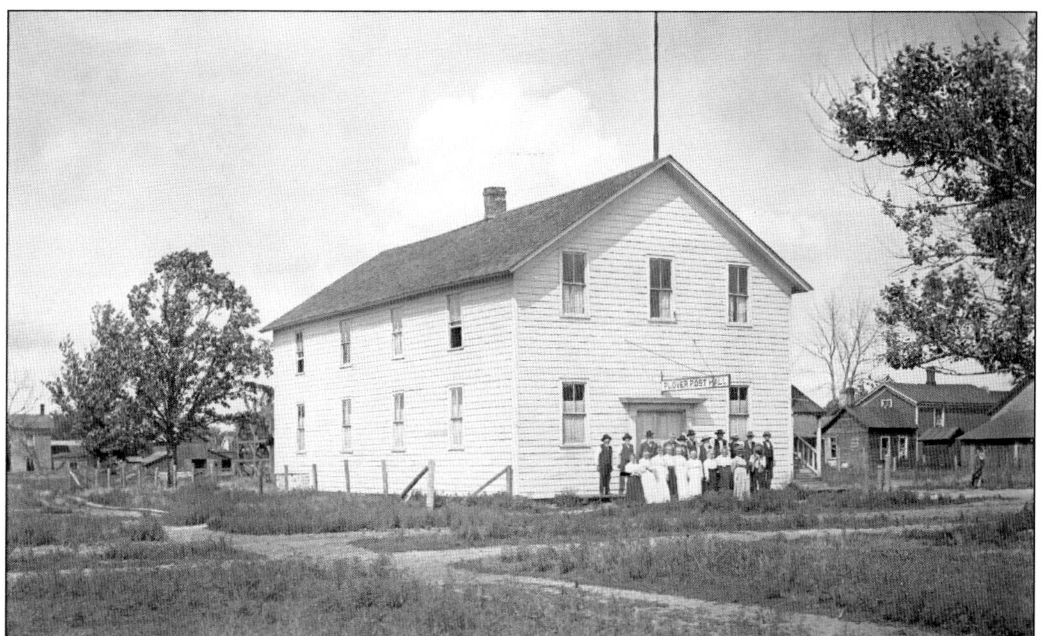

This photograph shows one of many social gatherings at the Grand Army of the Republic's Plover Post Hall. The hall was located on the northeast corner of Green and Second Streets (current Earhart Avenue) and was also used as the town hall. The hall was built around 1885 and destroyed by fire in 1945. The former town hall was built on this site, and currently, the Plover Town Hall Center is there.

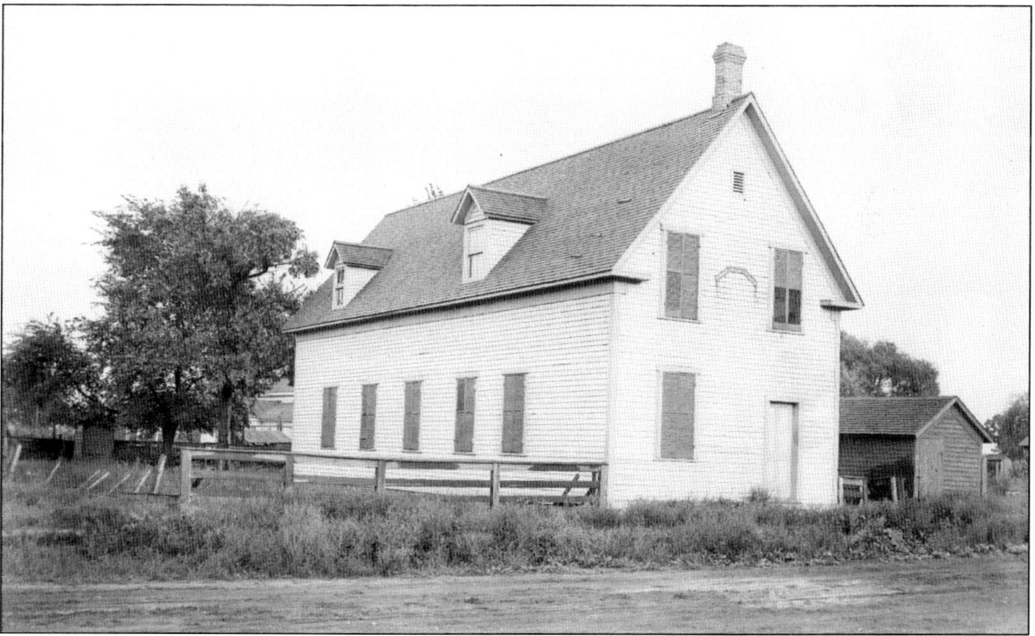

The Odd Fellows Hall of the Independent Order of Odd Fellows (IOOF) was located on the east side of First Street between Willow and Walnut Streets. Many of the early residents of Plover were members of the IOOF. The hall used to be the old Plover graded school, which was built prior to 1858, and was later purchased by Jay Phelps and used as part of his house and business.

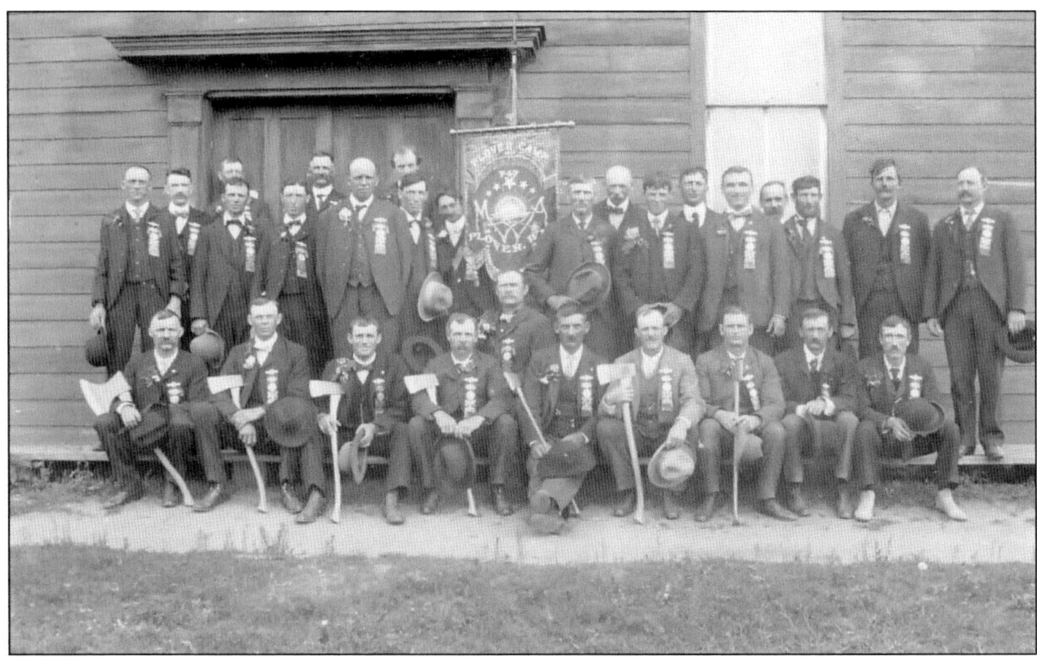

Plover Camp 747 of the Modern Woodmen of America was organized on October 16, 1888, and was a fraternal benefit society established to provide life insurance benefits for its members. The 10 names on the charter list include: F.H. Bahner, H.H. Moore, L.H. Cowles, E. Woodbury, D.V. Bean, W.C. Wiley, E.J. Jentsch, S.F. Durga, Frank Tyler, and Henry A. Marlatt.

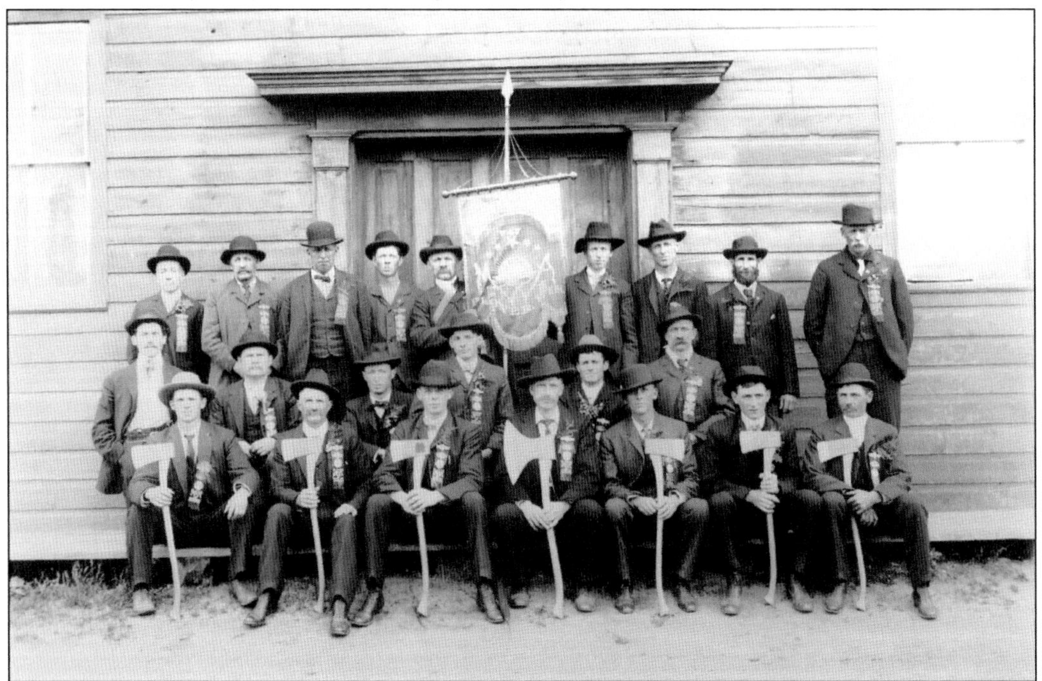

The Modern Woodmen of America Plover Camp No. 747 stands in front of Bourn's Hardware Store dressed in full regalia to participate in the 1904 Decoration Day. The woodmen occupied the hall over the store starting in 1895.

In 1910, there were eight different camps of the Modern Woodmen of America in Portage County. These camps raised money to build a cottage at the Modern Woodmen Sanatorium at Colorado Springs, Colorado, to be used for Modern Woodmen of Portage County who might be afflicted with tuberculosis.

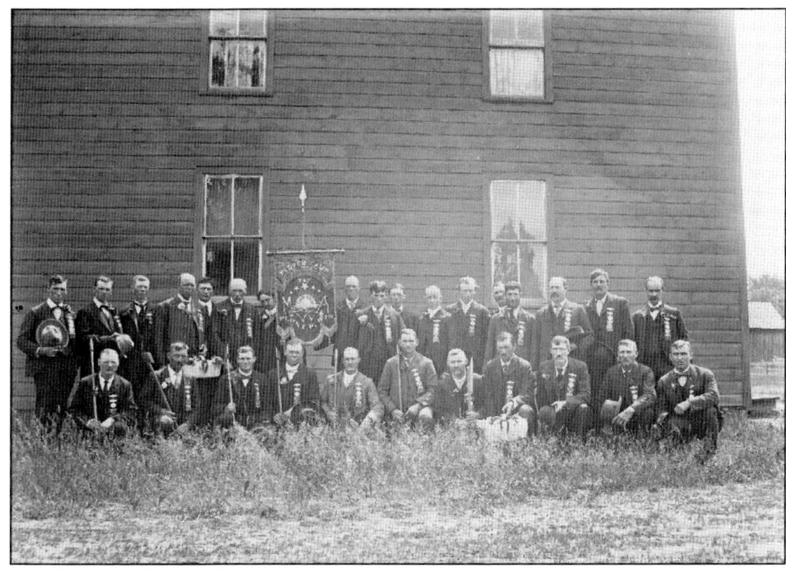

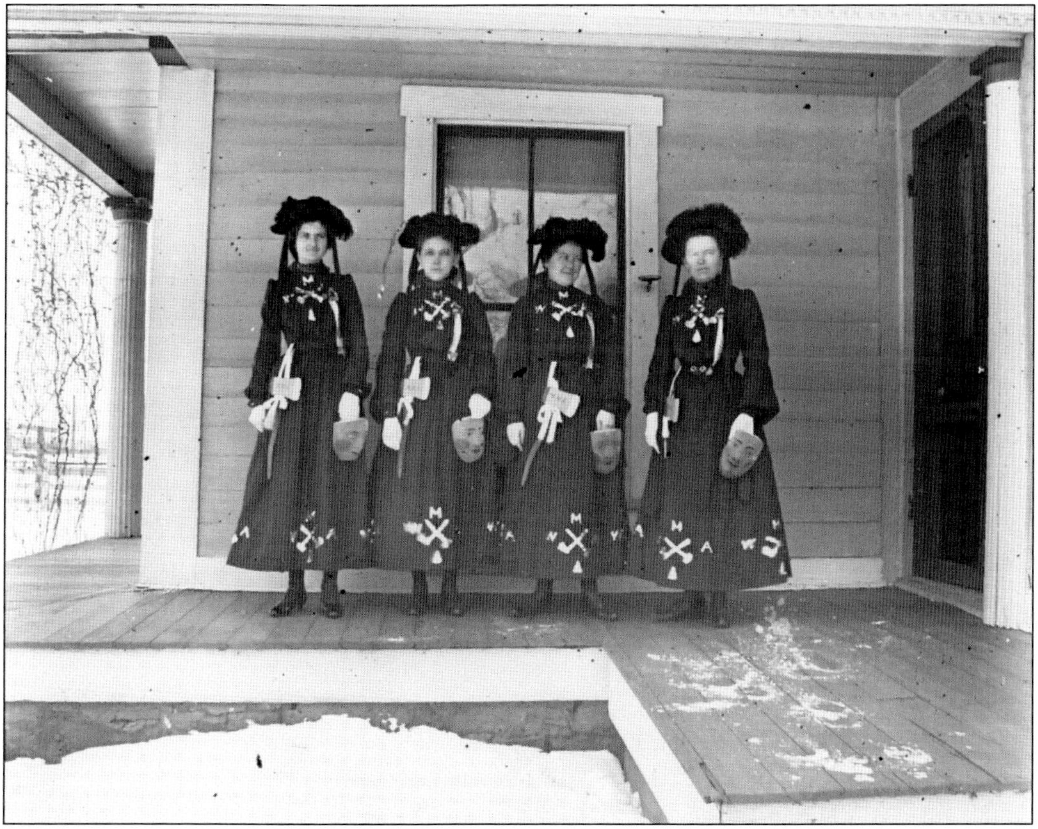

Four ladies stand on the porch of the Potts house dressed in Modern Woodmen of America regalia and holding masks. A ladies' auxiliary of the Modern Woodmen was created nationally in 1888 called the Royal Neighbors of America, and Plover organized the St Patrick's Camp No. 4127 on March 17, 1905. Every year, they held a celebration with entertainment and dinner around St. Patrick's Day.

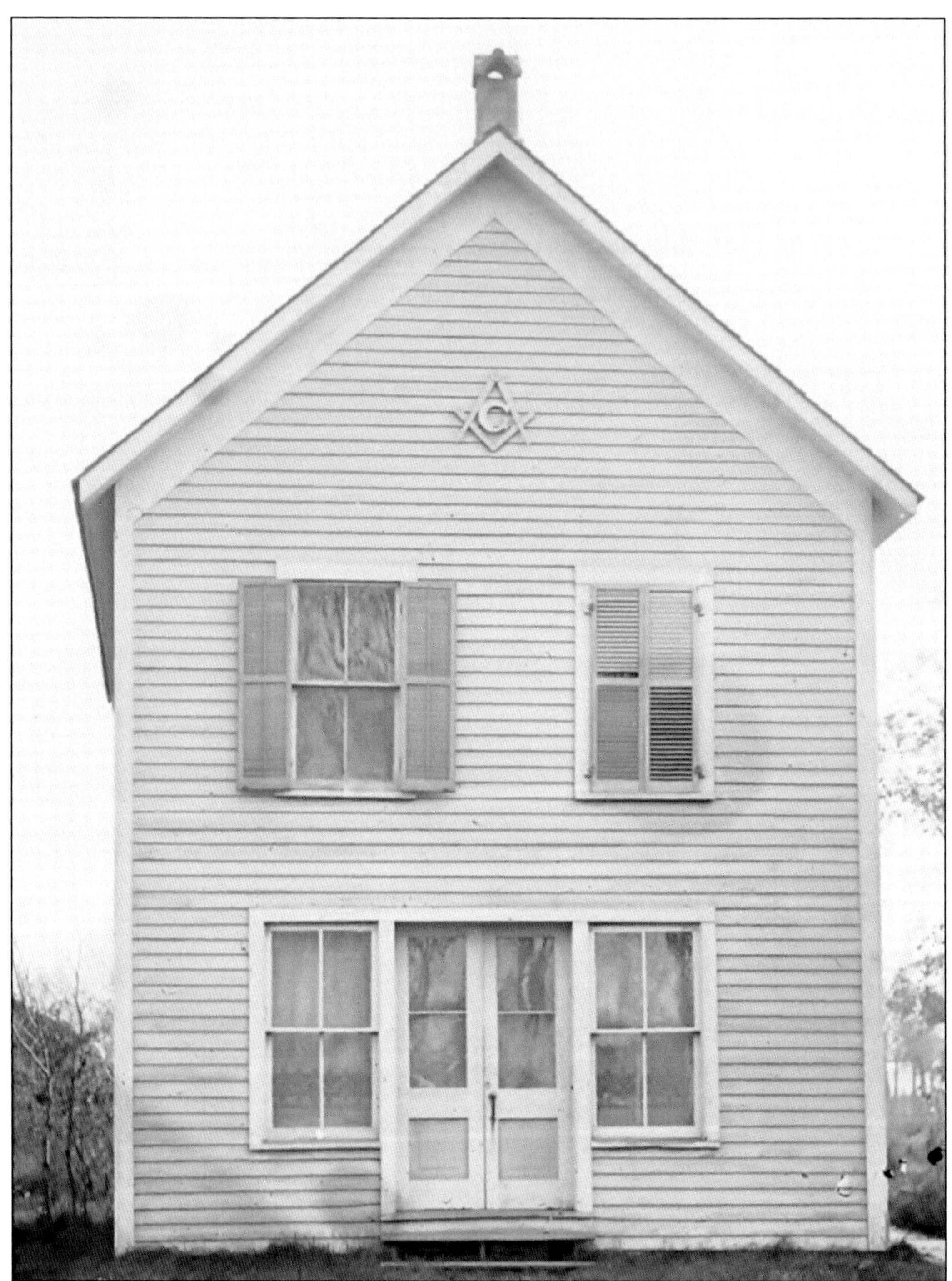

Plover Masonic Hall of Lodge No. 76 was located on the northeast corner of South and First Streets. Many of the early prominent residents of Plover were masons including Luther Hanchett, James A. Alban, F.E. Halladay, J.O. Raymond, and James W. Pierce. The lodge was granted dispensation in 1854 and organized under charter in 1856. In 1875, this building replaced the original masonic hall, which was originally the courthouse, after it burned in 1872.

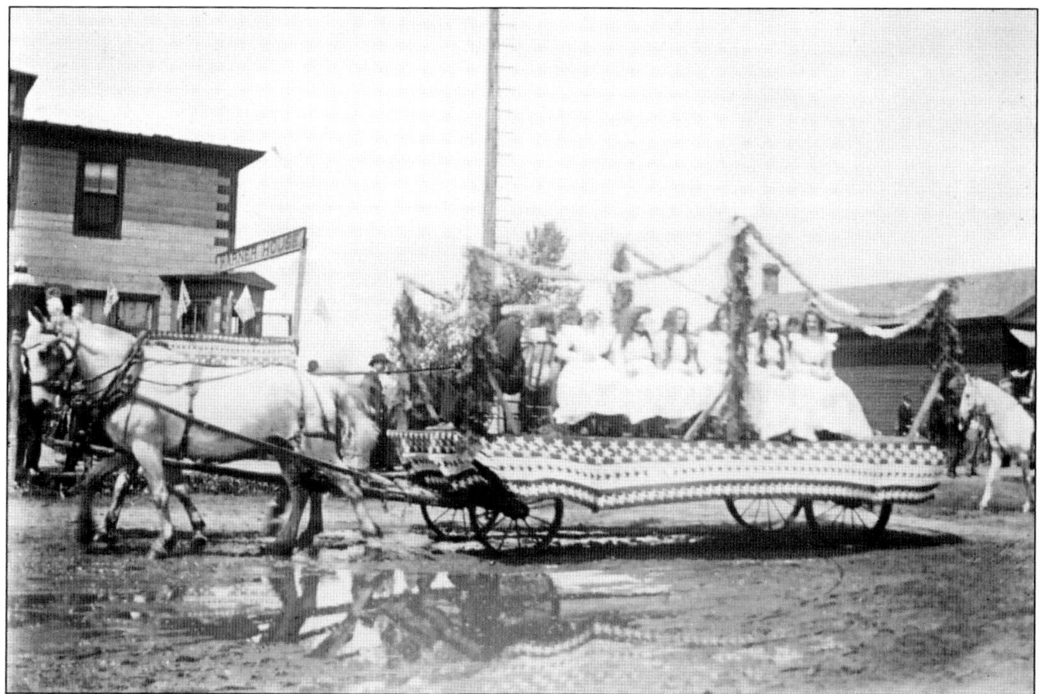

A float for the 1900 Fourth of July parade crosses the intersection of Willow and First Streets in front of the Warner House and liberty pole. This float contains young ladies, each dressed in a white dress, representing the 13 original states. The 1900 celebration included baseball, a pigeon shoot, foot and bike races, tug of war, and fireworks.

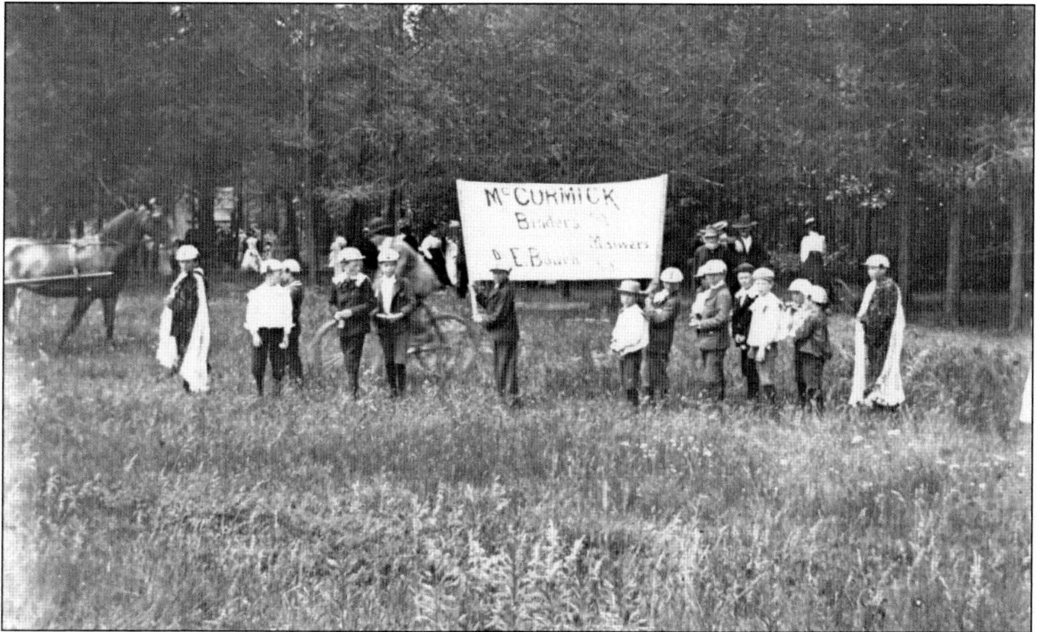

A group of children line up for a parade holding a sign advertising McCormick Binders and Mowers sold by Algie E. Bourn, a purveyor of farm machinery and hardware in the village of Plover until he was elected to county sheriff around 1903 and moved to Stevens Point.

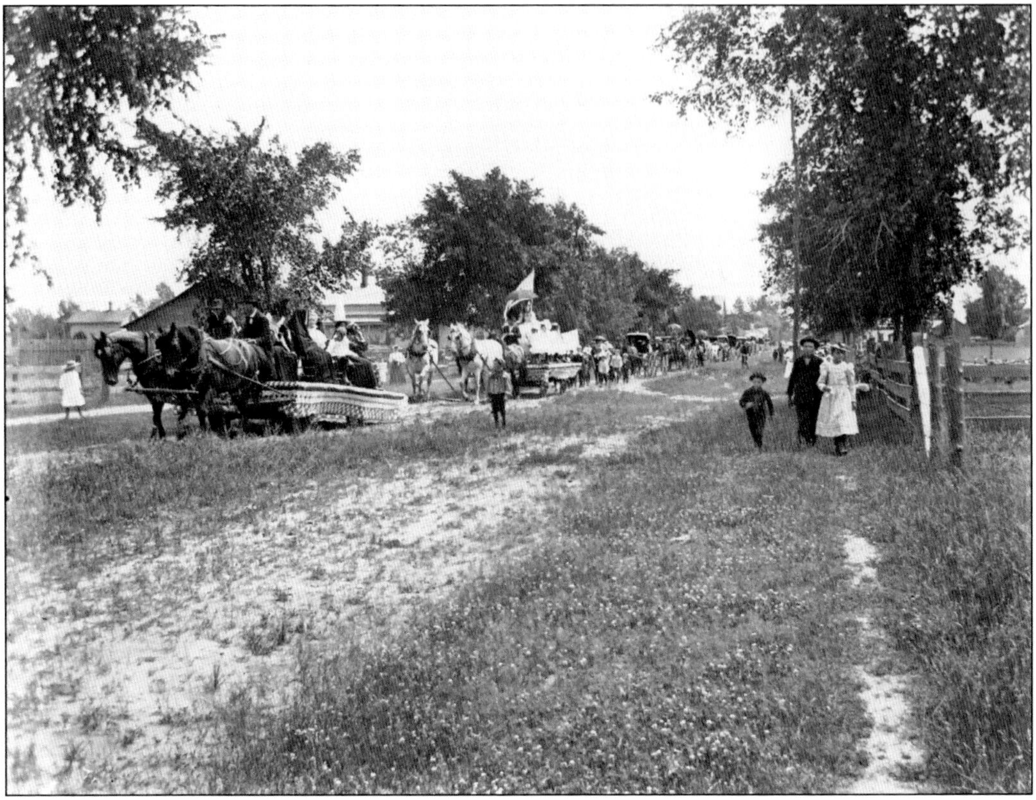

The village comes together to observe Decoration Day. As a precursor to Memorial Day, Decoration Day was commemorated by parading to the local cemetery and decorating the headstones of soldiers. The event in Plover included a parade leading out of town to the Plover Cemetery, where a speaker would deliver a speech.

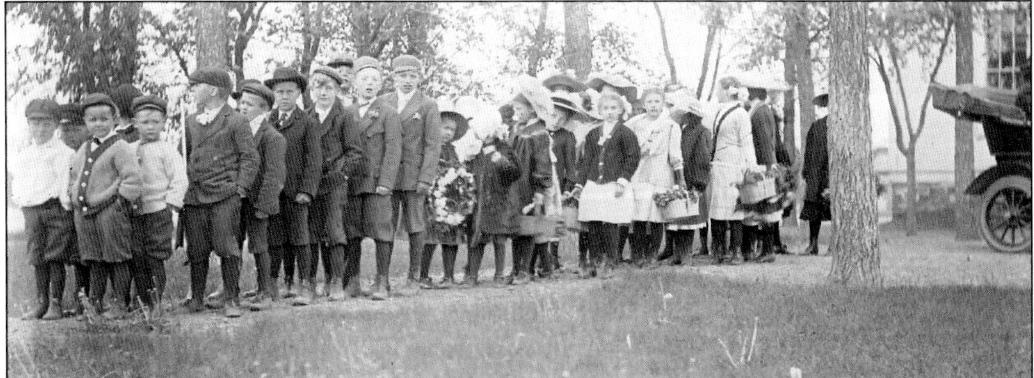

A group of schoolchildren line up at the Plover school for Decoration Day. Many children carry flowers that will be used to decorate headstones of veterans at the Plover Cemetery. According to Pat Collins, writer of the long-running "Tap Snilloc" and "Sportscope" columns in the *Stevens Point Journal*, Decoration Day was an annual event that schoolchildren looked forward to.

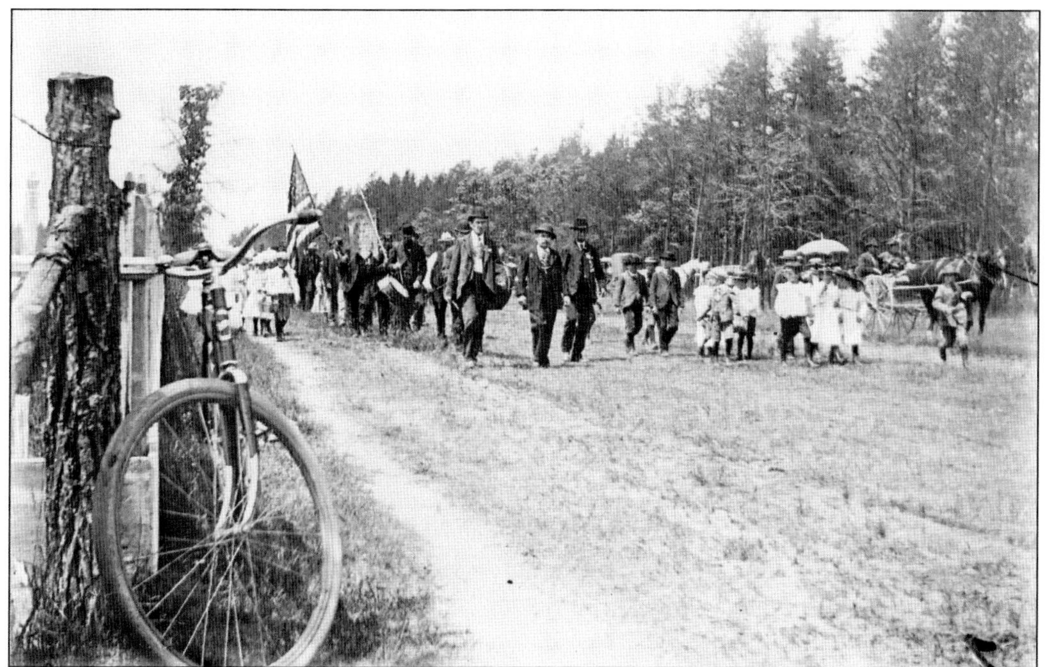

The Decoration Day parade marched from the GAR Hall to Harroun Corner (First Street and River Drive), where the schoolchildren joined, being escorted by the Sons of Veterans as a guard of honor, and continued to the Plover Cemetery. Generally, Decoration Day participants included the GAR post, Sons of Veterans, Woman's Relief Corps, citizens, and a drum corps.

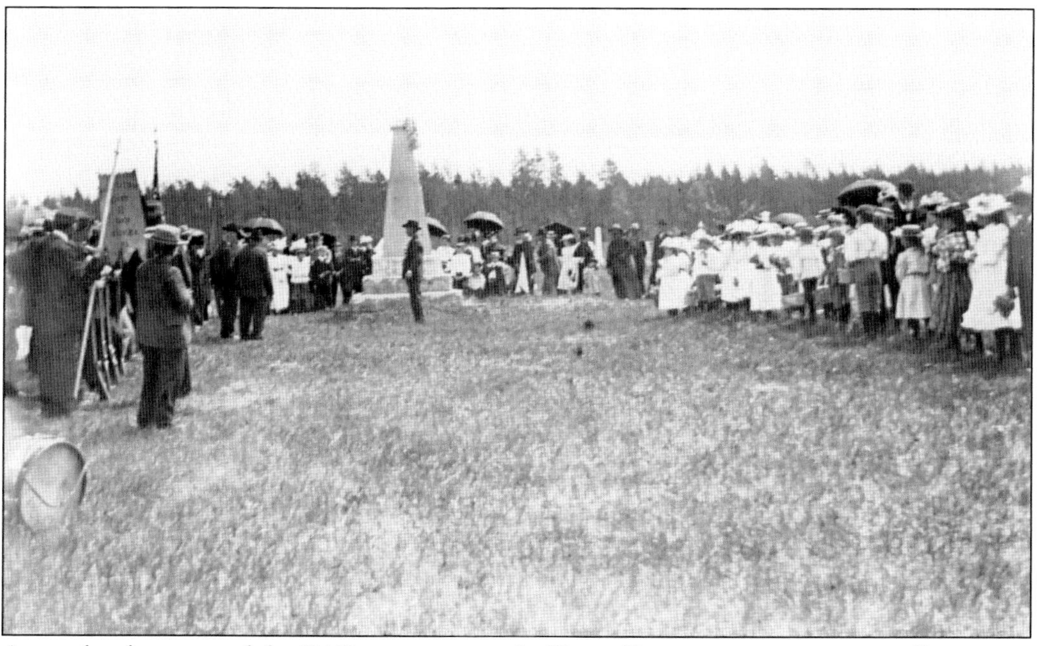

A crowd gathers around the GAR monument at the Plover Cemetery to commemorate Decoration Day. On the left are members of the A.J. Welton Camp 83, Sons of Veterans group. Events of the day included singing, children decorating the soldiers' graves, speakers, and dining and entertainment after leaving the cemetery.

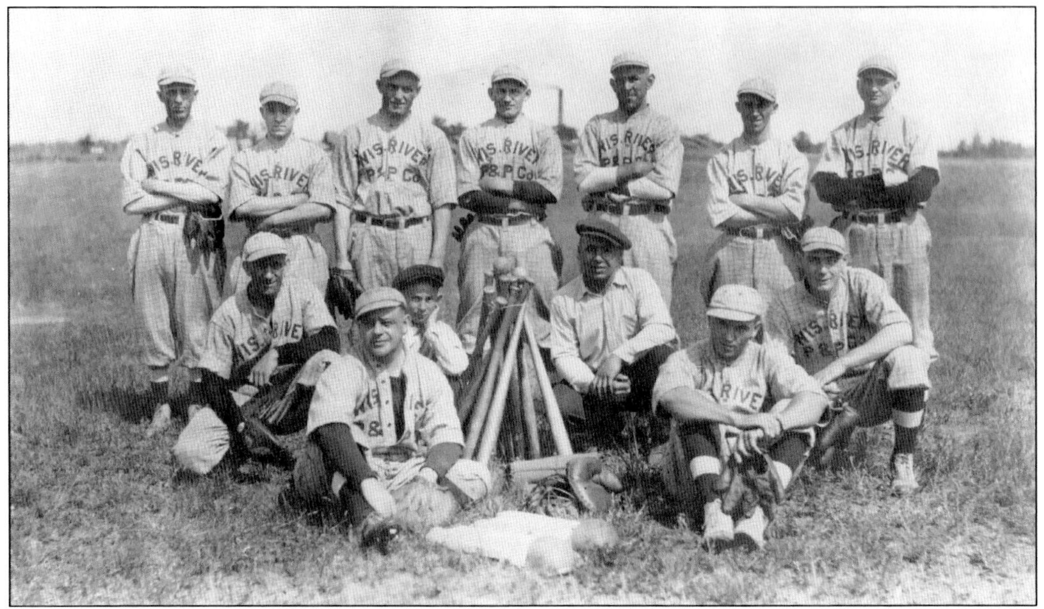

The Wisconsin River Pulp & Paper Company baseball team, or "upper mill team," poses for a c. 1920 photograph. There were several different leagues at the time, with different skill levels and seriousness of play. Businesses would organize teams to play each other, and many towns organized their best players to play against other towns.

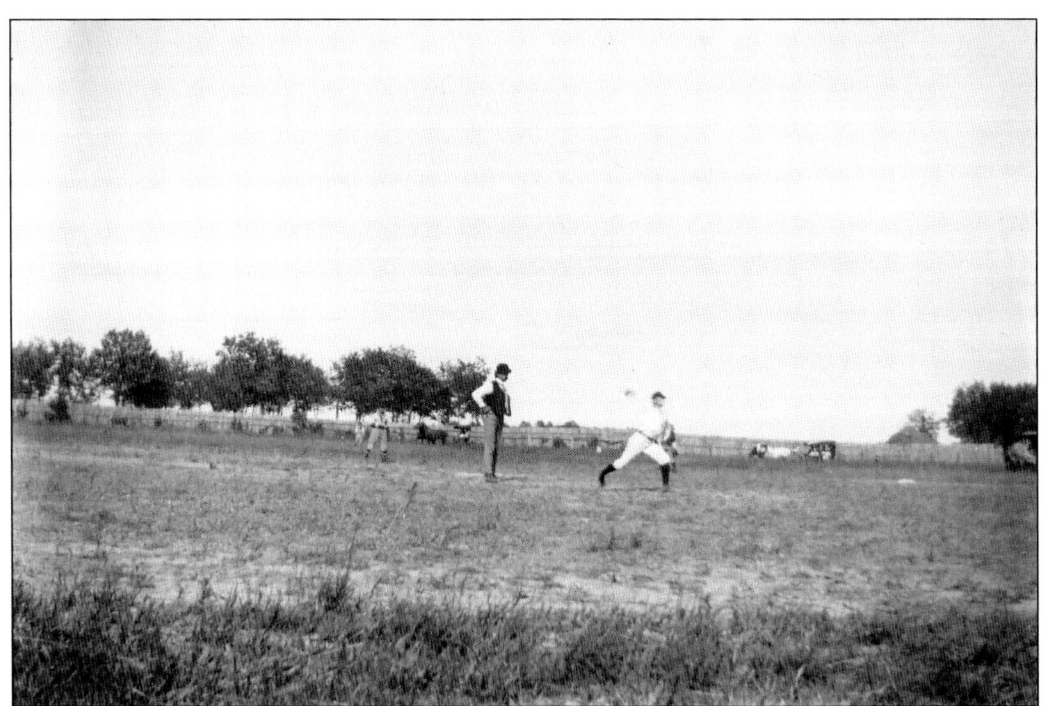

A classic American scene unfolds on a Plover baseball field in the early 1900s. In the distance, spectators sit in their carriages watching the game. The first game played in Portage County was in 1876, with Stevens Point beating Almond by a score of 25-9.

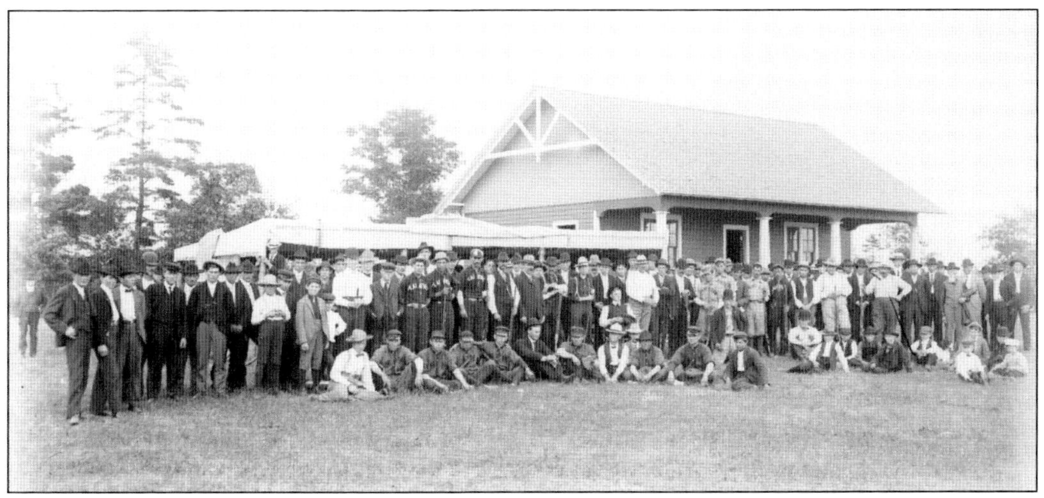

It is unclear where this photograph was taken, but it is plausible that it was taken at the Whiting-Plover Paper Mill Gun Club due to some of the competitors wearing "WPM" (Whiting Plover Mill) jerseys. Other members from area gun clubs competing included Plainfield, Bancroft, and Wautoma. In 1919, the Whiting-Plover Paper Mill Gun Club built a new clubhouse on the island opposite the Whiting-Plover Paper Mill, where they met weekly for competition and recreational shooting.

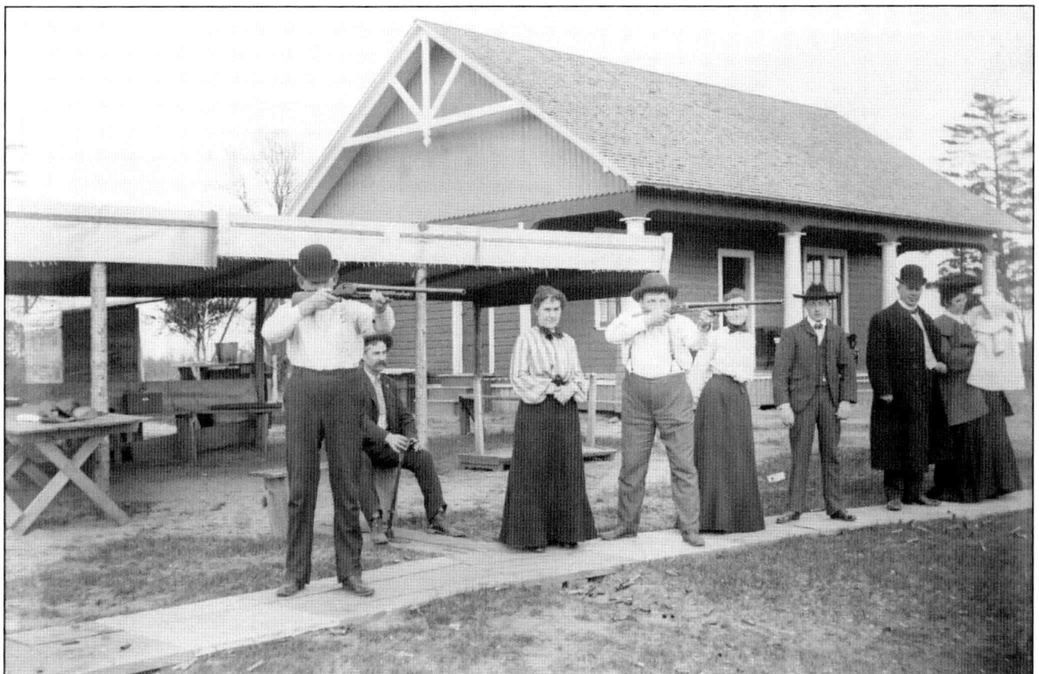

There were several gun clubs in the area in the early 20th century, including the Plover Gun Club, Stevens Point Gun Club, Wisconsin River Gun Club, and Whiting-Plover Gun Club. Many towns in central Wisconsin also had their own club and competed against each other.

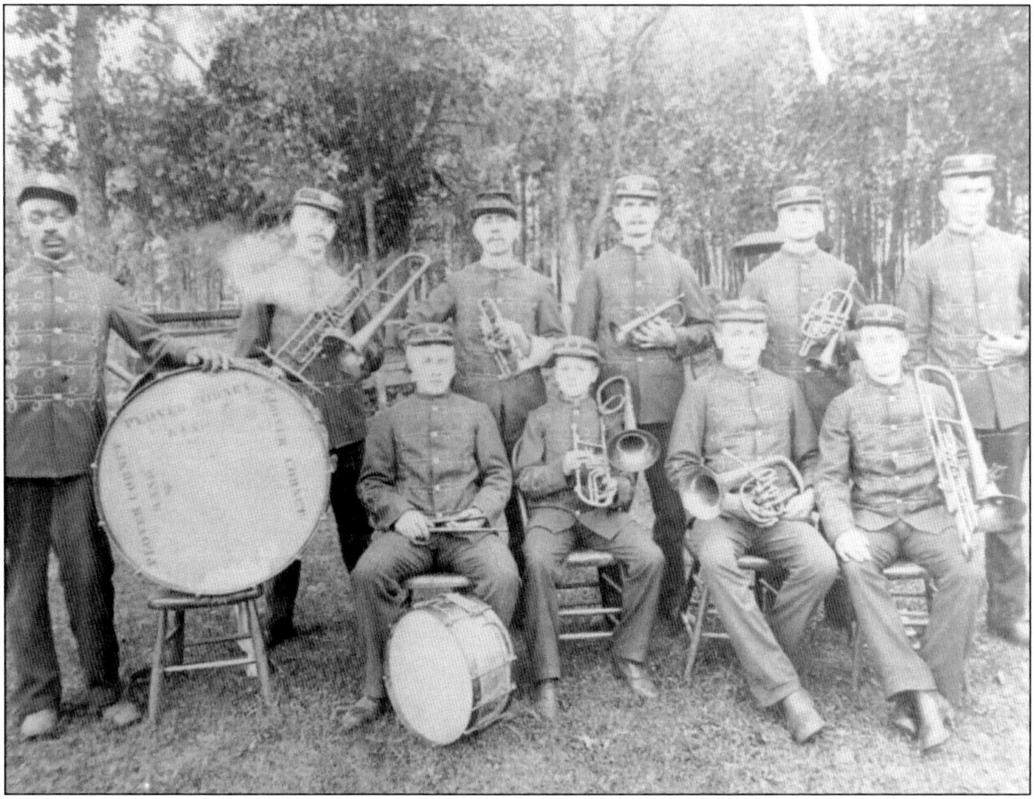

The Plover Cornet Band poses for a photograph during the 1891 Fourth of July celebrations in Plover. Events included a greased-pig contest and banquet dinner at the hall of the Grand Army of the Republic. Band members, from left to right, included Lou ?, Harry Yorton, unidentified, "Bammers" ?, unidentified, Edward Norton, William Shannon, William Allen, Merc Banner, and Charley Shannon.

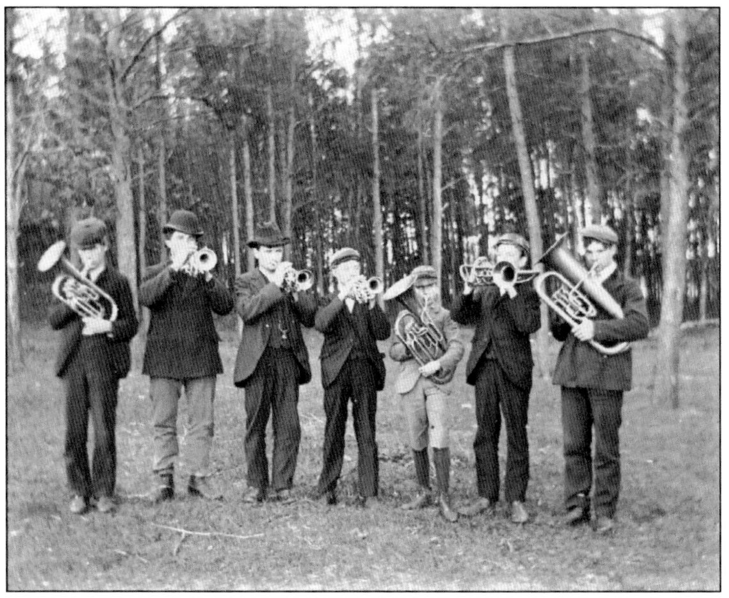

This group of Plover musicians is identified as "Cass Beach Group," but little is known about them. There may be a connection to Plover resident Lewis Cass Beach, but nothing conclusive could be found.

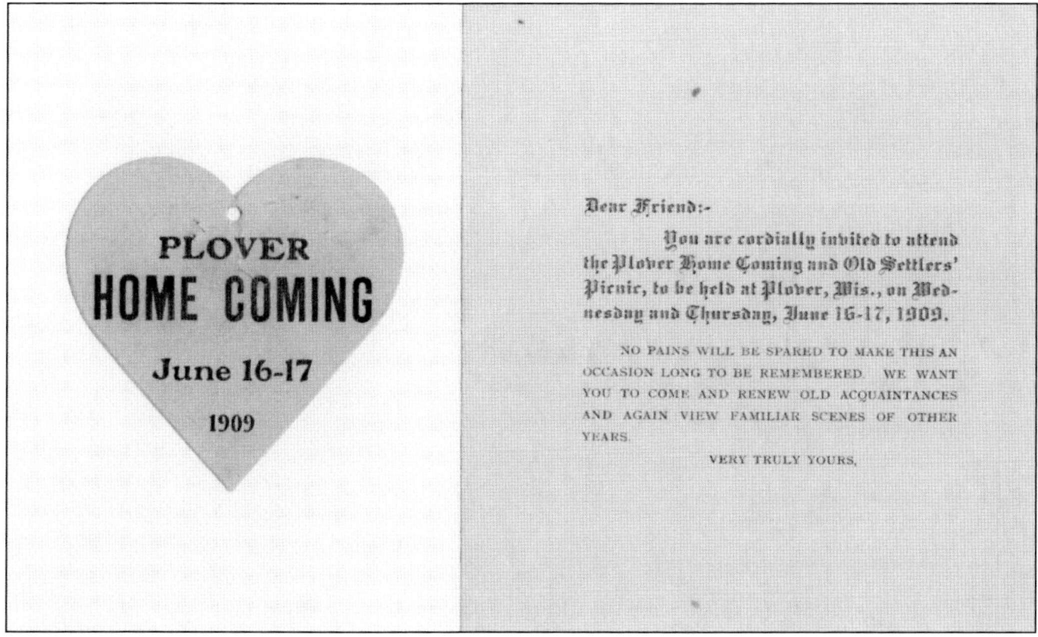

PLOVER
HOME COMING
June 16-17
1909

Dear Friend:-

You are cordially invited to attend the Plover Home Coming and Old Settlers' Picnic, to be held at Plover, Wis., on Wednesday and Thursday, June 16-17, 1909.

NO PAINS WILL BE SPARED TO MAKE THIS AN OCCASION LONG TO BE REMEMBERED. WE WANT YOU TO COME AND RENEW OLD ACQUAINTANCES AND AGAIN VIEW FAMILIAR SCENES OF OTHER YEARS.

VERY TRULY YOURS,

The Plover homecoming of 1909 attracted the largest number of people that the village of Plover had ever seen. Events included a large free feast that was held in the empty lot next to the GAR Hall, remembrances, music by the Union Band, singing, musical performances, baseball games, a gun club shooting contest, a partial solar eclipse on June 17, dancing in the GAR Hall, poetry readings, and a comedy act.

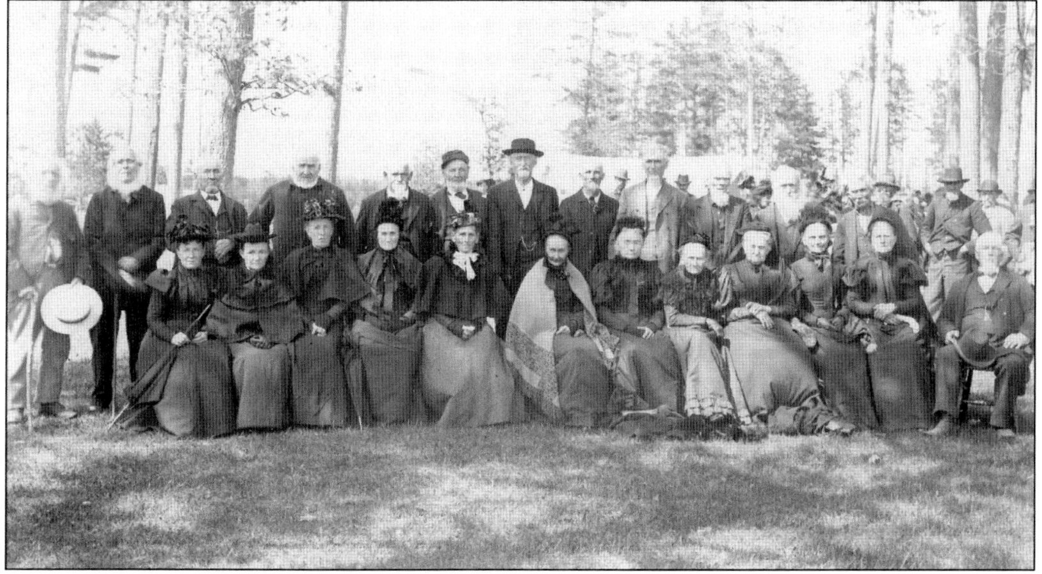

The Old Settlers Club meets at S.A. Sherman's grove in 1898. Pictured are those who settled in Portage County in or before 1848. From left to right are (first row) Arvesta Derozier, Alvina Precourt Puariea, Sarah Myers, Phyletta Eckels, Lovina Newby, Lydia Dawley, Mandana Hale Bliss, ? Metcalf, Maria Anson, unidentified, Mary Boursier, and S.A. Sherman; (second row), Mr. Coats, Leander Trudell, Antoine Precourt, John Eckels, Oliver Bigelow, Jesse A. Martin, Matthew Slutts, Dave Porter, Ed Metcalf, James O'Brien, George W. Franklin, and two unidentified.

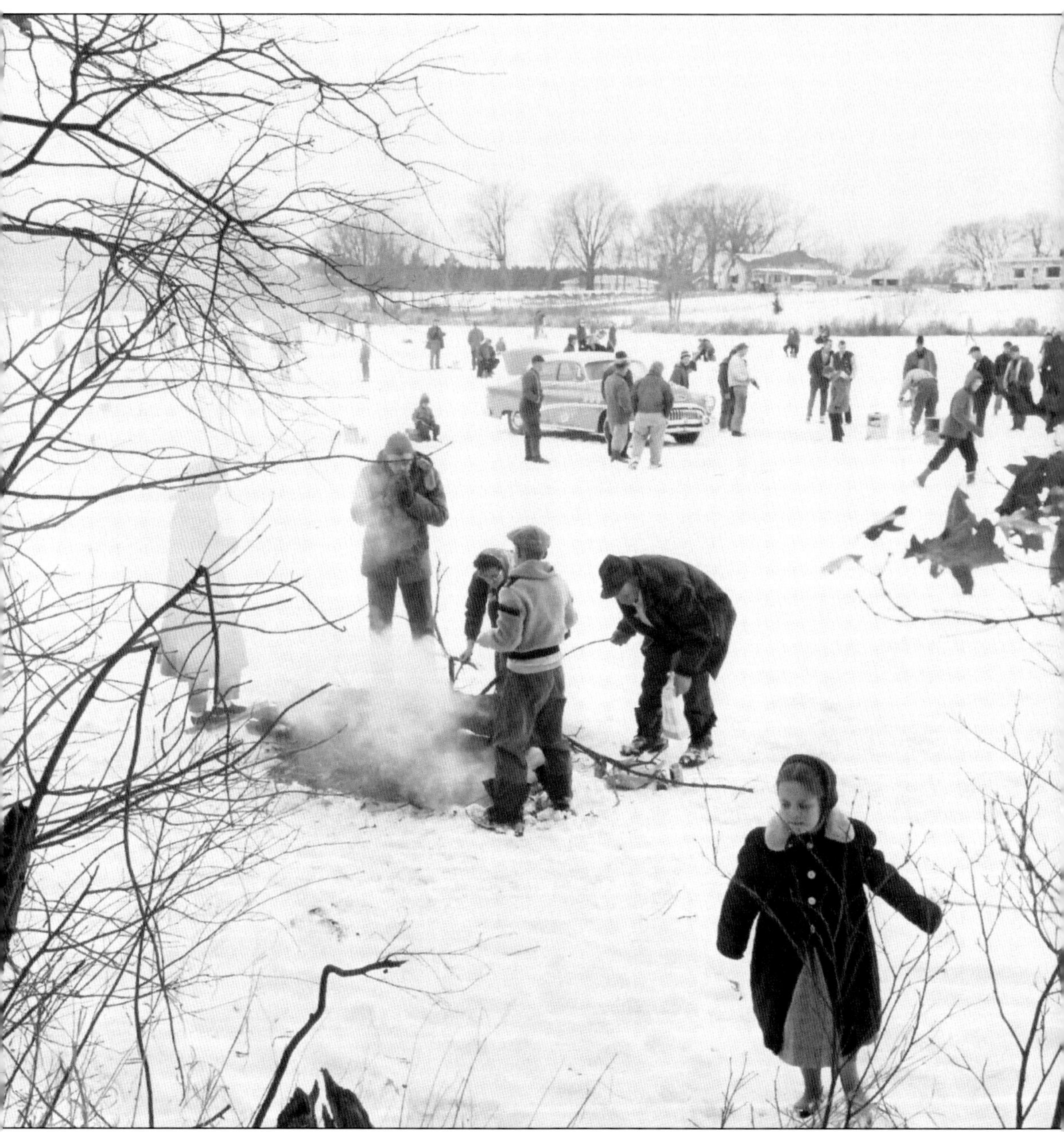

People take to the ice on the Springville Pond as the Springville Fisheree gets underway in 1961. The Springville Fisheree was sponsored by the Plover Fish and Wildlife Conservation Committee and was established in 1955. Each year, the event was held at either Springville or McDill, and profits went toward the improvement of the McDill Pond. Garold Coulthurst served as the 1961 fisheree chairman.

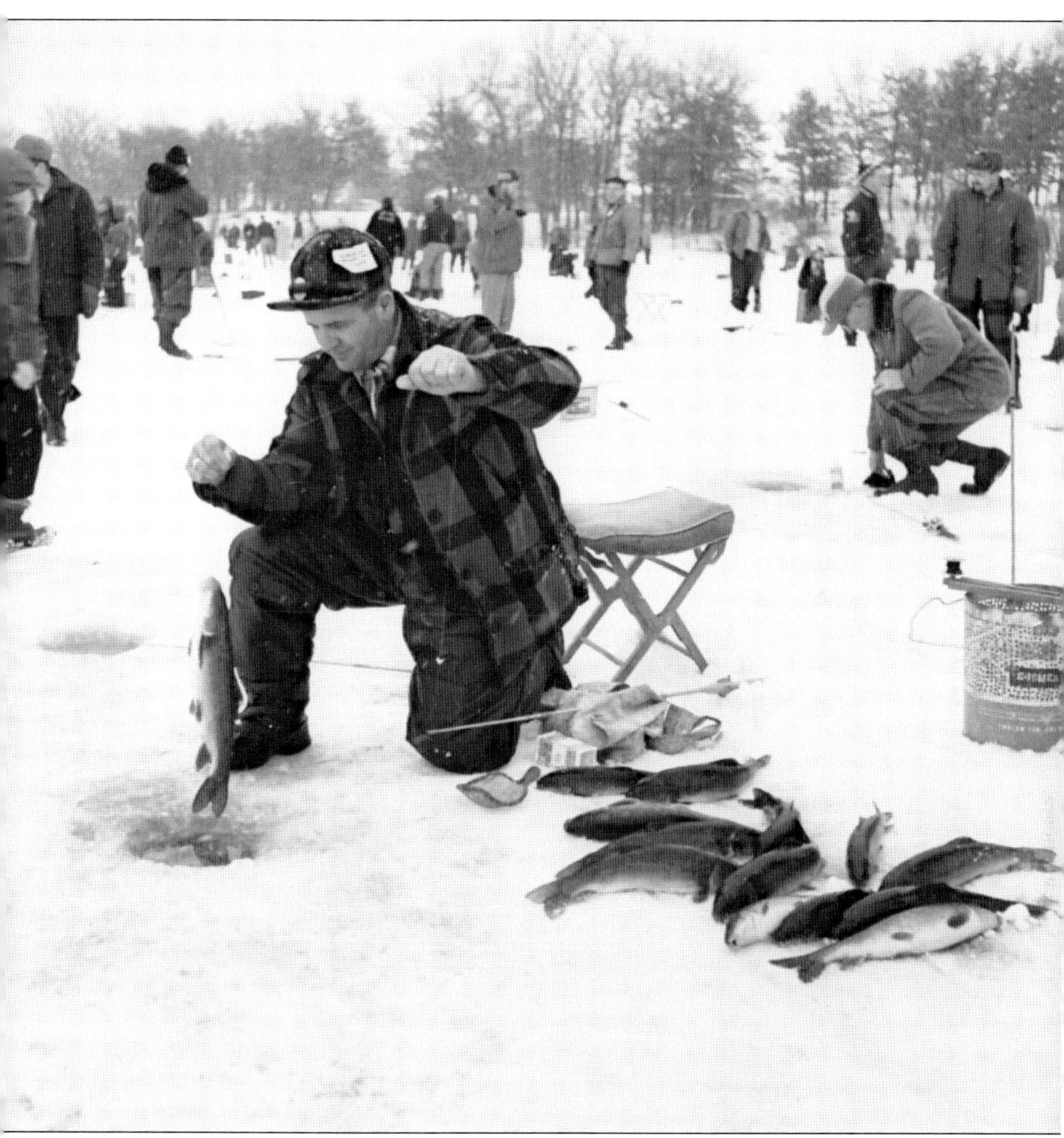

A man pulls his catch up through the ice at the Springville Fisheree in 1961. The event attracted an estimated 600 participants. At this year's event, the first-prize winner was Joe Firkus, with a 12-pound 5-ounce northern pike. The youngest competitor was Kathryn McGinley of Stevens Point at two years and five months, and the oldest was R.G. Newby of Plover at age 76.

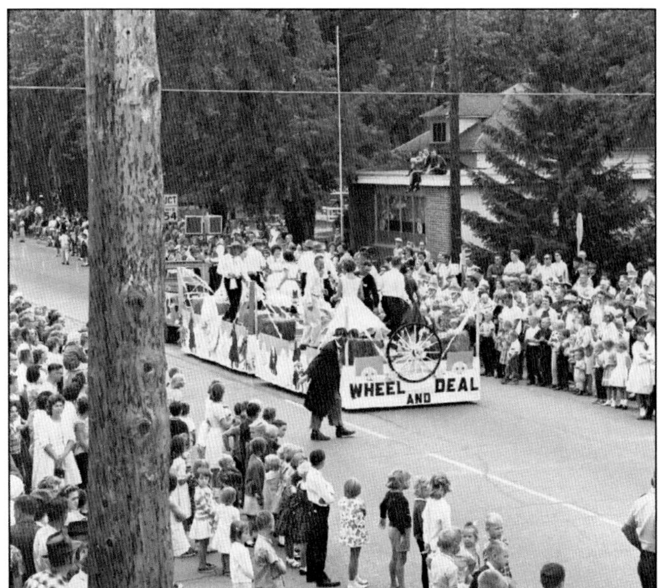

The third annual Golden Sands Festival was held on August 7–9, 1964. The parade was remembered as the most memorable event of the weekend with the Wheel and Deal Square Dance Club float being the highlight of the parade. It was reported that this float won the trophy for most humorous entry, with its two squares performing as the float moved along the parade route.

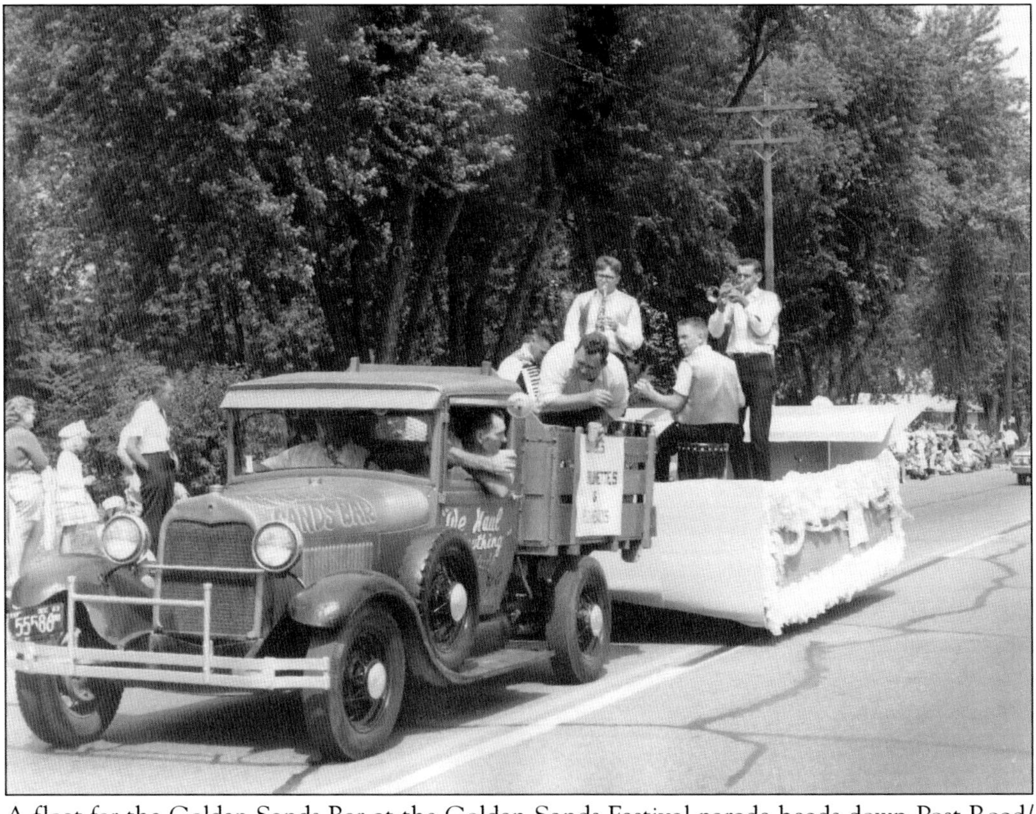

A float for the Golden Sands Bar at the Golden Sands Festival parade heads down Post Road/Highway 51. Since this was the main north-south artery, the parade blocked all weekend traffic moving through Plover. This year's festival featured carnival rides set up in the area around the Plover Community Hall, the coronation ball, Silver Dollar Days, a youth baseball game, a street dance, the parade, a band concert, and a square dance.

Pictured at the third annual Golden Sands Festival in 1964 are queen contestants, from left to right, Carol Tuskowski, Jean Van Beckum, Joan Newby from Whiting (seated), Jeanette Weber, and Patricia Harris. The man is unidentified.

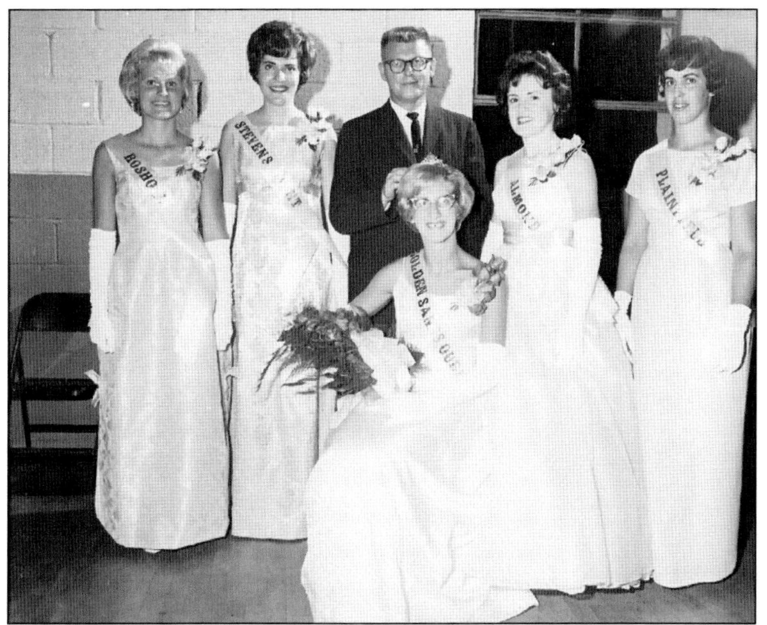

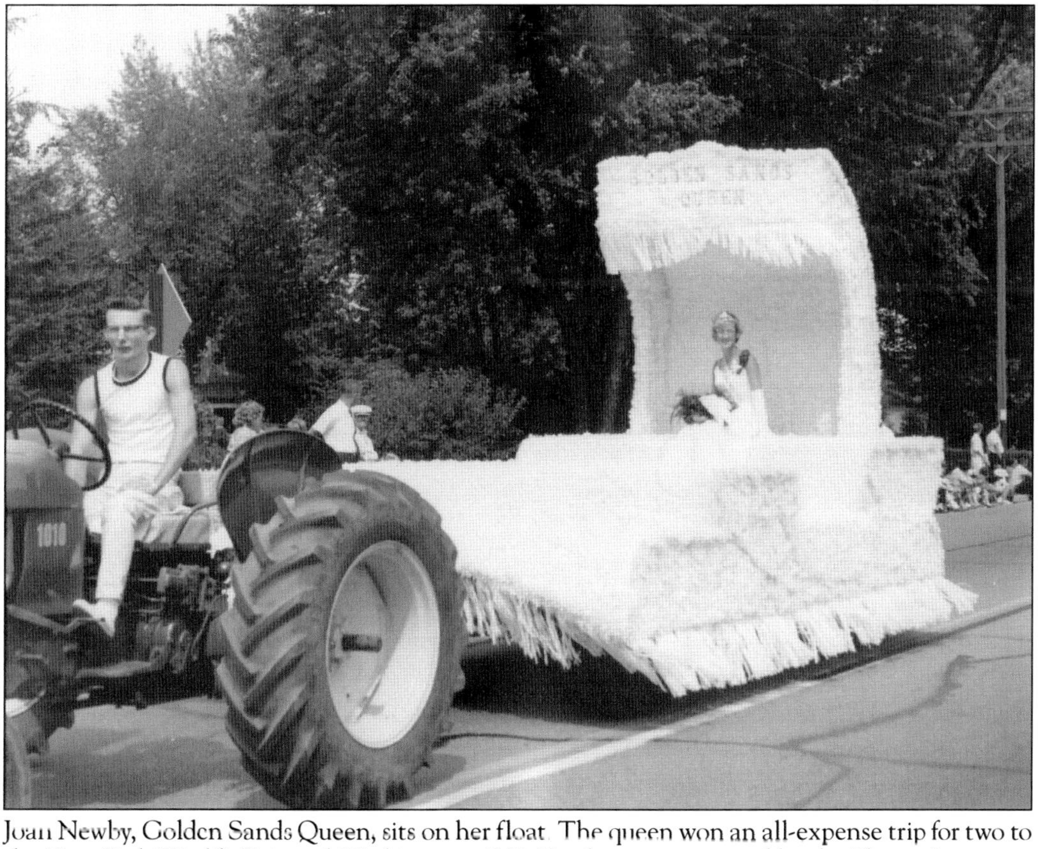

Joan Newby, Golden Sands Queen, sits on her float. The queen won an all-expense trip for two to the New York World's Fair and Washington, DC. Newby was sponsored by the Plover American Legion and the Plover Volunteer Fire Department. Her parents are Claude and Mabel Newby.

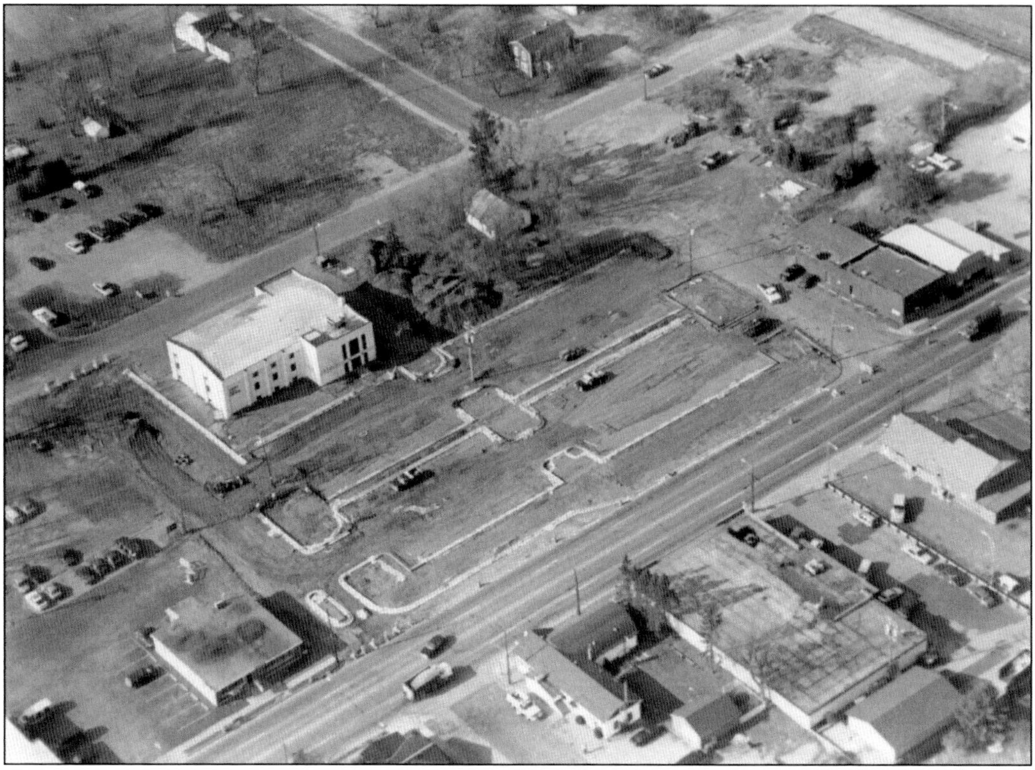

This view looks northwest at Post Road where a new parking lot is being built for the former Plover Memorial Center/Town Hall/Village Hall and eventual professional building. Also visible on the lower edge of the photograph is the Plover post office and Sandy's Bar.

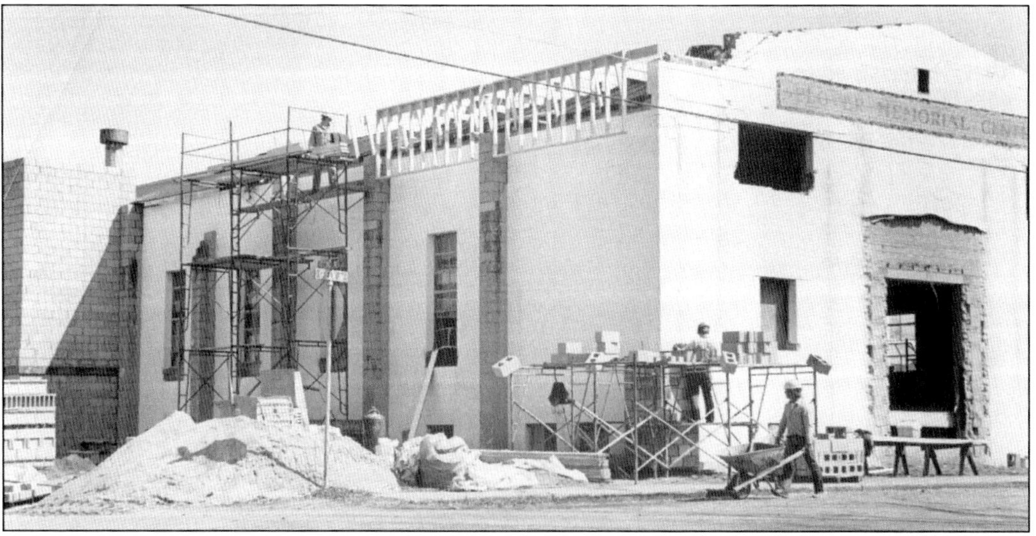

The Plover Memorial Center was built in the early 1950s on the same spot that the GAR Hall once stood on the northeast corner of Green and Second Streets (current Earhart Avenue). This building would be used as both the Town of Plover Hall and also the Village of Plover Hall. In this photograph, work crews are renovating the building into a professional building in 1983. (*Stevens Point Journal.*)

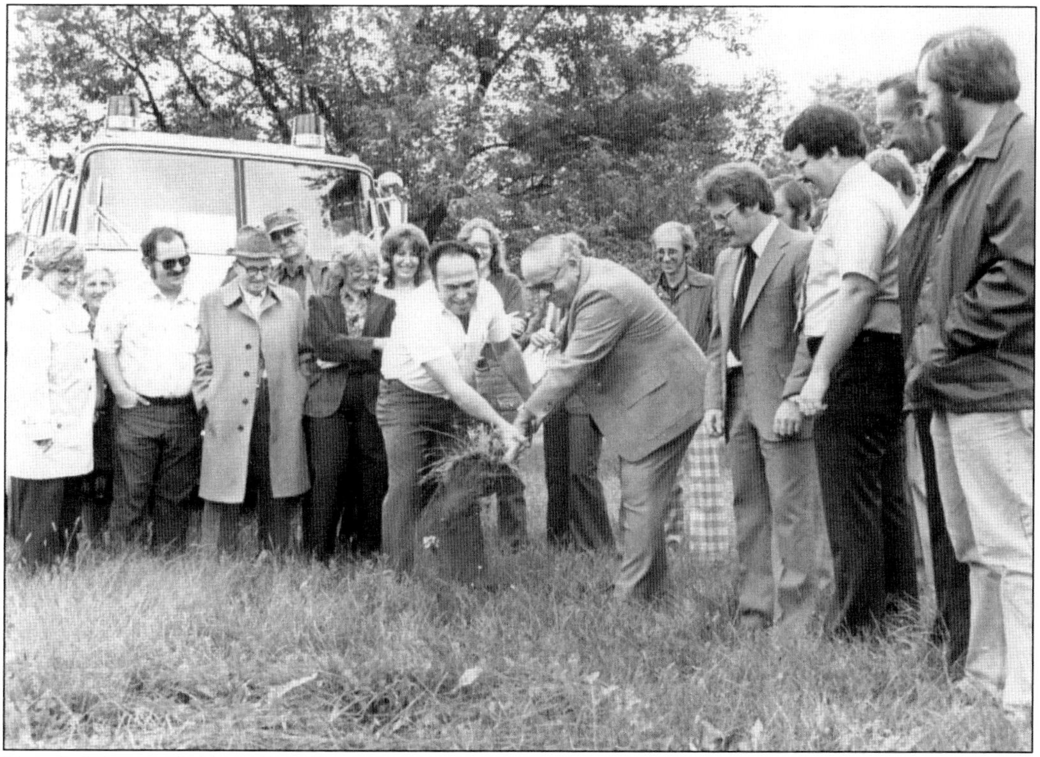

Dan Schlutter (left) and William Adams work the shovel on the ground breaking for the new Village of Plover Municipal Center in 1978. Also pictured are Debbie Sniadajewski, Pat Ladecki, and Philip Idsvoog. This building is located at 2400 Post Road. (*Stevens Point Journal.*)

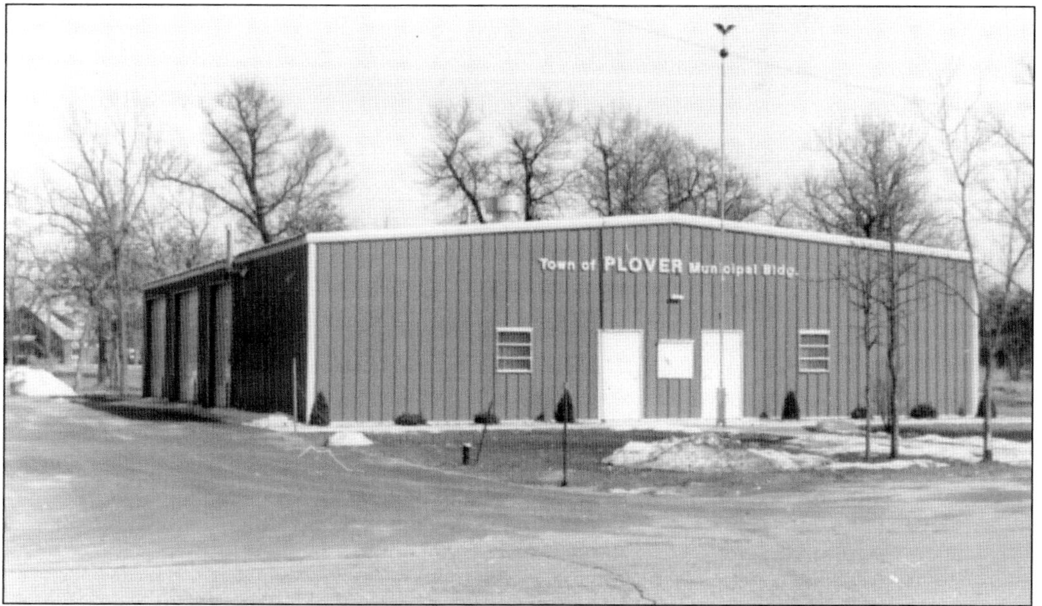

This Town of Plover municipal building was erected in 1972 at a cost of $36,000 and is located on south Hoover Road, just south of Highway 54. This building has been used as a garage since the new town hall was built.

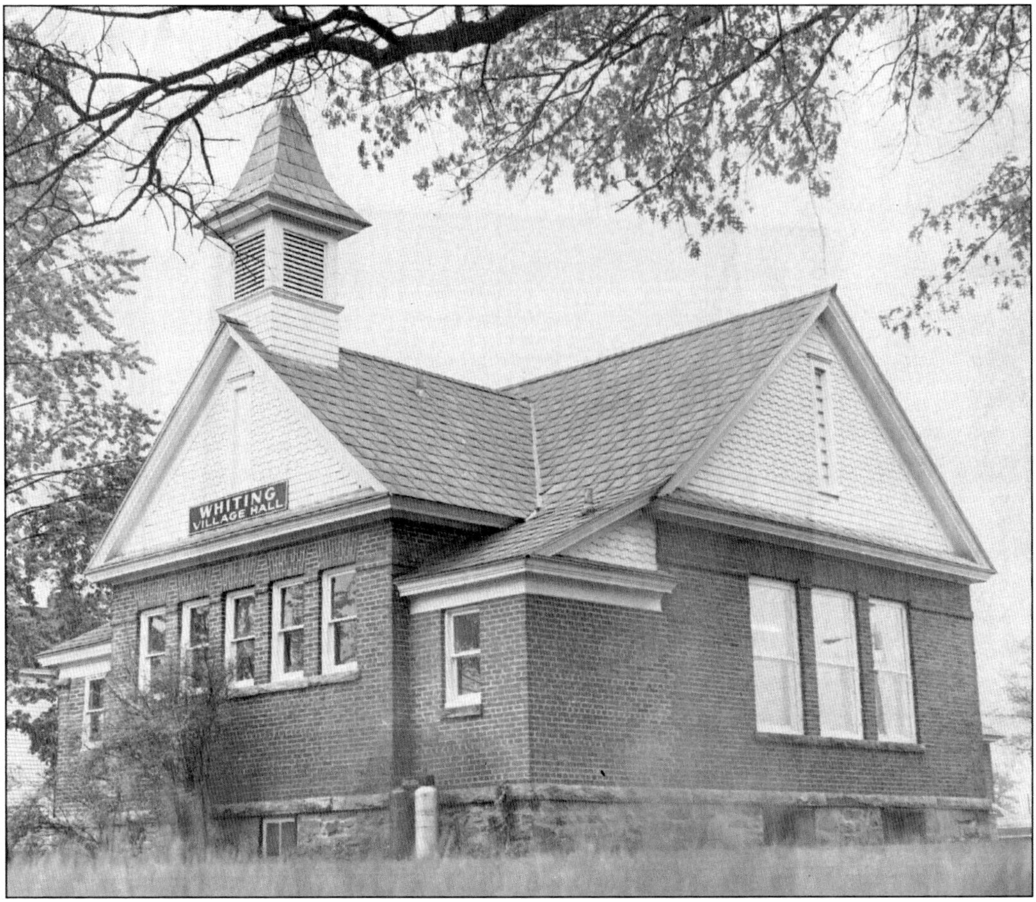

This schoolhouse was built on Charles Abrecht's land on lots 3–6 of block 69 of the original 1888 plat of Conant Rapids. The architect was William Waters, and it was built by George Potter of Stevens Point at a cost of $1,509.00. The school opened on October 15, 1896, with an enrollment of seven students, and the teacher was Mary Catlin. The Village of Whiting used the hall shortly after being incorporated in 1947, and it was later used as a credit union for the employees of the Consolidated Paper mill.

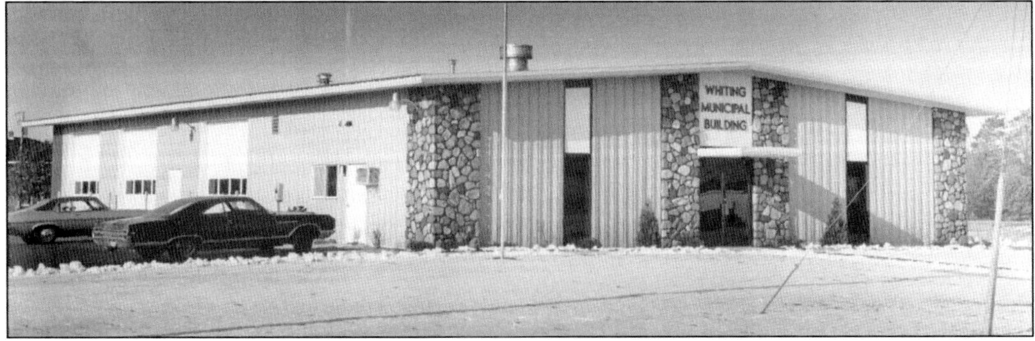

The Whiting municipal building is shown here as it looked in 1974. This building was constructed by Davis Steel Building Company of McFarland with a bid of $54,171 and was located at the corner of Church Street and Sherman Avenue. It was used for village offices until the spring of 1999, when they were moved into the current village hall. (*Stevens Point Journal.*)

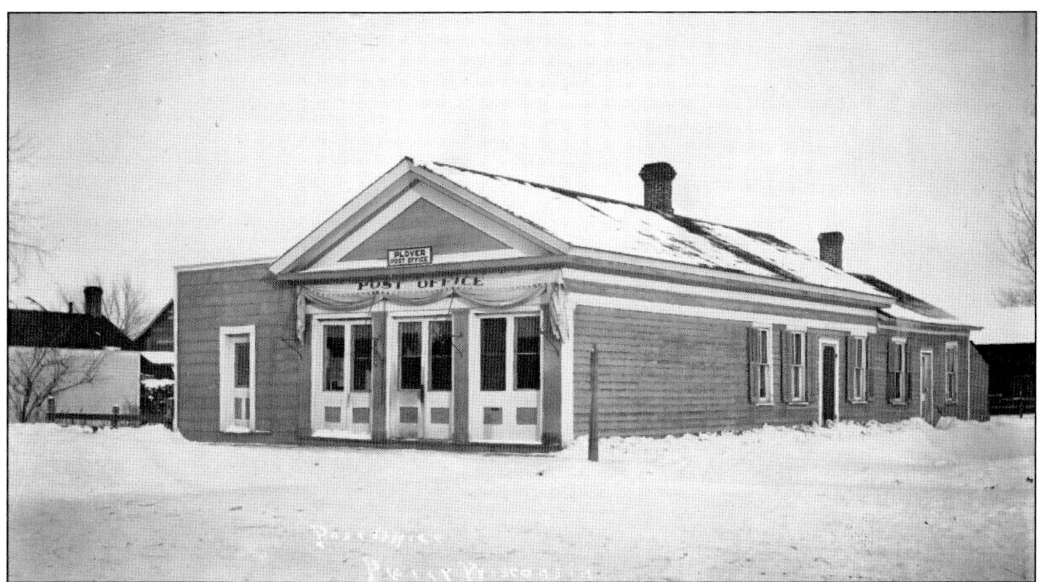

The first Plover post office was established on January 14, 1845, as Plover Portage. The post office pictured was located on the northeast corner of Green and First Streets and is now in Heritage Park in Plover. The back part of the building was used as a doctor's office, and in later years, the building served as a restaurant, waterbed store, and other various businesses.

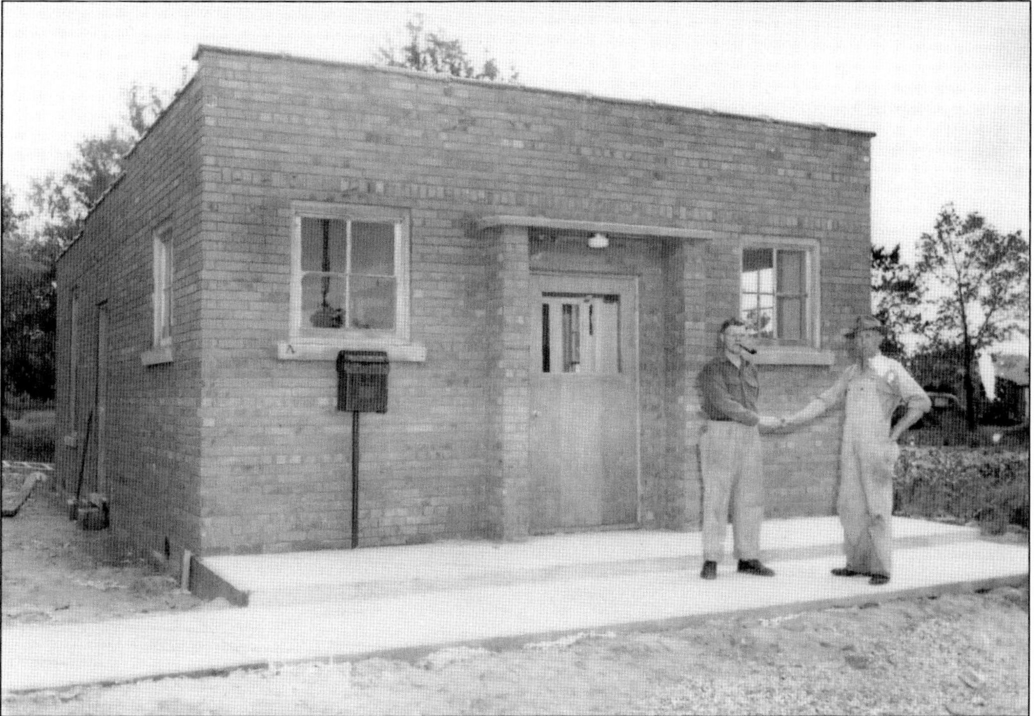

This new Plover post office was built around 1951 and was only used for seven years before a new post office was built to facilitate increased volume. Postmasters up to this point included George Wyatt, Charles Lane, Harriet Lane, Charles Dunaven, Amelia Dunaven, Mary Weinholt, Kate Barnsdale, Frank Barnsdale, Bernice Lampman, Della Wherritt, and George Sterling.

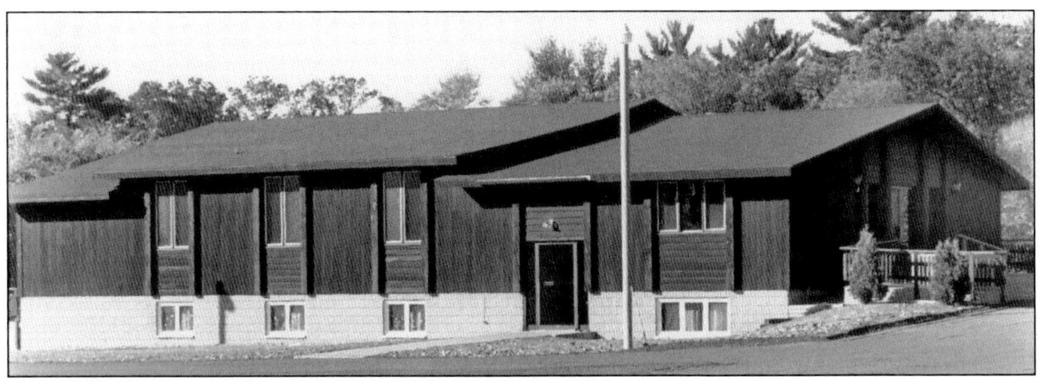

The Plover branch of the Portage County Public Library was originally housed in the village municipal center. The library moved to this building, the former Grace Baptist Church, and opened on September 30, 1991. The fire department moved all the books and furniture to the new library using a truck from Okray Family Farms, completing the task in only six hours. (*Stevens Point Journal.*)

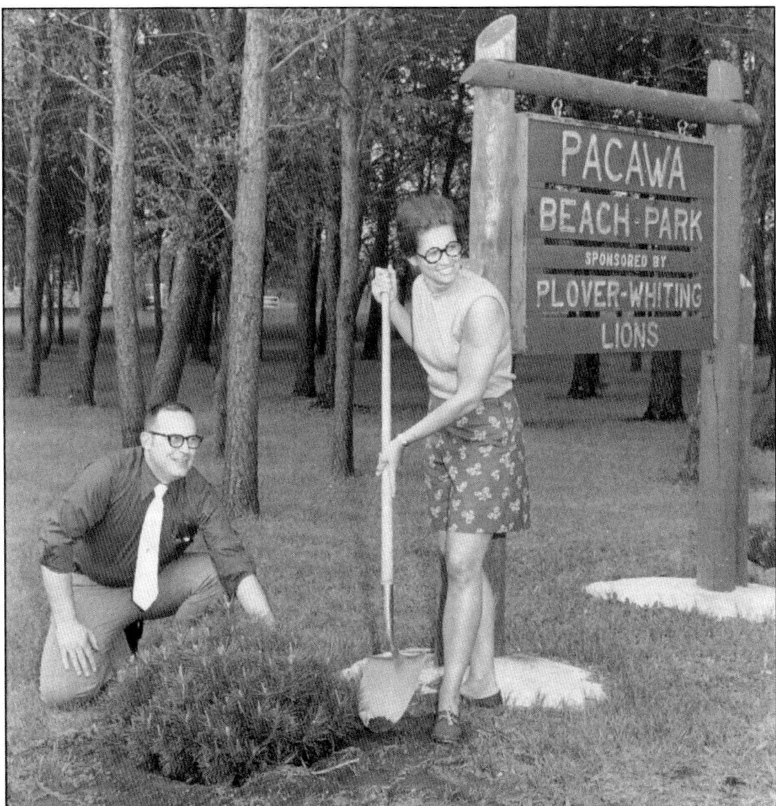

Gary Lutz (left), president of the Plover-Whiting Lions Club, and Sally Murwin, president of the Plover Woman's Club, plant trees at Lake Pacawa in May 1974. Clarence and Regina Worzella leased 18 acres of land for $1 a year to the Lions Club with the stipulation that the land could be used by the Lions Club as long as it was used as a public park. The Lions Club subsequently purchased another 16-acre parcel in the late 1970s. (*Stevens Point Journal.*)

Five

BUSINESSES

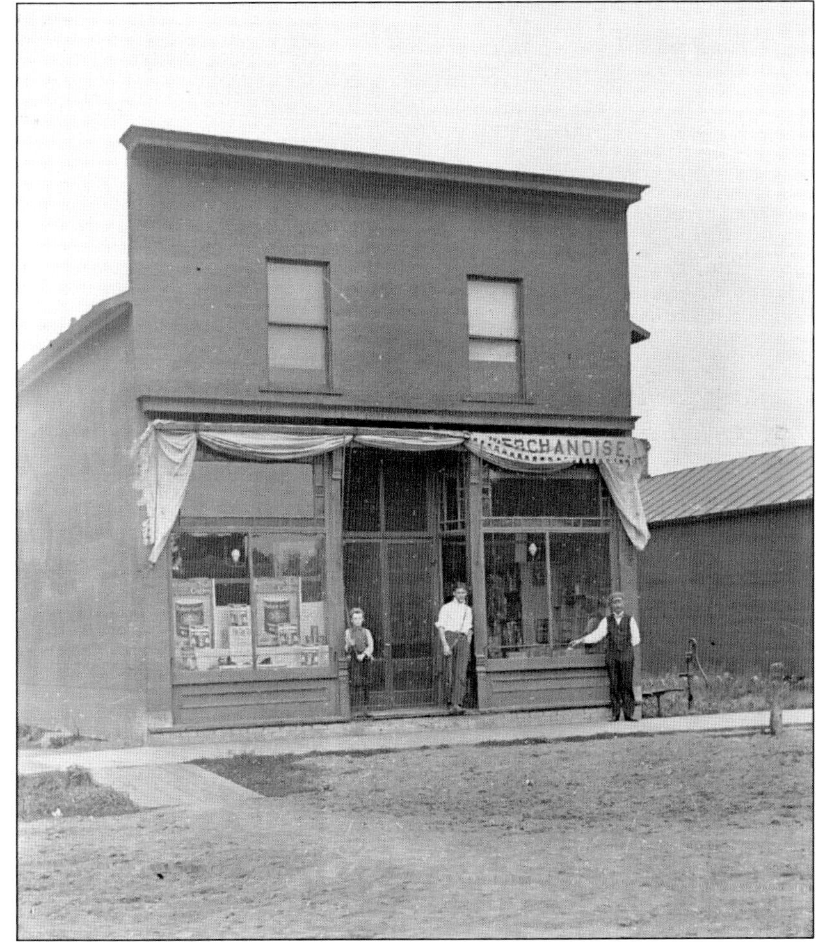

The Pierce grocery store stood on the northwest corner of First and Green Streets and was across the street from the Frank Lila store. Standing in front of the store are, from left to right, unidentified, Leo Pierce, and James W. Pierce. The Portage County Historical Society moved the building to Heritage Park in 1990.

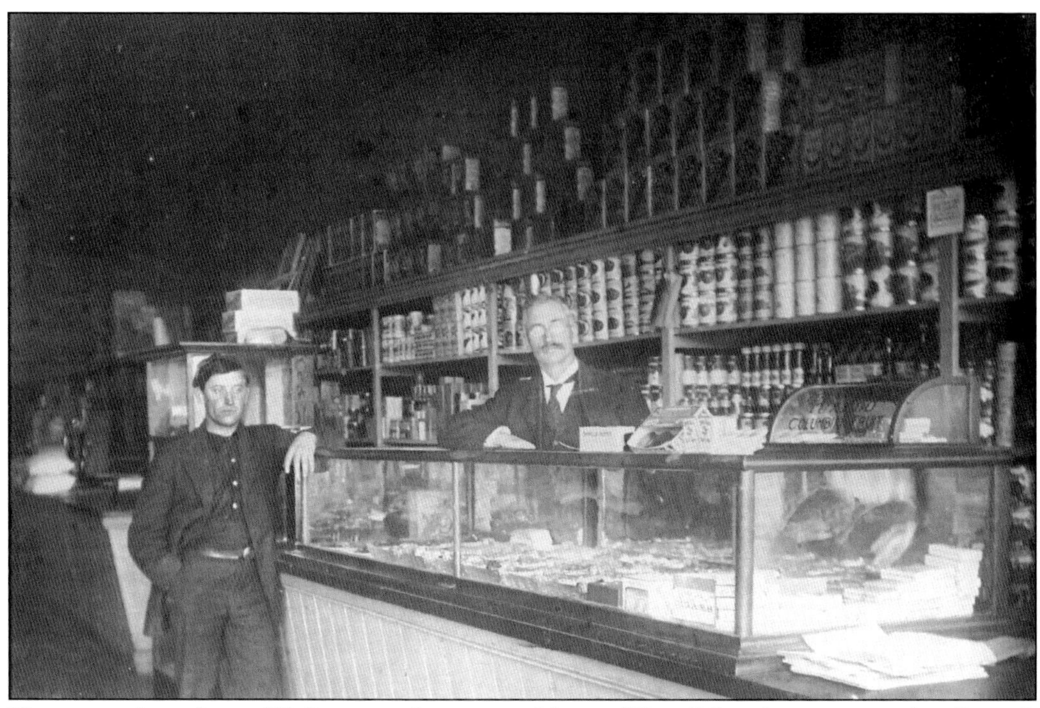

Plover merchant James W. Pierce and customer Martin "Tune" Booth are pictured in Pierce's grocery store around 1910. The first owner of the store was James Pierce Sr., and it was owned by four generations before closing in October 1967.

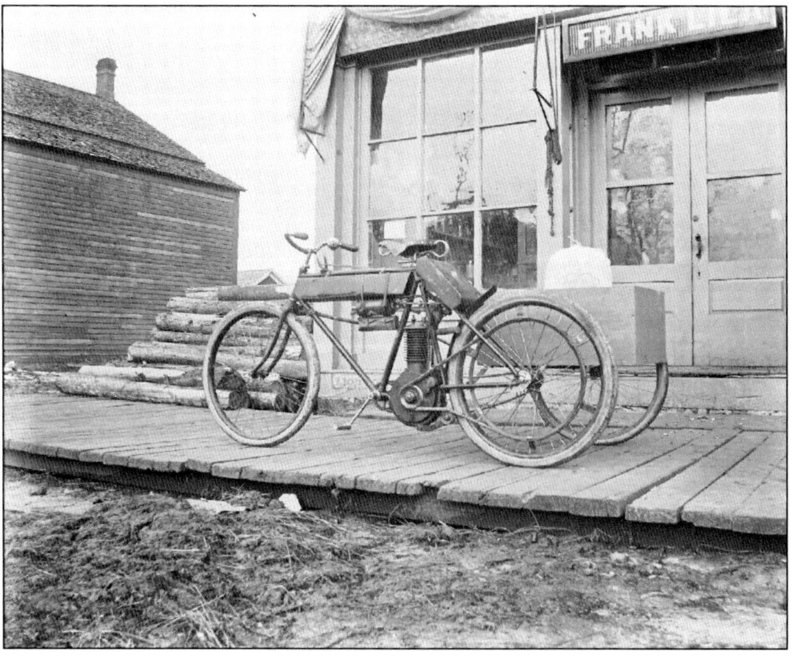

A three-wheeled motorcycle is parked outside the Frank Lila general merchandise and grocery store. Frank Lila operated the store from 1902 to 1913 before it passed to his sons. It was located on the east side of First Street between Green and Willow Streets.

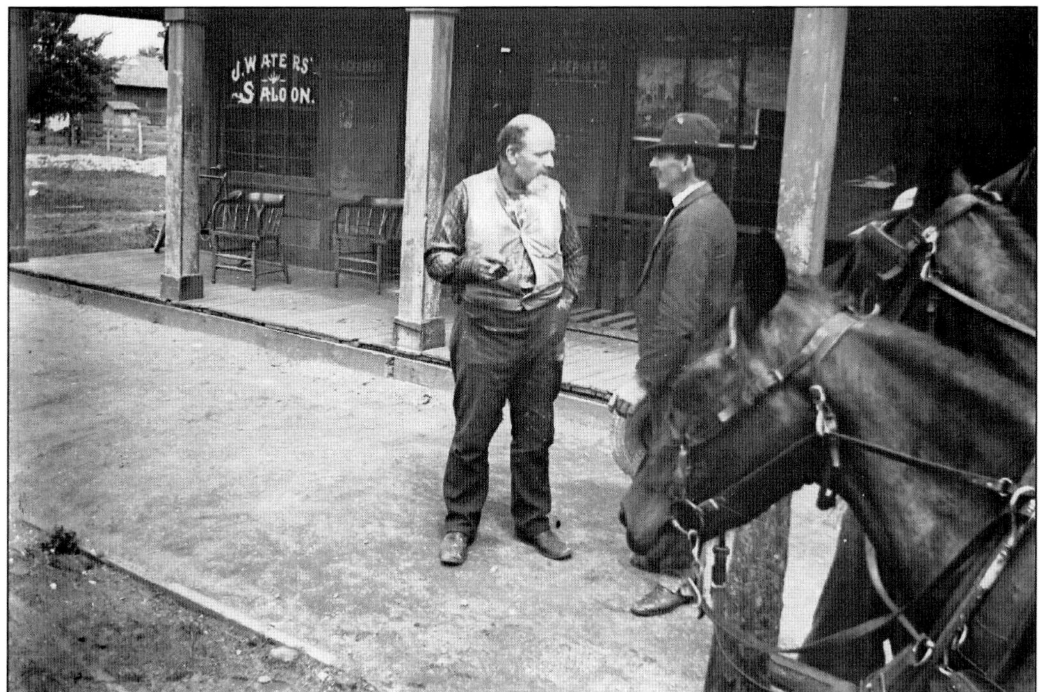

James Waters talks with Jake Herring outside the J. Waters' Saloon. The saloon was located on First and Willow Streets where Jeepers Gin Mill used to stand. This location has had a series of saloons, taverns, or bars since the late 1800s.

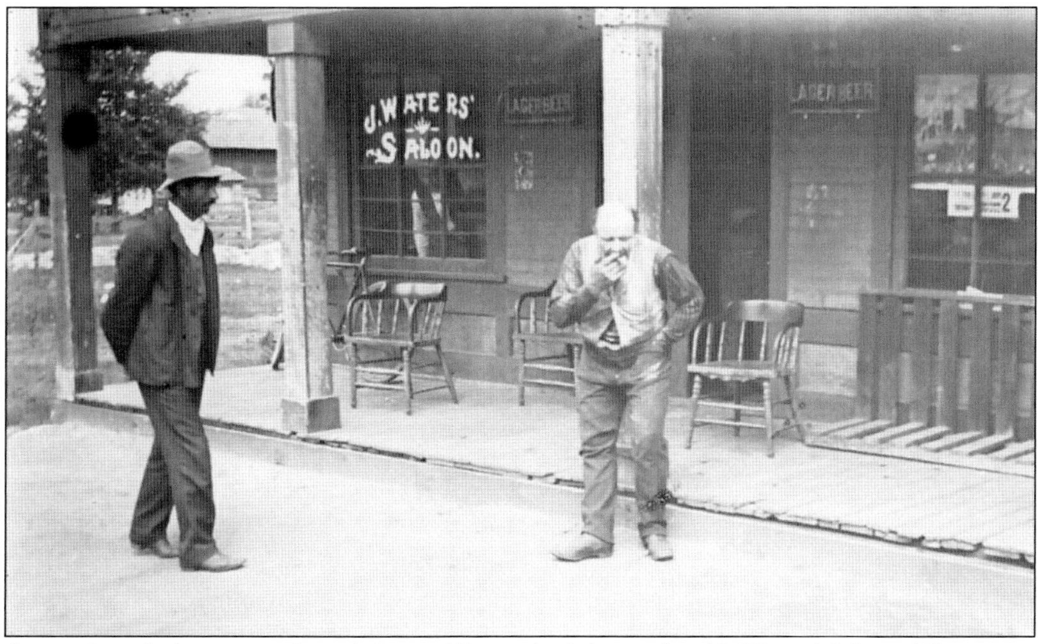

An unidentified man stands with James Waters (right) outside of J. Waters' Saloon. Waters was an immigrant from England and a Plover and Portage County pioneer who lived in the village for over 60 years. C. Eslinger became the proprietor of the saloon in the early 1900s and sold it to William Adams in 1909.

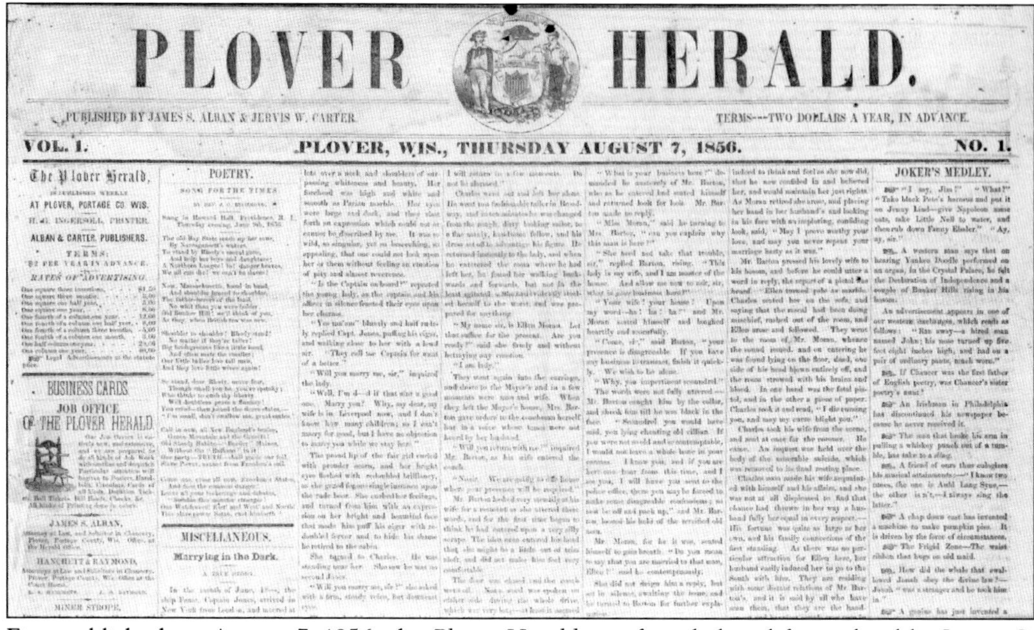

PLOVER HERALD.

PUBLISHED BY JAMES S. ALBAN & JERVIS W. CARTER

TERMS---TWO DOLLARS A YEAR, IN ADVANCE.

VOL. 1. PLOVER, WIS., THURSDAY AUGUST 7, 1856. NO. 1.

The Plover Herald, AT PLOVER, PORTAGE CO. WIS. ALBAN & CARTER, PUBLISHERS.

POETRY.

JOKER'S MEDLEY.

BUSINESS CARDS

JOB OFFICE OF THE PLOVER HERALD

JAMES S. ALBAN,

MISCELLANEOUS.

Marrying in the Dark.

First published on August 7, 1856, the *Plover Herald* was founded and first edited by James S. Alban and Jervis W. Carter and published by H.G. Ingersoll. The newspaper only had this title for the years 1856 and 1857 and went through a couple of name changes before becoming the *Plover Times* in 1863. Alban and Carter started the paper as a means to oppose slavery, support the Republican candidates for the 1856 election, and provide local and state news.

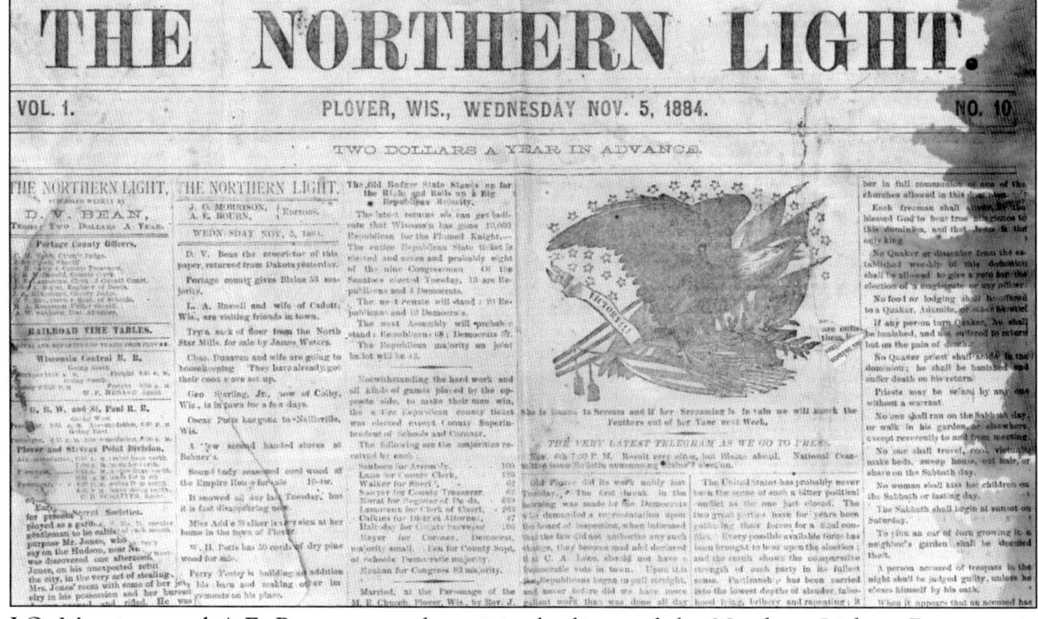

THE NORTHERN LIGHT.

VOL. 1. PLOVER, WIS., WEDNESDAY NOV. 5, 1884. NO. 10

TWO DOLLARS A YEAR IN ADVANCE.

THE NORTHERN LIGHT, D. V. BEAN,

THE NORTHERN LIGHT. J. O. MORRISON, A. E. BOURN, EDITORS.

RAILROAD TIME TABLES.

J.O. Morrison and A.E. Bourn were the original editors of the *Northern Light*, a Democratic newspaper. This November 5, 1884, issue is one of the few surviving issues of this newspaper. It was reported in the February 23, 1884, issue of the *Stevens Point Journal* that "H.H. Moore of Plover has a press and the type on the road, with which to start a Democratic paper in that village, to be called the Northern Light."

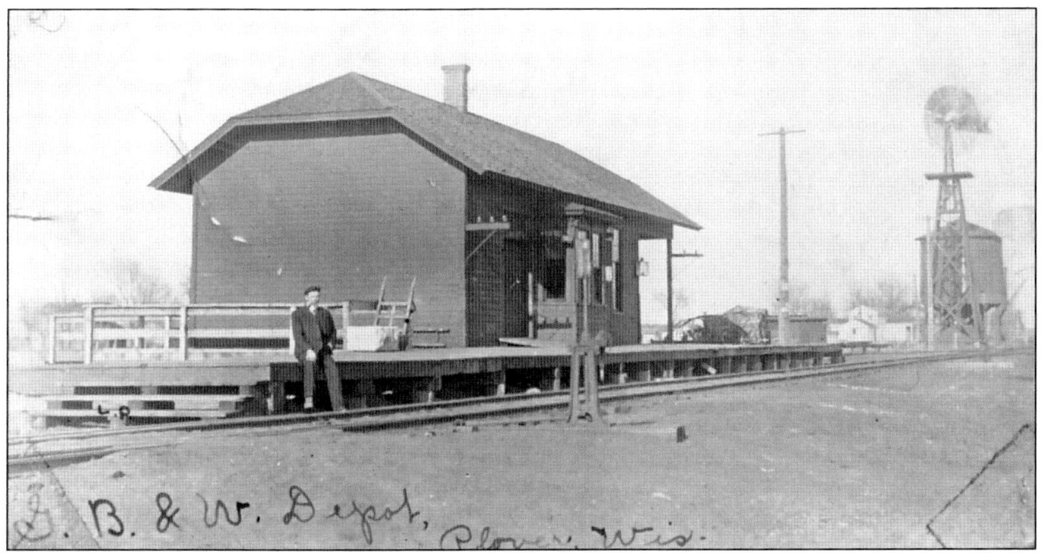

The Green Bay & Western depot at Plover, located at the west end of Walnut Street, burned and was rebuilt in 1923. This was one of two depots located in the village of Plover, with the other being the Wisconsin Central (later Soo Line), which was part of the Portage Line. In 1881, the Green Bay & Western built a spur line that connected Plover to Stevens Point in direct competition with the "P-Line." (UWSP Archives.)

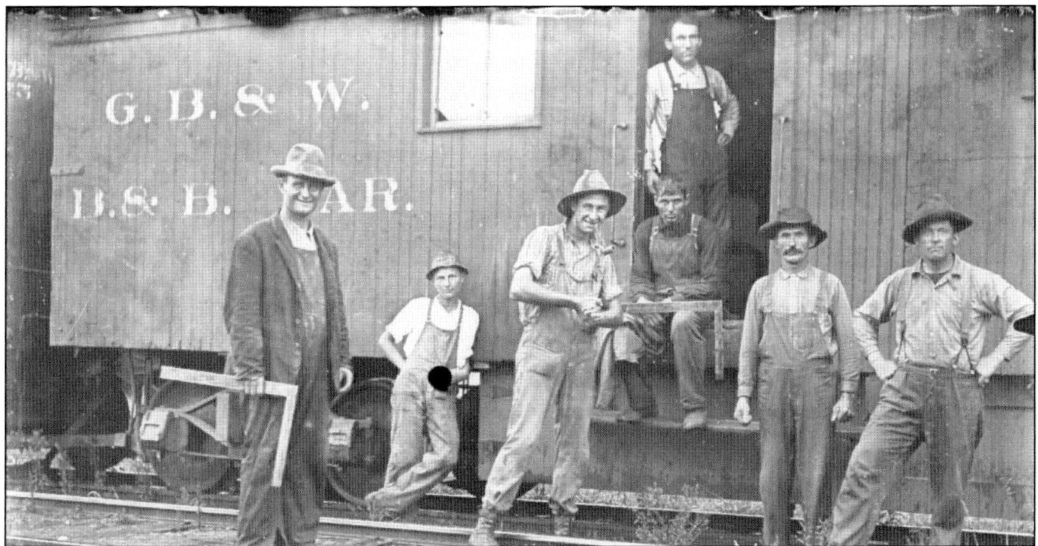

Green Bay & Western Railroad employees, most likely part of the bridge and building gang, stand in front of a railroad car. The crew may have been in town in February 1923, rebuilding the Green Bay & Western depot that burned to the ground several weeks earlier. The railroad connected Green Bay to Winona, Minnesota.

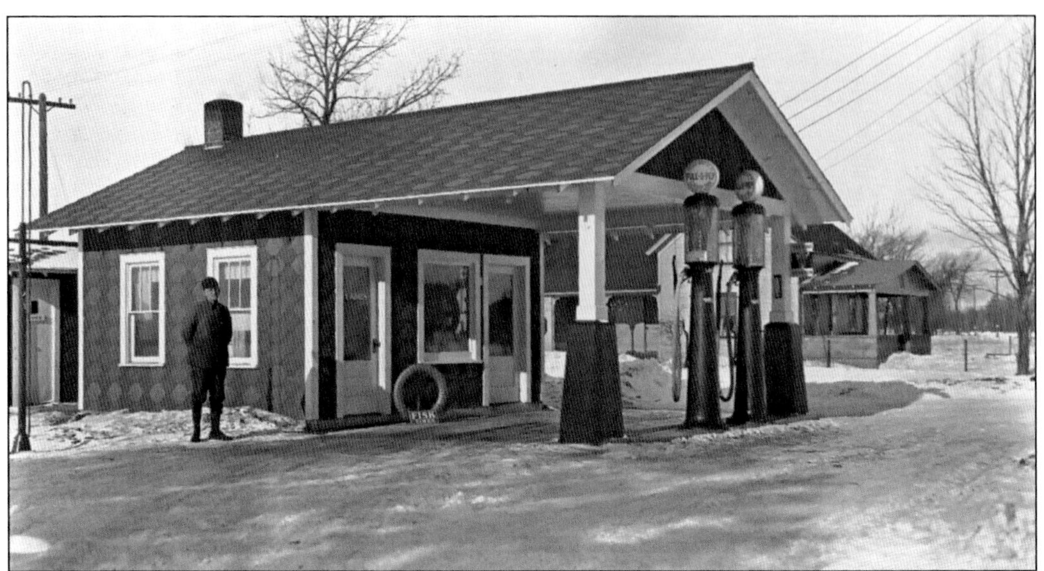

Frederick G. Halladay stands next to his filling station on the east side of Highway 51, one mile north of Plover. This is a nice example of two Wayne 1920s-era visible gas pumps. The Halladay station later became a Valvoline filling station.

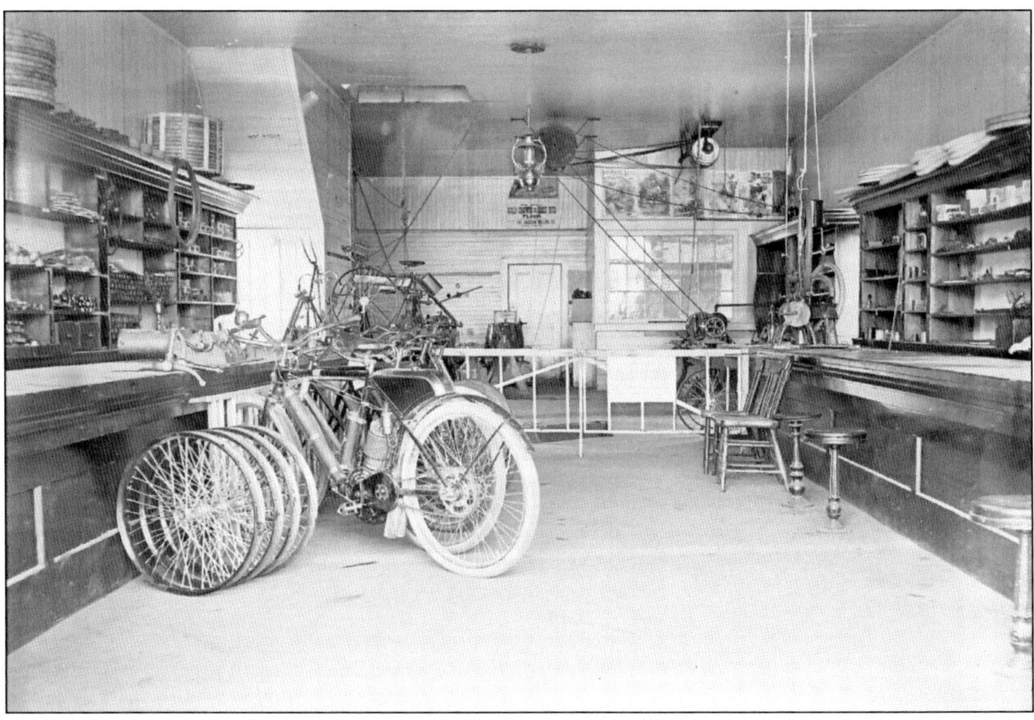

Shown here is the interior of Walter Barnsdale's bike shop, located near his house on the corner of First and Elm Streets (current Sumac Lane), in May 1904. Bicycling became popular in the late 1800s and at the turn of the 20th century. This shop also sold motorcycles only three years after Indian began production and one year after Harley Davidson. Barnsdale sold his shop in 1911 so he could focus on his moving pictures.

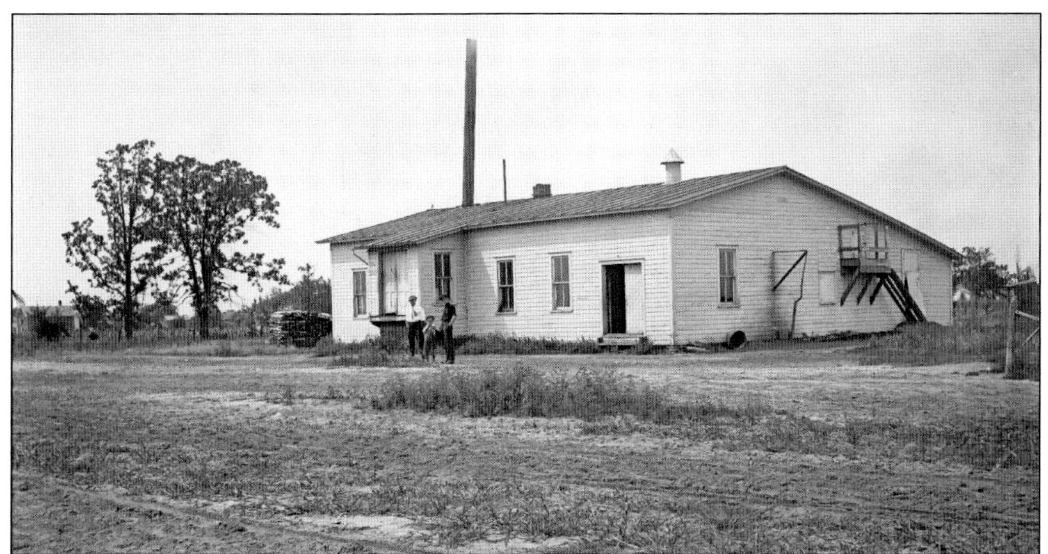

The Plover Creamery was built on the north side of Post Road just east of South Drive in 1900 by Marcus F. Pierce. In 1906, Pierce sold to Maurice Rasmussen, who operated the business until 1909. Rasmussen then sold to an organization of local farmers named the Plover Creamery Company, which operated until about 1918. In 1925, the creamery was resurrected when Otto McCormick, Otto Weller, and Leo Pierce purchased the building and reorganized as the Plover Gold Butter Company. This final incarnation only lasted a few years before the business disbanded and the building was turned into a residence.

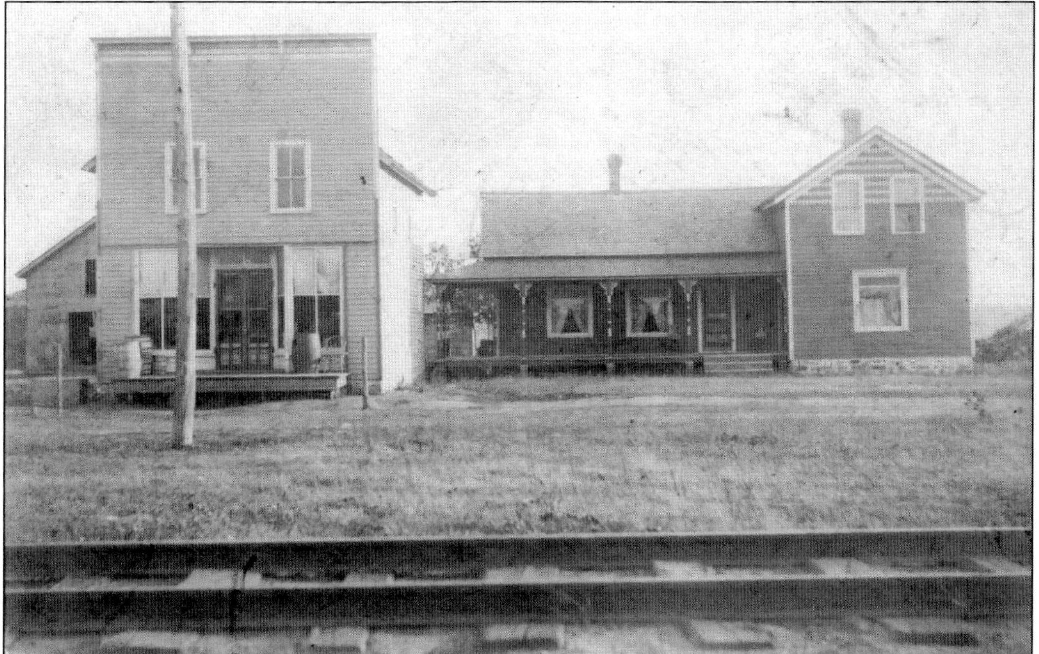

The Lutz general store (left) in Meehan was owned by Henry Lutz. On the first floor behind the store was the Lutz residence, and the second story was used as a community center. On the right is the house of William Clussman. These buildings were to the right of the Meehan church when looking south. (Ryan Berren collection, Gordon Fox.)

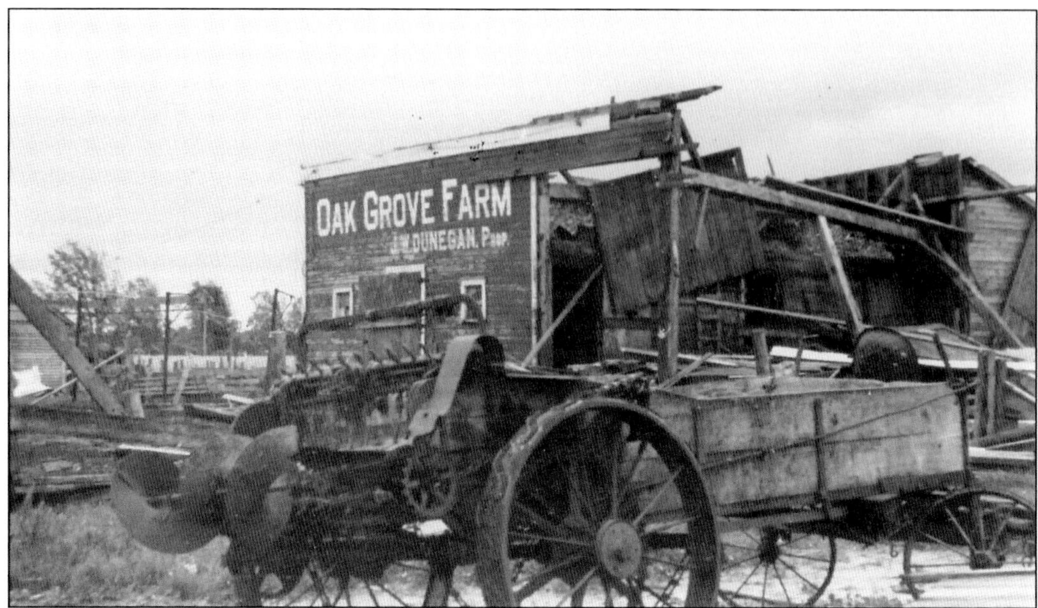

J.W. Dunegan was the proprietor of these damaged buildings on Oak Grove Farm, which was located south of the village on the south side of Highway 54. George Somers managed the farm in the 1910s, and William Brooks managed it in the late 1920s and early 1930s. The farm was auctioned off in 1948.

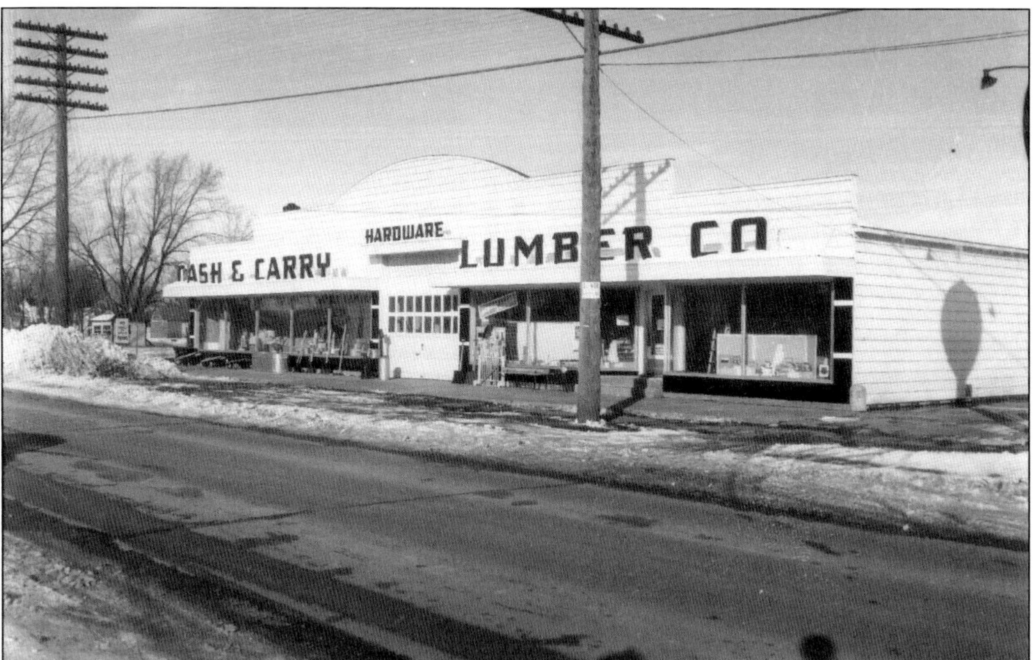

This photograph of the Cash & Carry Lumber Company was taken in 1951. Original owners were the brothers Emil and Victor Mansavage. Located on the east side of Post Road just south of the Green Bay & Western Railroad tracks, this building was later occupied by St. Vincent de Paul. The building was torn down in September 2015 in order to make way for a Post Road expansion project. (*Stevens Point Journal.*)

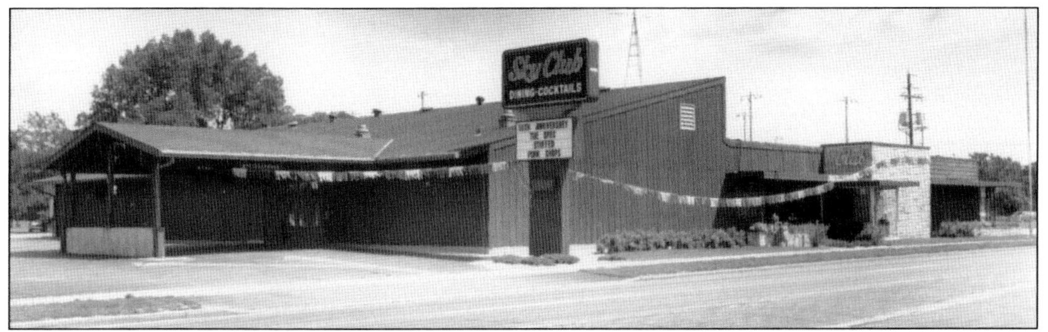

The Sky Club supper club, a longtime Plover landmark, was established in 1935 by George Armstrong as Army's Restaurant, and in 1940, Marion Nall bought it and renamed it the Sky Club. The business was purchased by Louis and Evelyn Schnittger in 1949 and then sold to John Freund in 1961. Since that time, Sky Club has been operated by the Freund family. The restaurant is credited with offering the first ever salad bar in 1950. (*Stevens Point Journal.*)

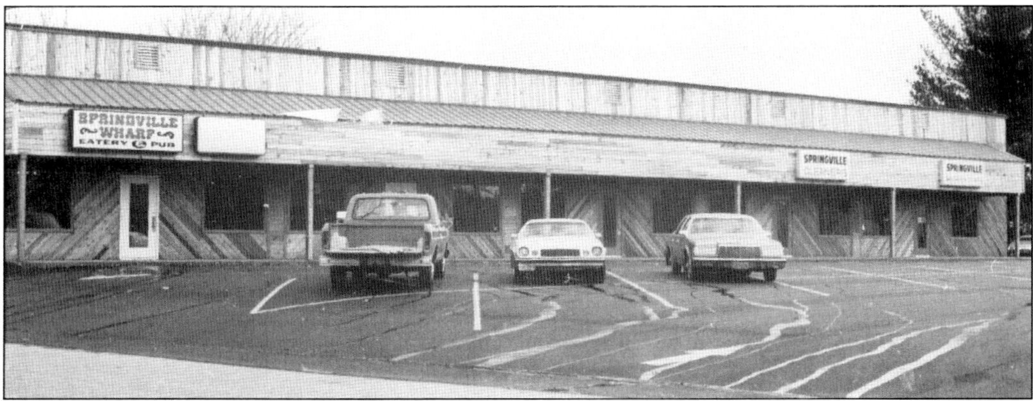

The Springville Wharf, a restaurant famous for its Italian cheese fries, is pictured here in 1981. In 2014, Springville Wharf changed its name to Springville Sports Grill and moved from this Post Road location to the Memories Banquet Hall on Plover Springs Drive due to the widening of Post Road and the destruction of this building. (*Stevens Point Journal.*)

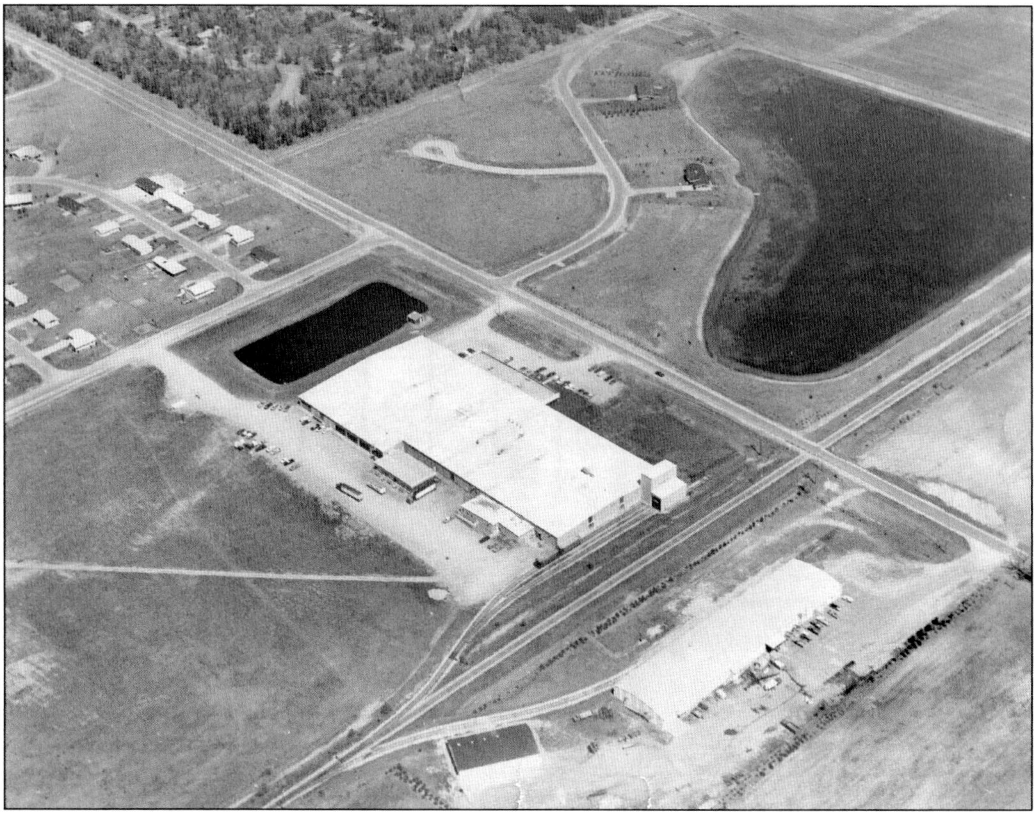

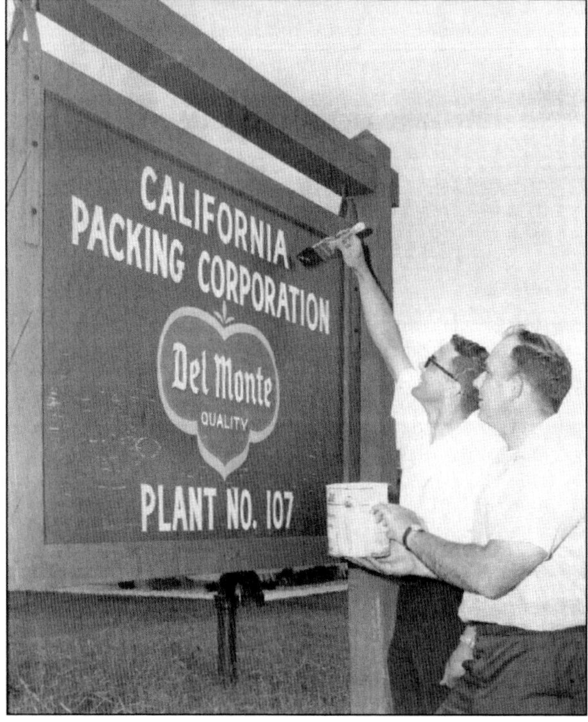

This is an aerial view of the Bake-Rite Bakery Company, which originally opened in the 1920s in Stevens Point. The company began building this new plant on Hoover Avenue in Plover in 1970 and began operation in 1972. Bake-Rite filed for bankruptcy in 1980, and after the trademarks and some equipment were purchased by Gardner Bakery, the plant closed in 1983.

Lee Bosche (left) and Laird Willson work on repainting a sign, changing it from California Packing Corporation (also known as "Calpak") to Del Monte. The plant, located on County Highway B, opened in 1966 as a bean-canning plant. Feeling that Calpak was no longer an appropriate name since they had packing plants across the country, the company changed its name to their top product line, Del Monte, in 1967. (*Stevens Point Journal.*)

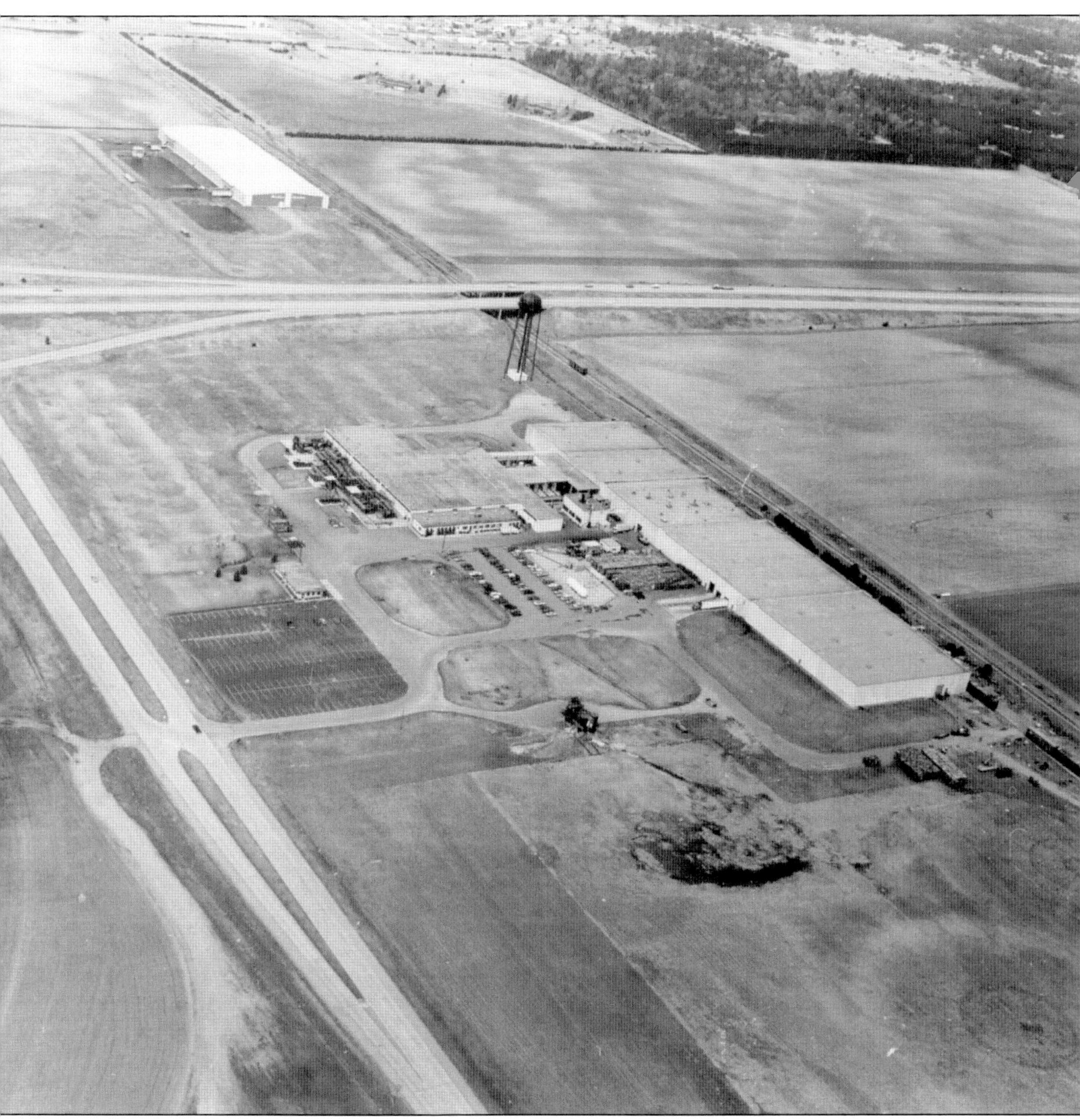

When this photograph was taken in 1984, the Plover Del Monte plant was the largest bean processor in the United States and the largest snap bean plant in the world at that time, producing about 10 percent of the nation's beans. In 1977, the plant was capable of processing 30 tons of beans per hour.

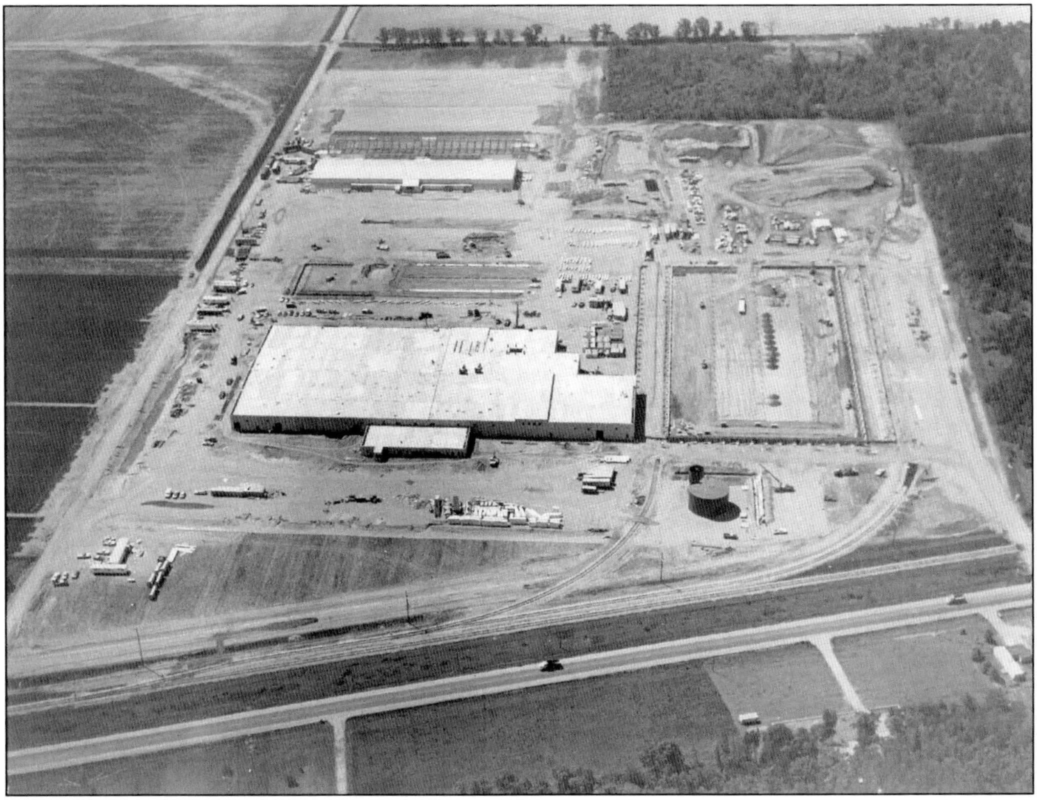

This view looks south at the Ore-Ida plant construction site in 1979. In the foreground is the main plant, and directly to the right are two train spurs going into the yet to be built area for Termicold, a cold storage warehouse, which changed its name to Americold in 1997.

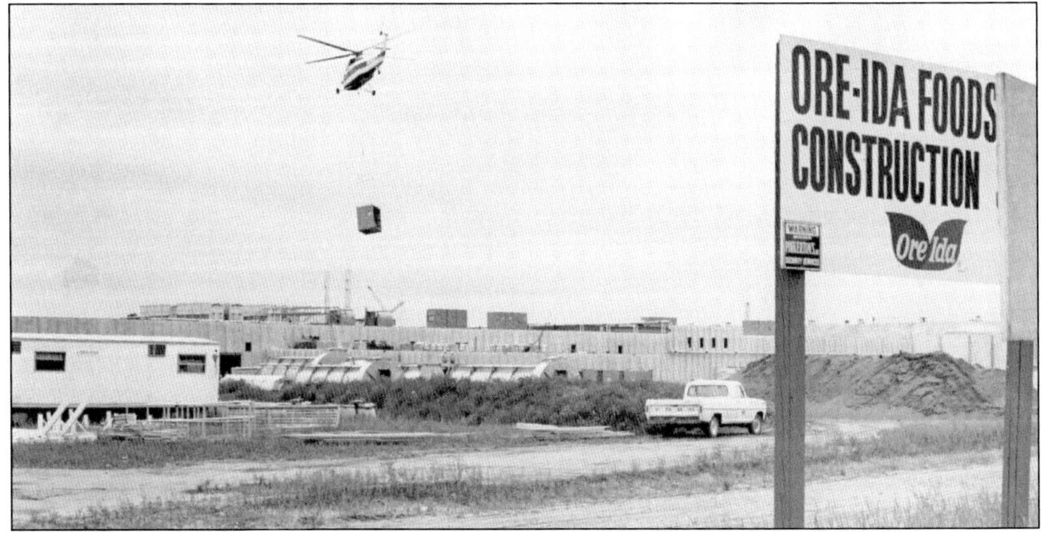

A helicopter is seen lifting part of an air conditioning unit to the roof of the new four-acre Ore-Ida plant in August 1978. In 1982, Ore-Ida completed a $30 million expansion that doubled the plant's capacity from 100,000 tons of potatoes per year to 200,000 tons. Ore-Ida was bought by the Canadian company McCain Foods in 1997. (*Stevens Point Journal.*)

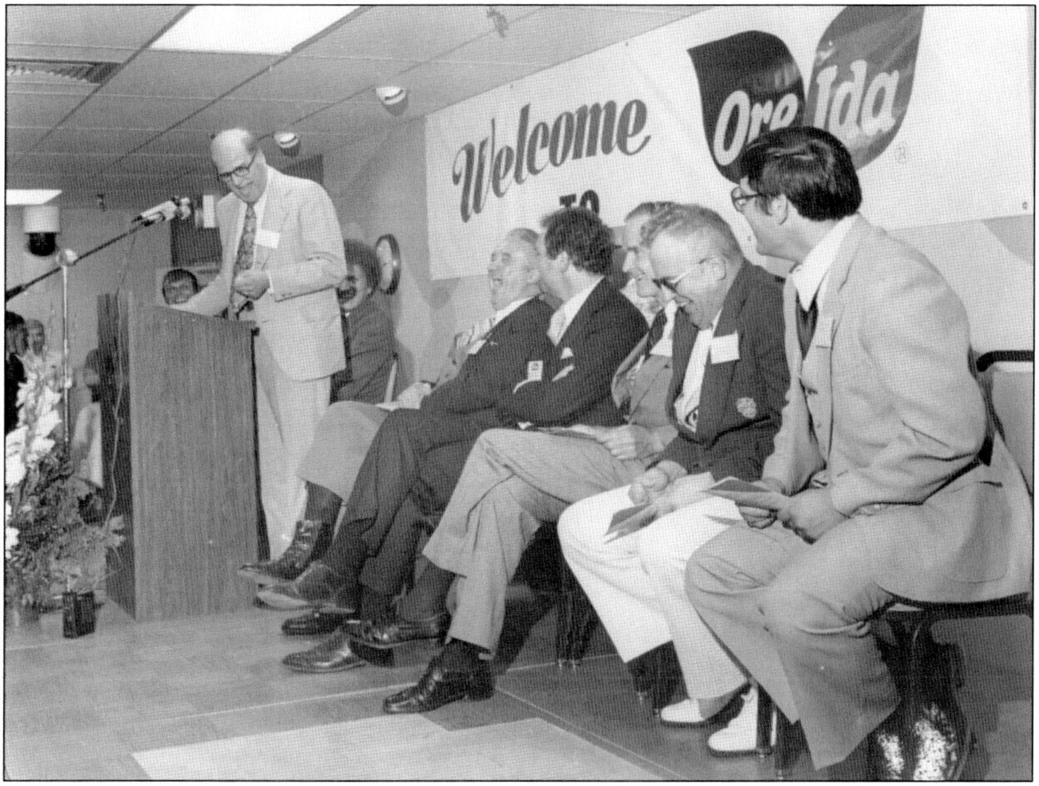

Guests of honor laugh at Sen. Gaylord Nelson's joke during the official opening of the new Ore-Ida Foods plant on June 8, 1979. Attendees for the event included, from left to right, Senator Nelson (standing) Gov. Lee Sherman Dreyfus, Pres. Anthony O'Reilly of the H.J. Heinz Company, Sen. William Proxmire, chairman Robert Steinke of the Town of Plover, and Mayor Michael Haberman of Stevens Point. (*Stevens Point Journal.*)

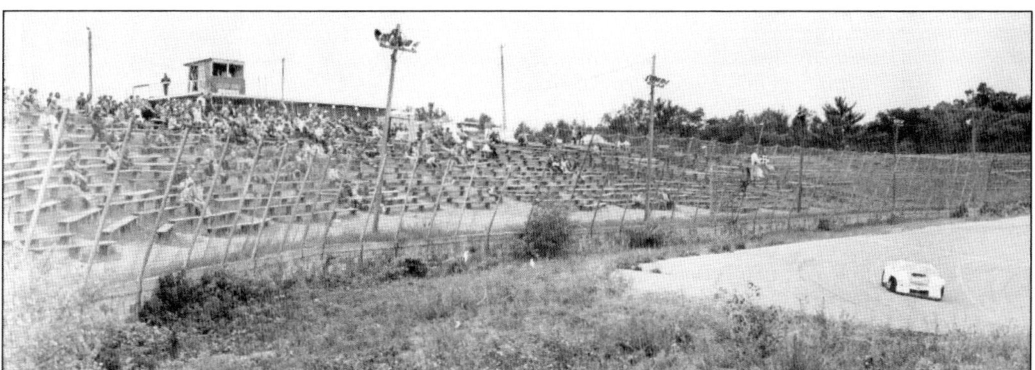

Golden Sands Speedway is located on Highway 54 across from McCain Foods. The Speedway was built in 1967 and closed in 1982 and saw its permit lapse when no races were held in 1983. In 1988, longtime owner Sam Bartus sold to Phil Bickley, who leased the track to Terry Prueser. The speedway reopened the next year after major renovations had been complete. This photograph is believed to have been taken around 1982. (*Stevens Point Journal.*)

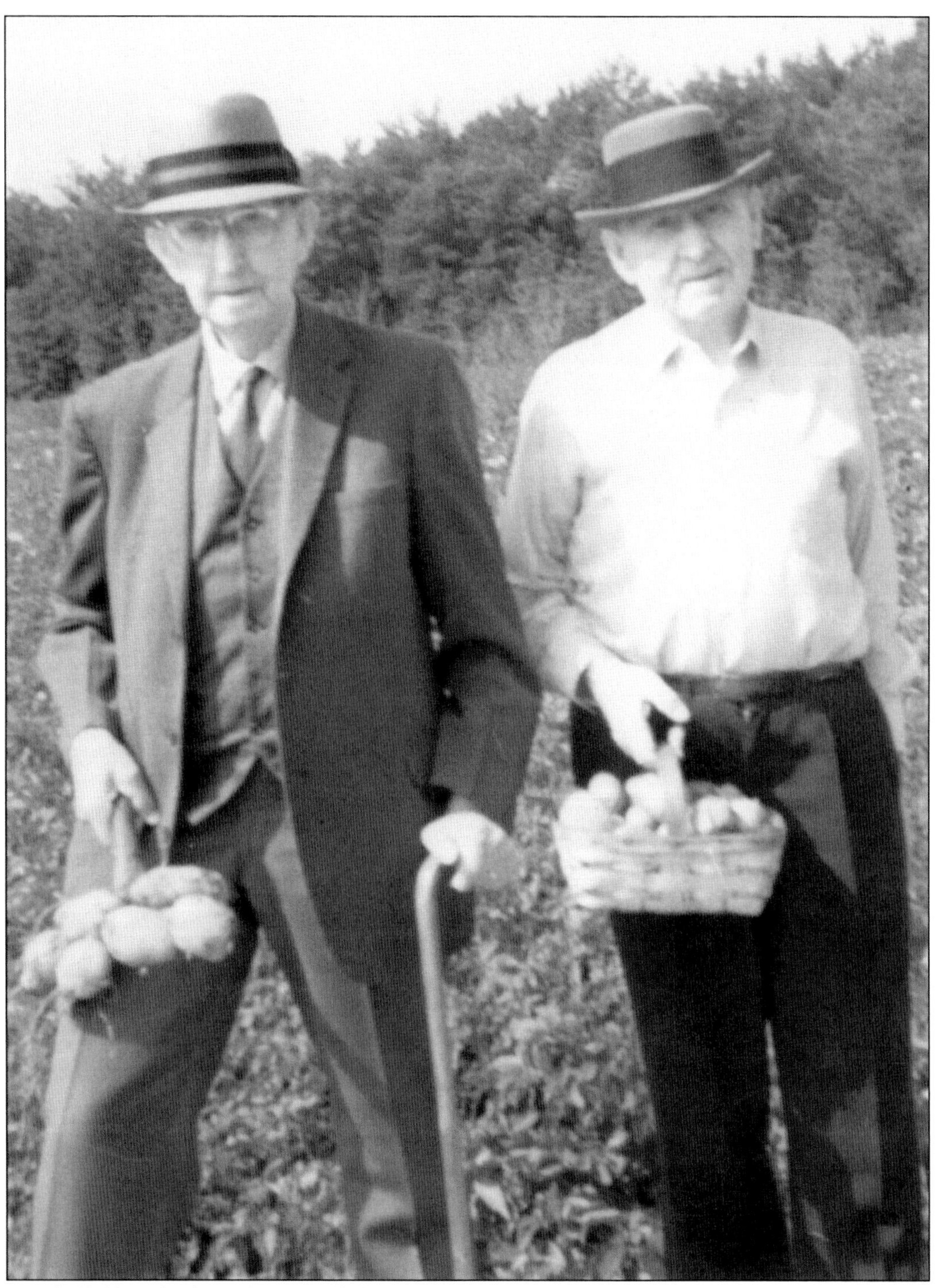

Joseph (left) and Alois Okray stroll through a potato field. The brothers founded Okray Family Farms in 1905. The company was based out of Stevens Point, but during the Great Depression, the Okrays purchased large tracts of land in the Plover area.

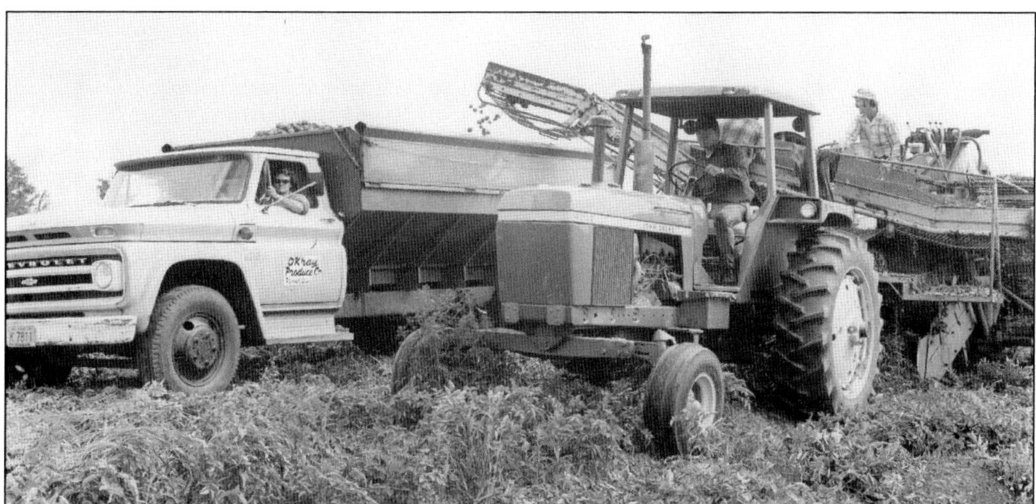

Okray employees use truck and tractor to harvest a potato crop. Prior to World War II, Okray Family Farms had planned to irrigate the land to facilitate better crop production, but the war made necessary materials, such as aluminum, scarce. After the war, they were able to begin irrigating fields, and although they were not the first farmers to do so, their contribution was substantial, helping to revolutionize irrigation in Central Wisconsin.

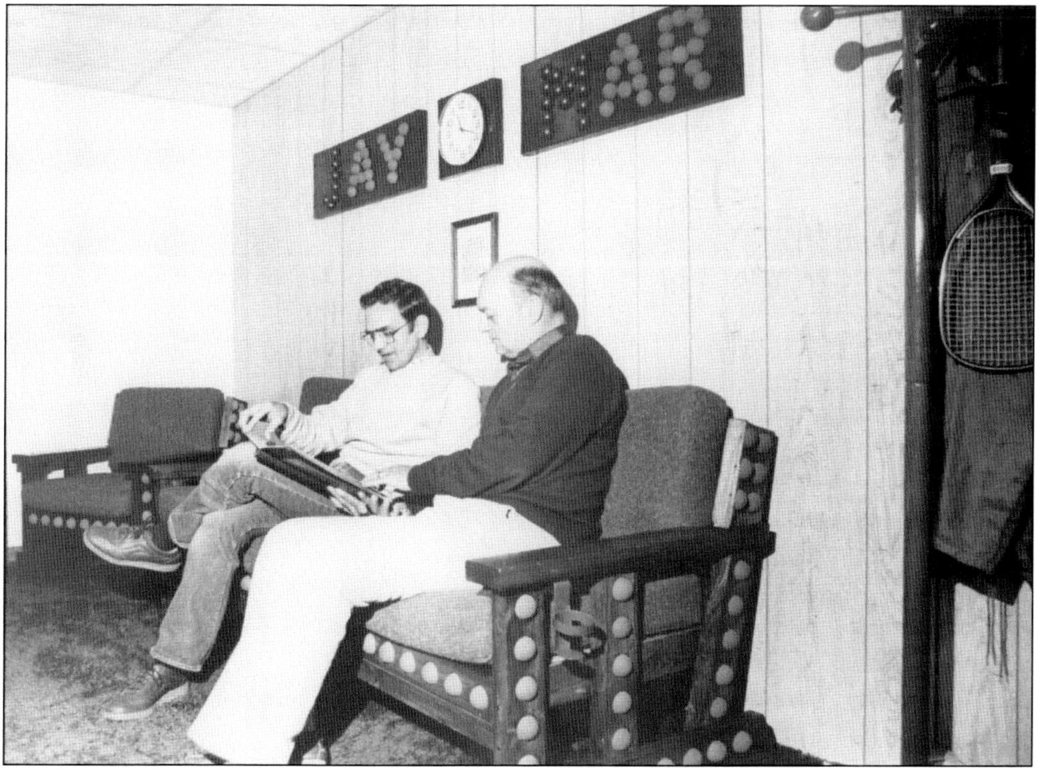

This photograph shows the inside of a Jay-Mar office, with Jay Warner Sr. seated on the right. The business was started in 1970 by Jay and Marilyn Warner, who sold boxes and bags to Wisconsin potato growers. Jay-Mar has since started selling farm seed, fertilizers, pet foods, bird seed, and lawn and garden supplies and is still a family-owned business.

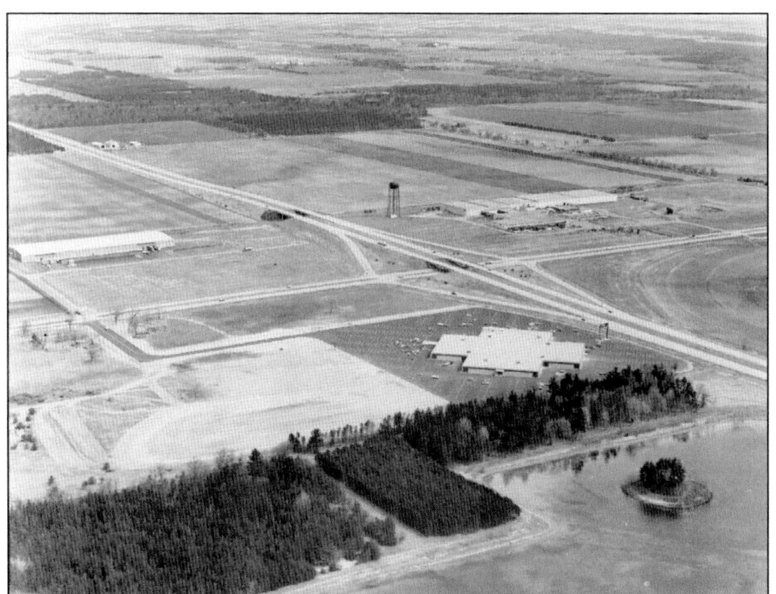

This 1984 aerial view looks northeast at Lake Pacawa, the Manufacturer's Direct Mall, and Del Monte Foods. Within a few years this area would explode with growth. New businesses would include Rainbow Falls, a hotel, gas station, and several restaurants.

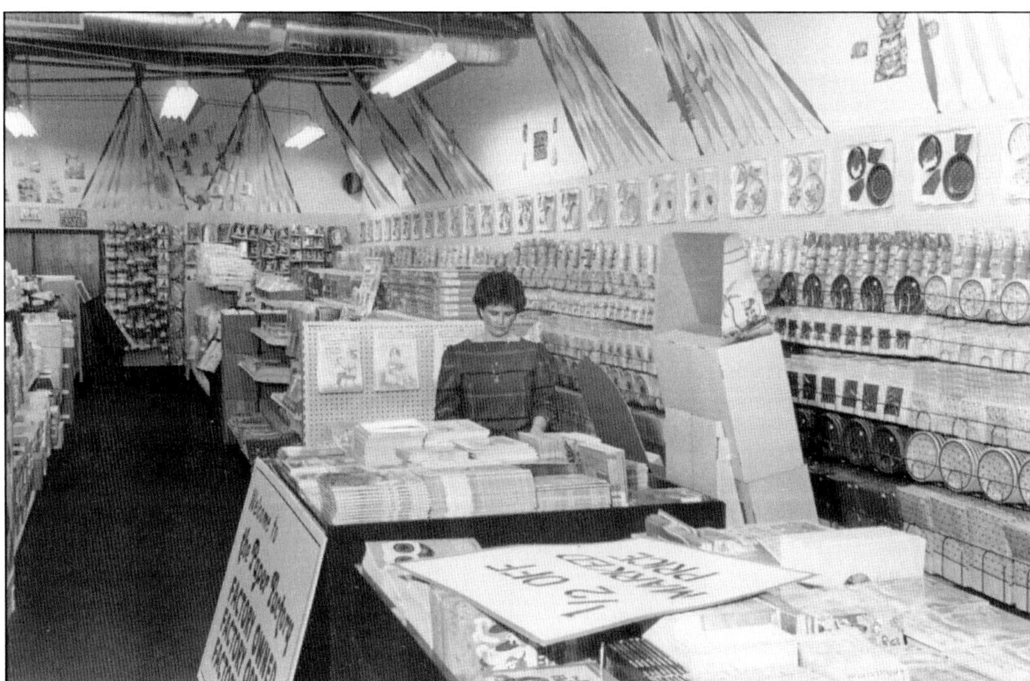

A woman browses the selection at the Paper Factory in the Manufacturer's Direct Mall and Outlet Center. The mall grand opening was on March 29, 1984, with businesses occupying 20 stores out of 30. Later, the mall was purchased by Lokre Development of Wausau, and late in 2002, the company got permission from the Village of Plover to demolish the building.

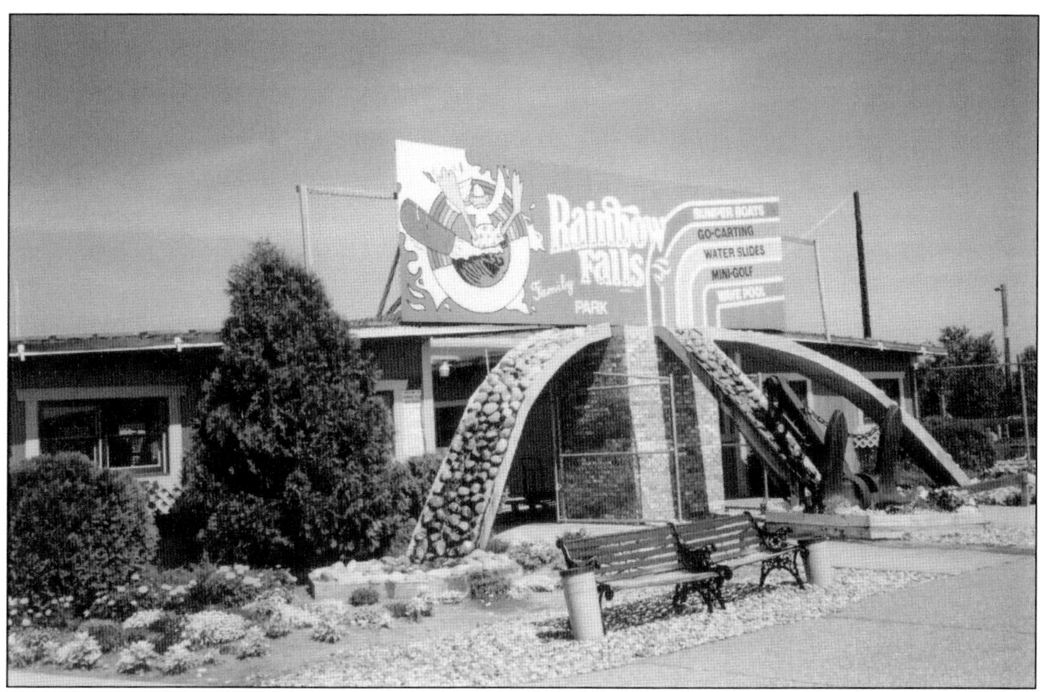

Rainbow Falls was opened in 1988 by Chester Skippy, who designed and constructed the park. The park started with bumper boats, three go-kart tracks, and five serpentine waterslides. Rainbow Falls was later owned by Lokre Development of Wausau, and the last season of attendance was 2003, when it was decided to not reopen in March 2004. The above photograph is of the entrance, and the view below looks west from the top of Zero Gravity toward the Wave Pool and the River of Rainbows.

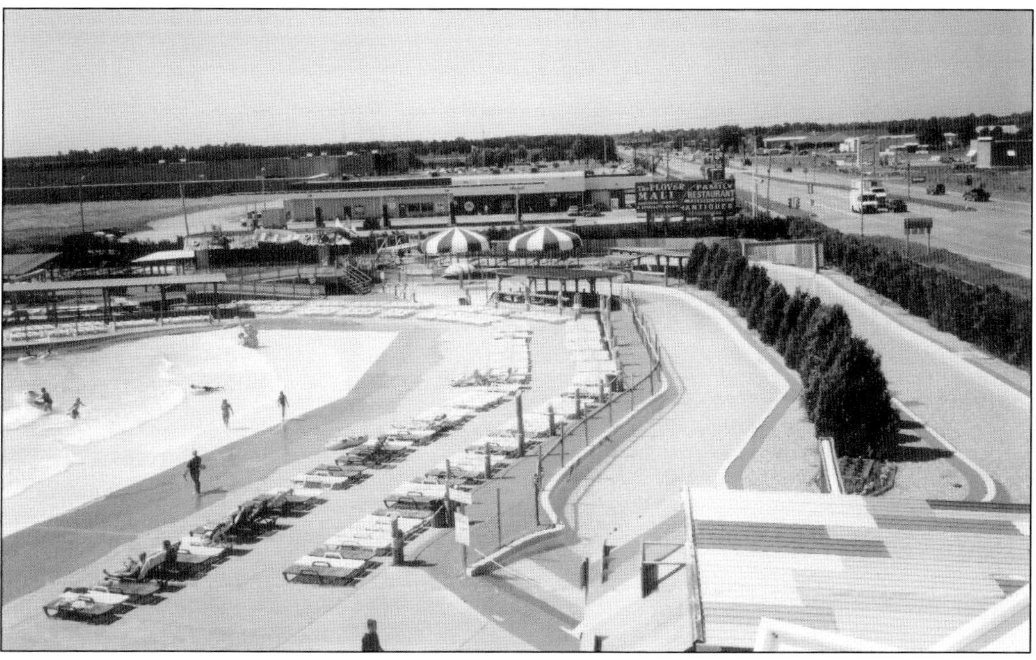

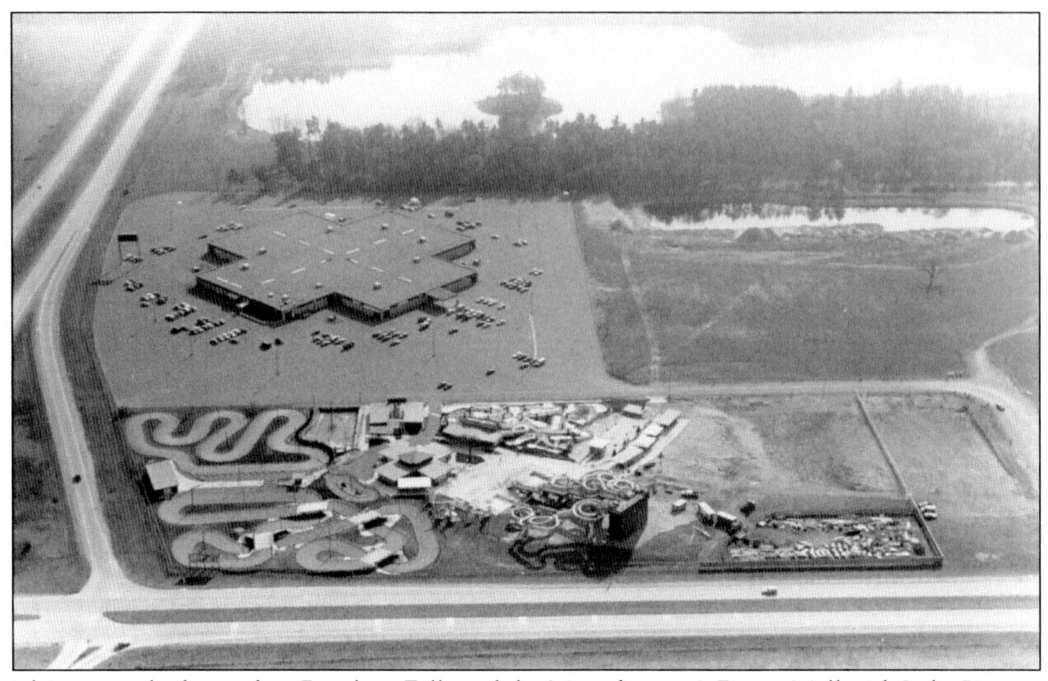

This picture looks south at Rainbow Falls and the Manufacturer's Direct Mall with Lake Pacawa in the background.

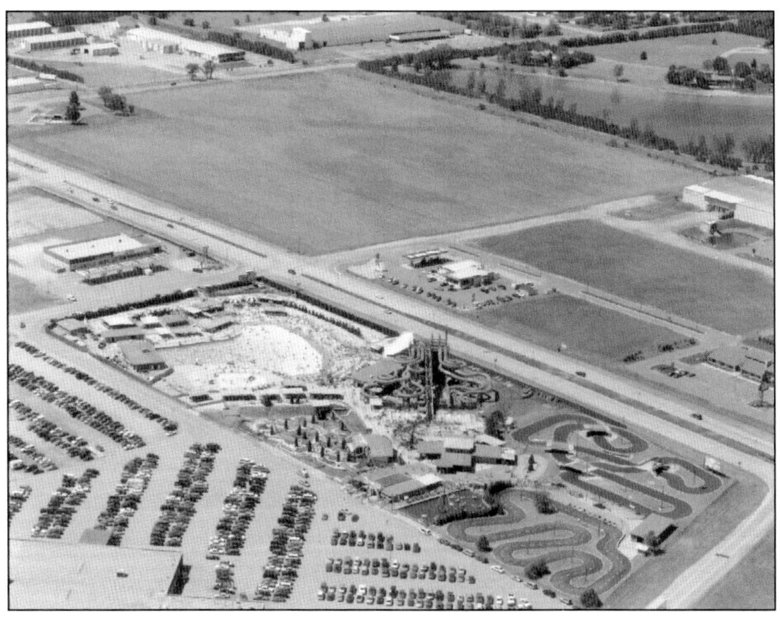

This view looks northwest at Rainbow Falls and the Manufacturer's Direct Mall. Notice the lack of retail development north of Plover Road where Copps, Shopko, and other retail stores stand today. At the top are Worzella and Sons Potatoes and the old Bake-Rite plant.

Six

THE RIVER AND MILLS

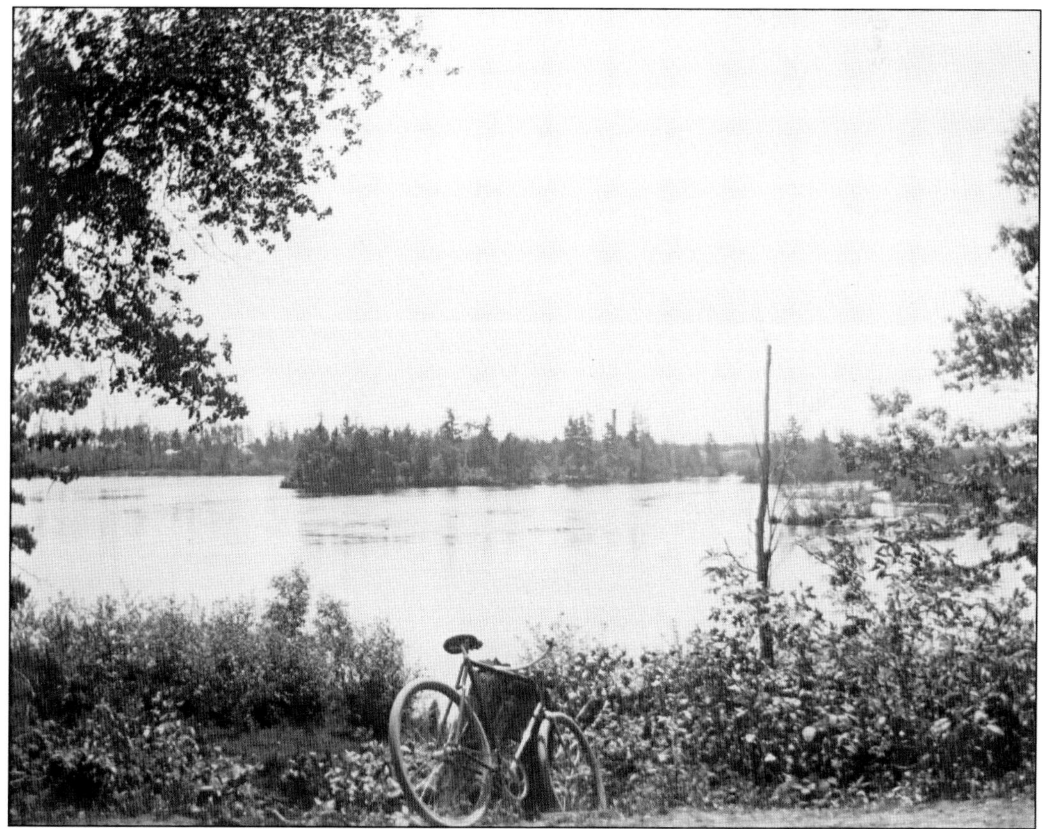

A bicycle leans on a stump next to the Wisconsin River at Plover. Referred to as the "hardest working river," the Wisconsin River runs 430 miles from the northeast to the southwest, nearly cutting the state in half. It starts in Lac Vieux Desert and empties into the Mississippi River at Prairie du Chien.

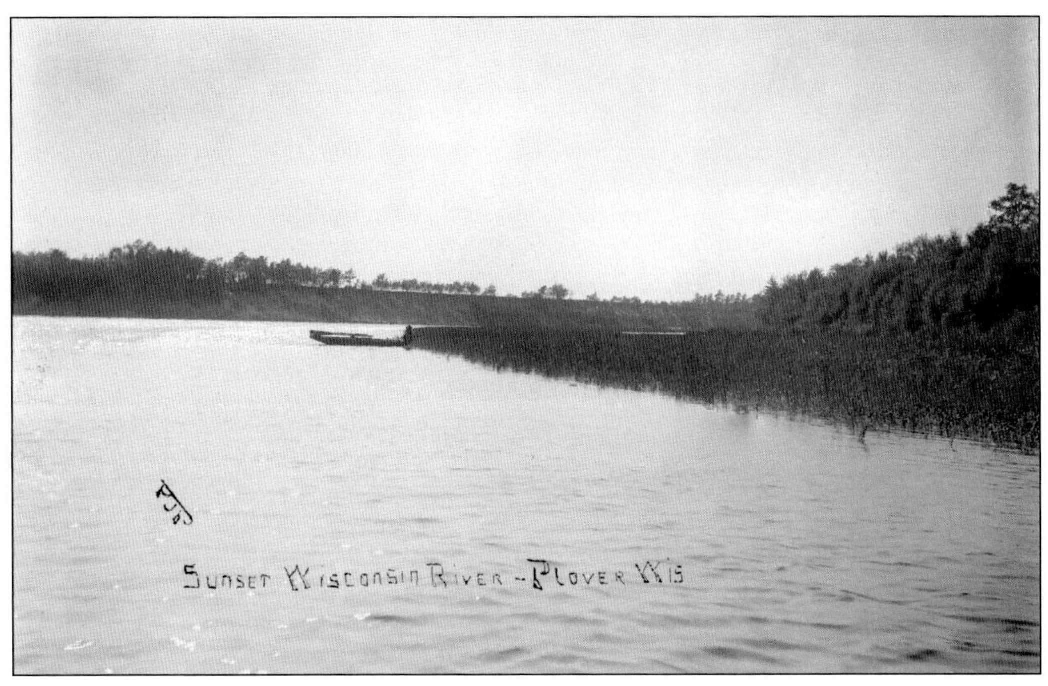

This view of the Yellow Banks of the Wisconsin River at Plover looks south at sunset. In the early days of Plover's history, this area would have seen the river clogged with fresh-cut timber being guided down the river as soon as the ice broke up in the spring. Raftsmen and river men negotiated the river as they drove the logs downstream to markets farther south.

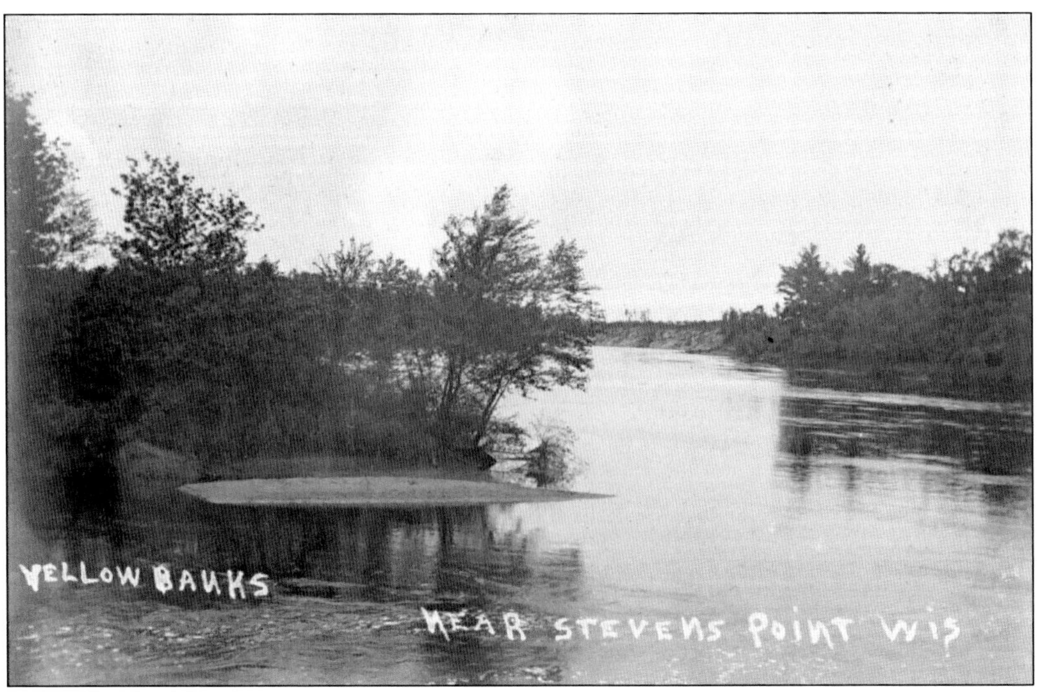

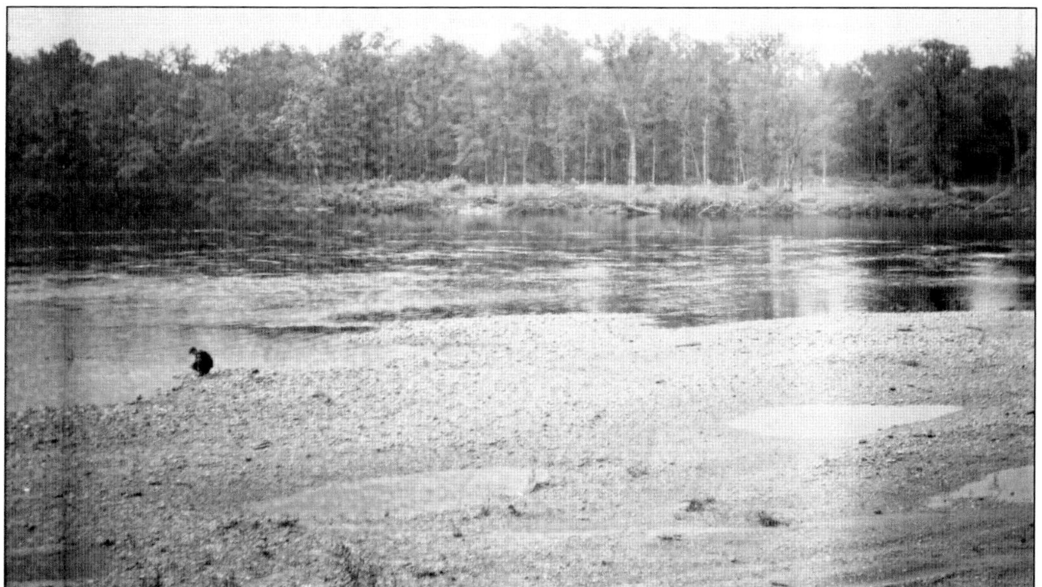

A boy crouches on the shore of the Wisconsin River north of the Yellow Banks at Plover. After the days when sawmills peppered the shoreline of the Wisconsin River, new industries popped up that harnessed the river's raw power. In this area, paper production became most popular, but the river is also used to generate electricity.

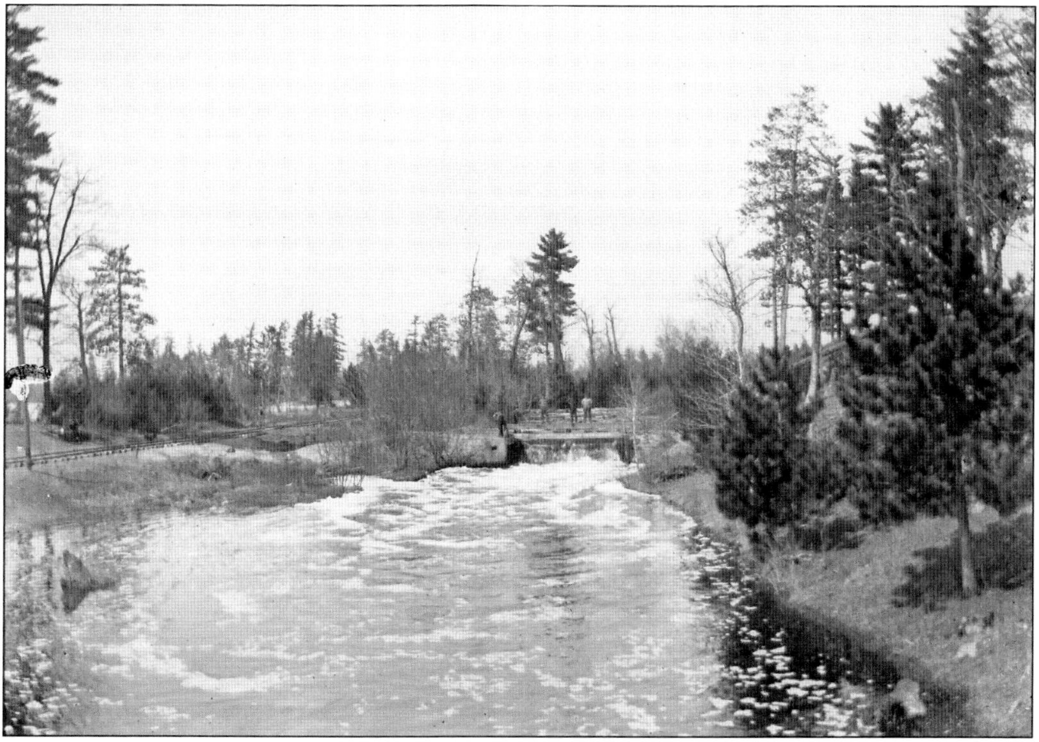

This photograph, identified as "Sherman's Cutoff," was located near the Whiting-Plover Paper Company. The Green Bay & Western spur leading to the mill can be seen on the left as five men stand on a small dam.

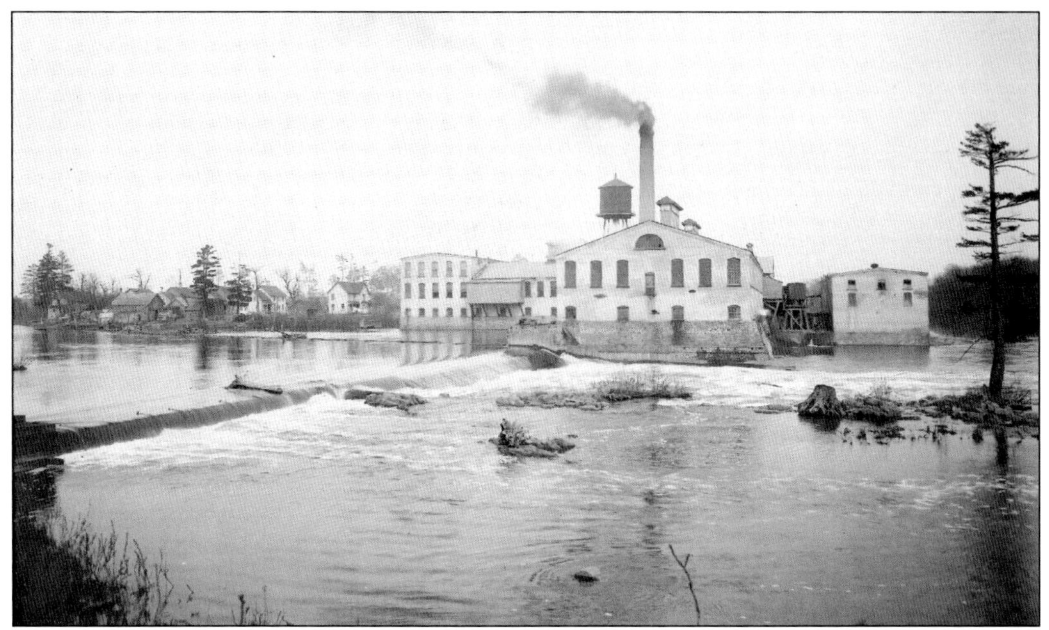

The Plover Paper Company mill was one of two mills built by George A. Whiting on the Wisconsin River, with the other being the Wisconsin River Paper and Pulp Company. The mill was built on land previously owned by Plover pioneer S.A. Sherman. Whiting would eventually team up with C.A. Babcock, R.H. Edwards, C.E. Edward, and Emmons Burr to create a stock company that was incorporated as the Plover Paper Company. Construction on the buildings was started on September 15, 1892, and the mill went into operation in early 1894. Whiting was president of the company from the beginning until his death in 1930. In 1912, the name of the mill was changed to Whiting-Plover Paper Company.

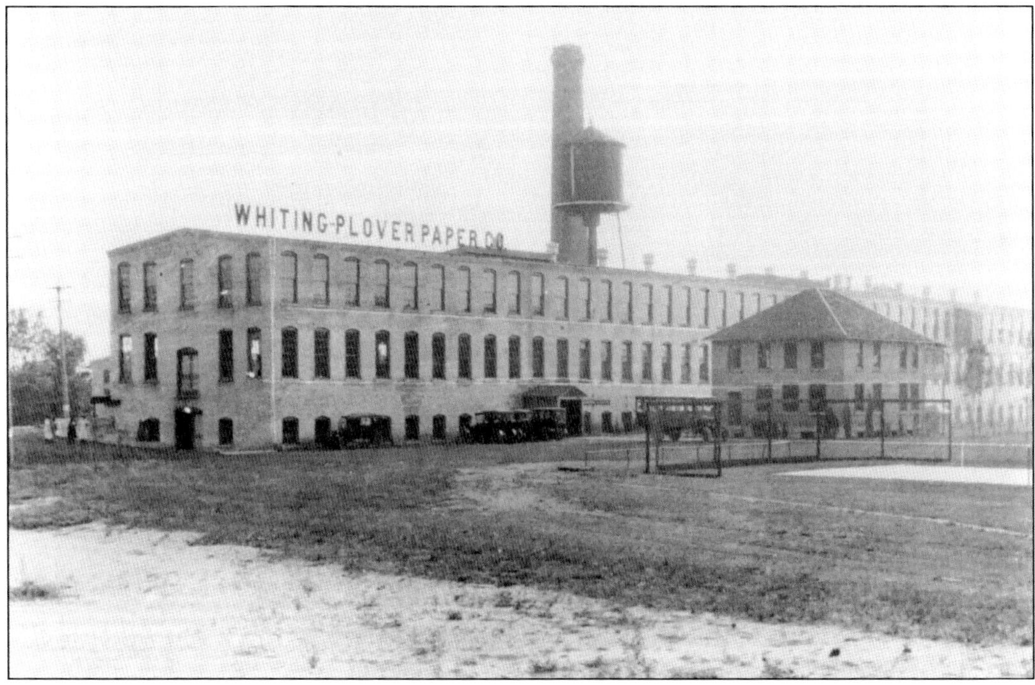

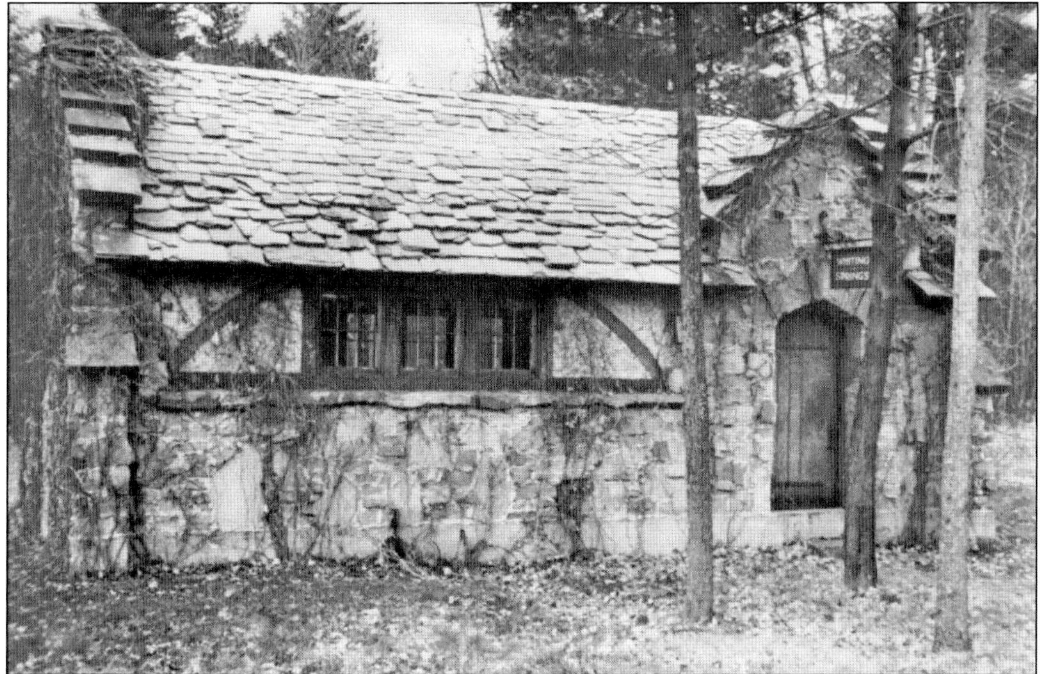

This spring house was built by the Whiting-Plover Paper Company to get water from a spring that was discovered in 1912 a couple miles away. Prior to this, the mill had a difficult time obtaining water that was clean enough to use in the paper-making process. This building was used for the Village of Whiting's town meetings for a short time after its incorporation.

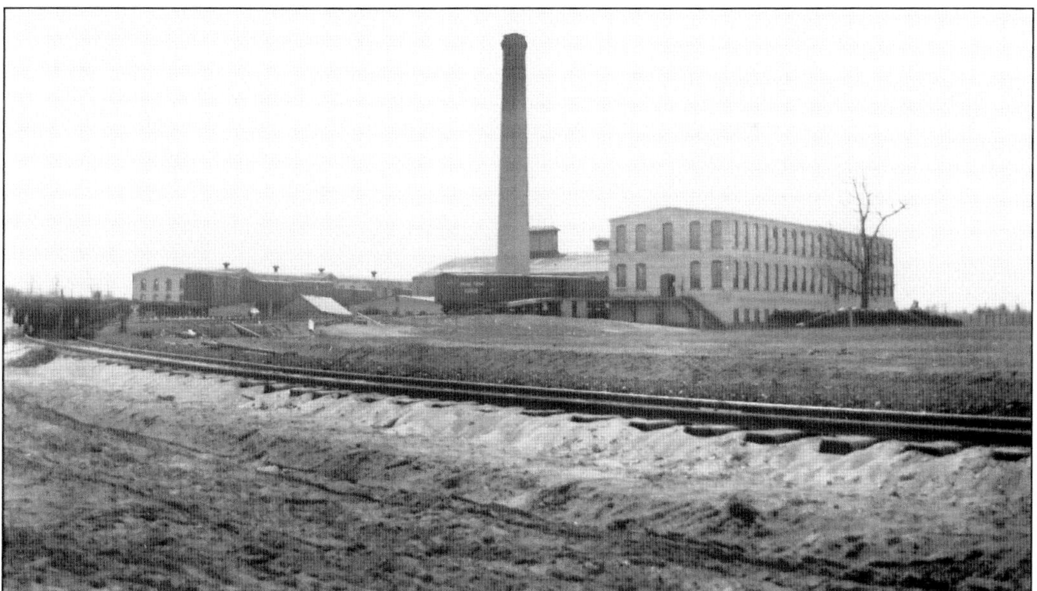

This image of the Whiting-Plover Paper Company shows the railroad spur leading to the mill. Commonly known by area residents as the "lower mill," this mill was originally established as the Plover Paper Company, and in 1912, the name was changed to the Whiting-Plover Paper Company. This mill has been operated by the Nekoosa Edward Paper Company, Great Northern, Kimberly-Clark, and currently, Neenah Paper.

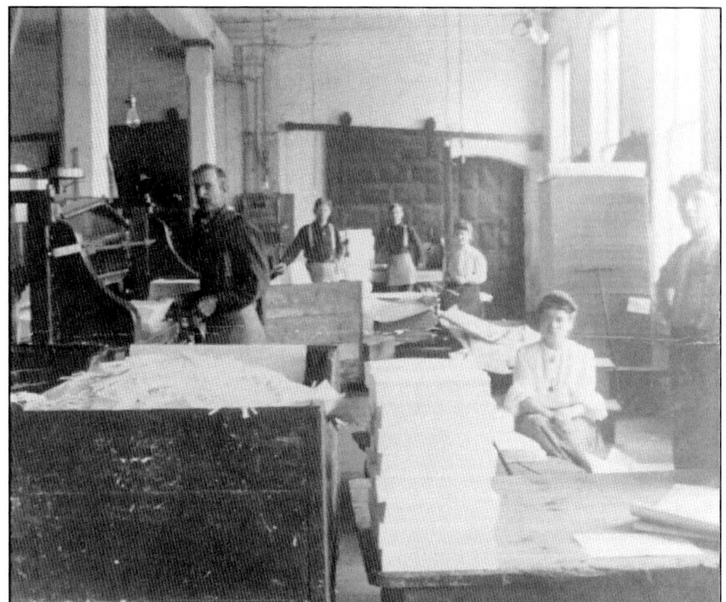

A group of employees are pictured working in the Plover Paper Company sorting room. The two women are Eva Booth Finnessey (background) and Eva Herman Booth (seated). Eva Herman Booth was married to Warren Booth and lived on Stockton Road in Plover.

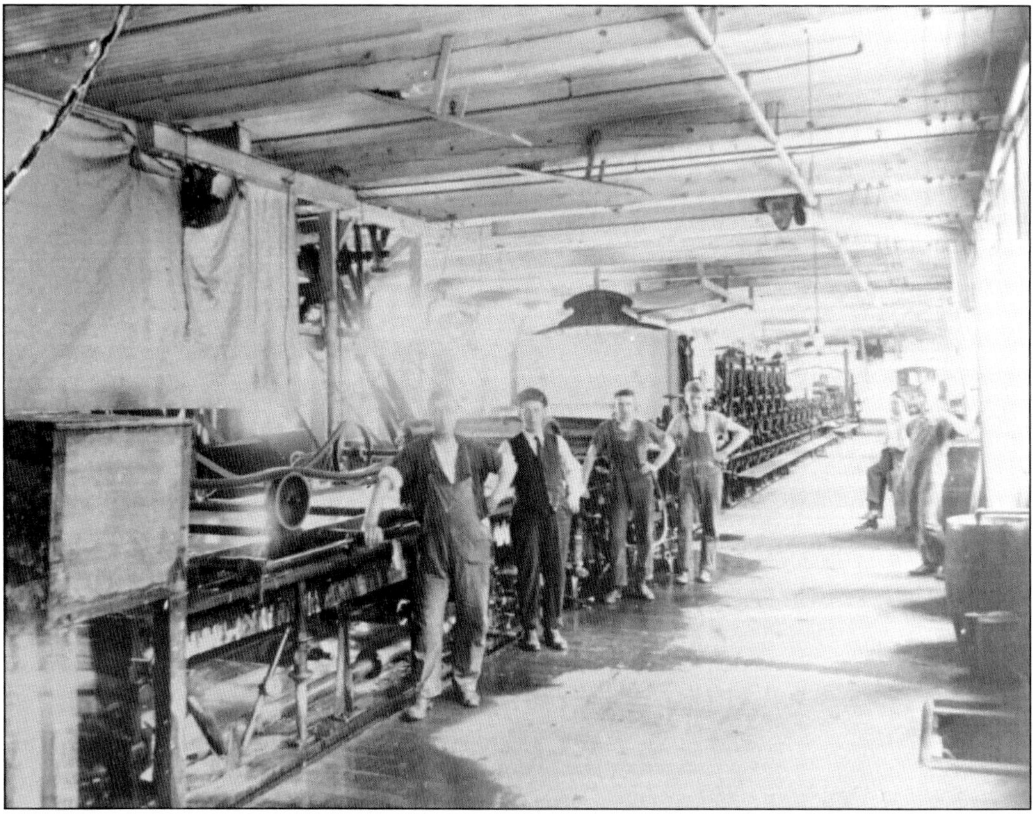

Shown here is the Plover Paper Company machine room, which measured 66 by 177 feet and was in the basement and first story. The Fourdrinier machine used in the mill had a daily capacity of 15,000 pounds of paper. Pictured are George Hager at far left, and his son Earl Hager, fourth from left. George was a paper maker, and Earl's profession was machine tender.

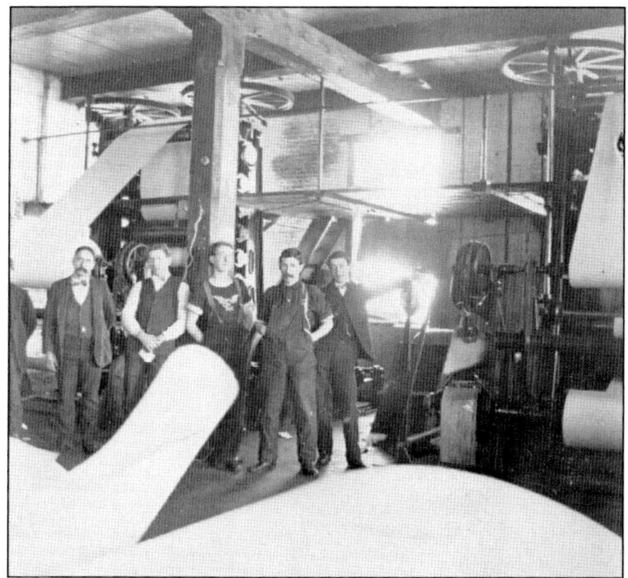

Employees are pictured in the finishing room of the Plover Paper Company in March 1901. The finishing room included two stories and a basement, and measured 40 by 80 feet. This was where the paper was calendared, cut, reamed, and made ready for shipment. Equipment at the time included two super calendars (visible on the left and right), three paper cutters, and one ream cutter.

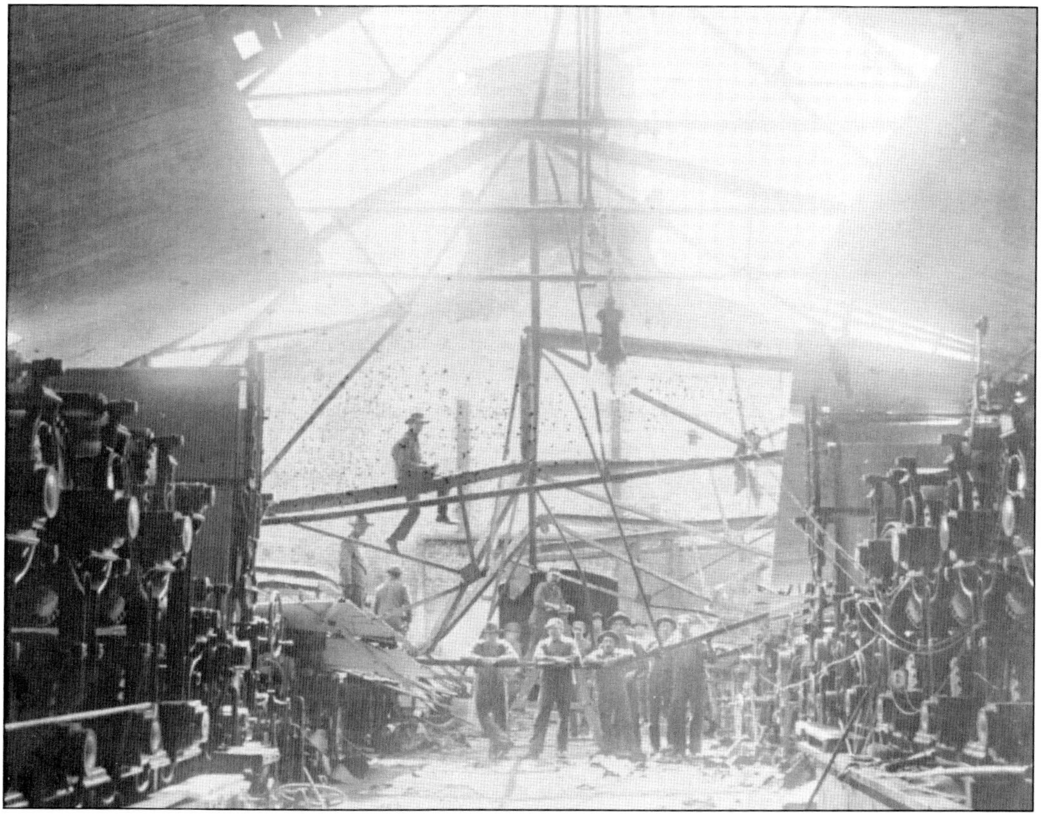

On July 4, 1900, the bales of rag on the third floor of the rag mill of the Plover Paper Company spontaneously combusted, causing a large fire with estimated losses of $75,000. The fire spread with incredible speed; luckily, the quick action of mill workers and the Stevens Point Fire Department saved the rotary boiler and other machinery in the west end of the mill. The fire kept 200 employees out of work for 30 days until the mill was rebuilt.

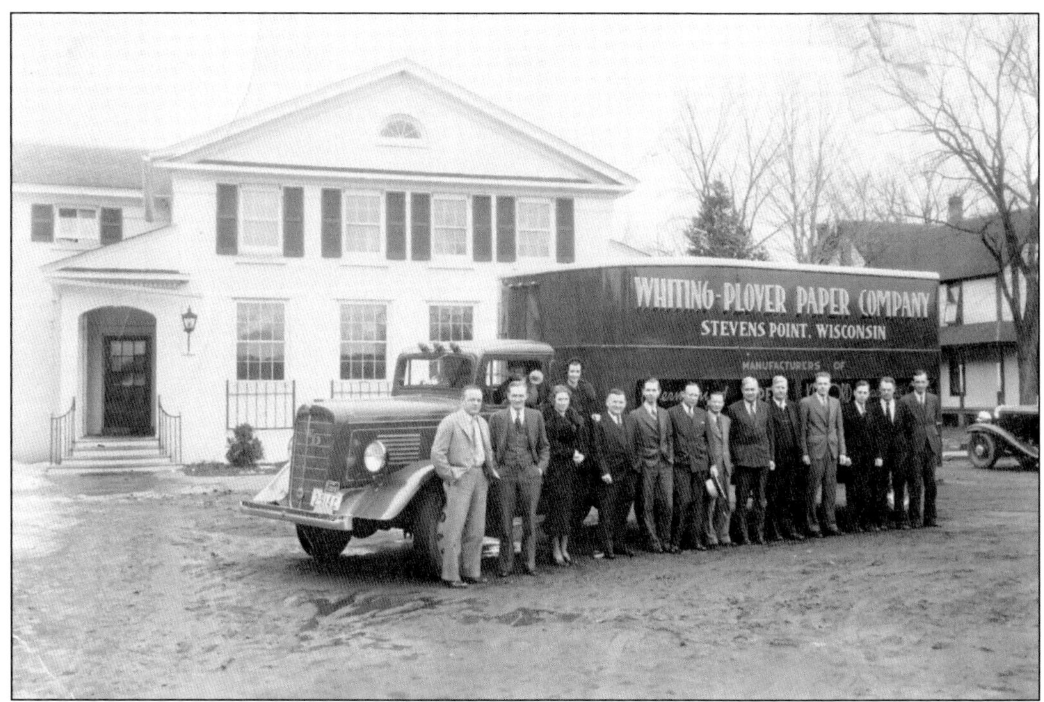

Employees of the Whiting-Plover Paper Co. pose with the company truck in front of the mill's office building. In 1932, the office building was completely remodeled, the exterior was whitewashed trimmed in green, and artistic porches and three new offices were added. Also, the company's laboratory was moved from the mill to the second floor of the office building due to the ability to control heat and humidity for more accurate paper testing.

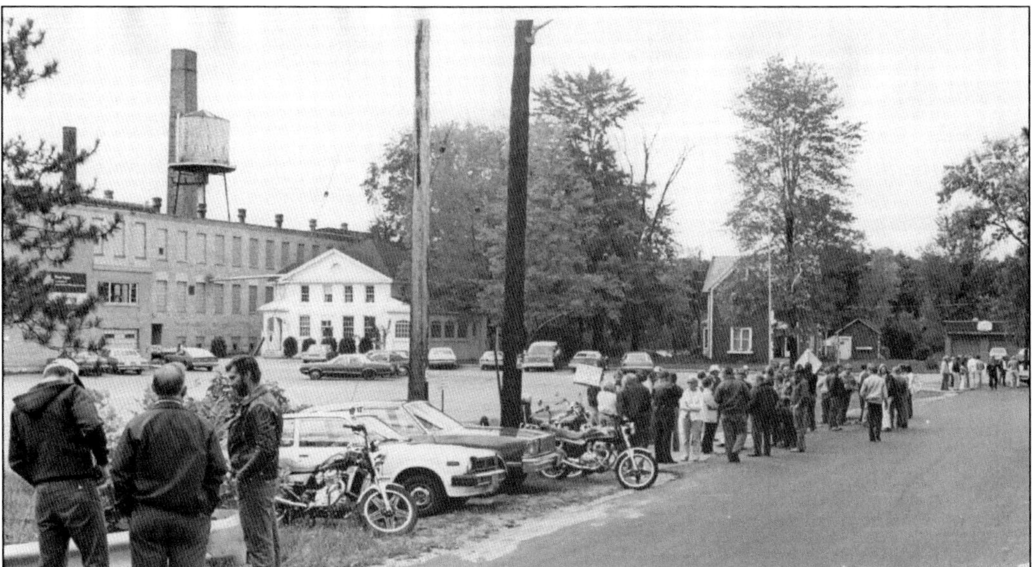

Pictured are employee protesters forming a picket line outside of Plover Papers over a wage dispute in 1980. Negotiations between Plover Papers and the employees had been ongoing from May 19 to August 10, when the union, representing 185 workers, rejected the new contract. The sign in the center reads, "Local 370 on strike against Great Northern Nekoosa." (*Stevens Point Journal.*)

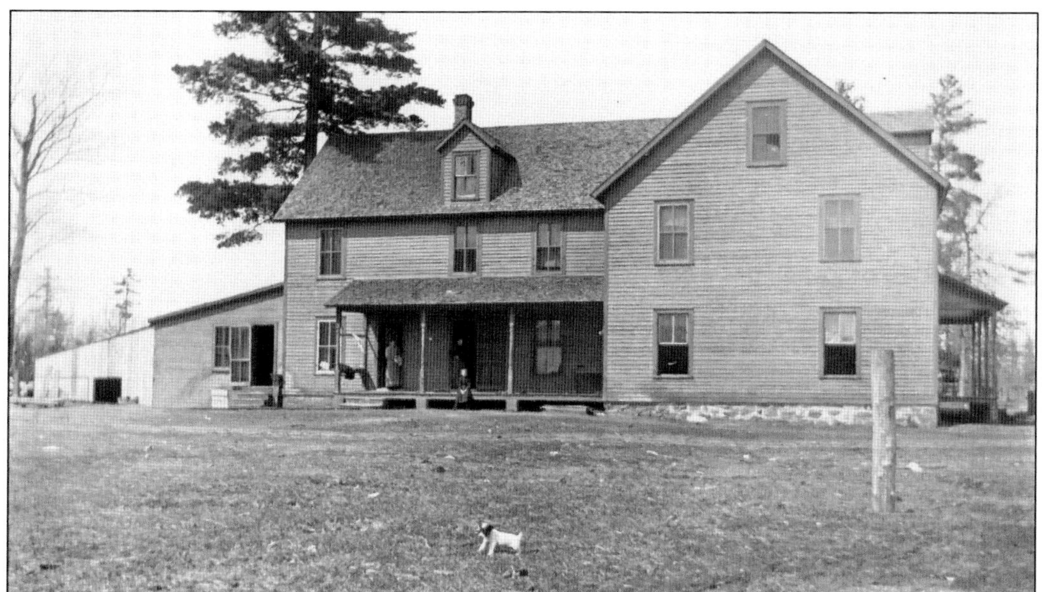

Several boardinghouses, such as the one pictured here, popped up around the paper mills in Whiting to board employees. Eventually, the paper mills would build company houses for individual families to live in around the various mills. Due to the influx of workers and families, the Whiting schoolhouse was built to accommodate the growing community.

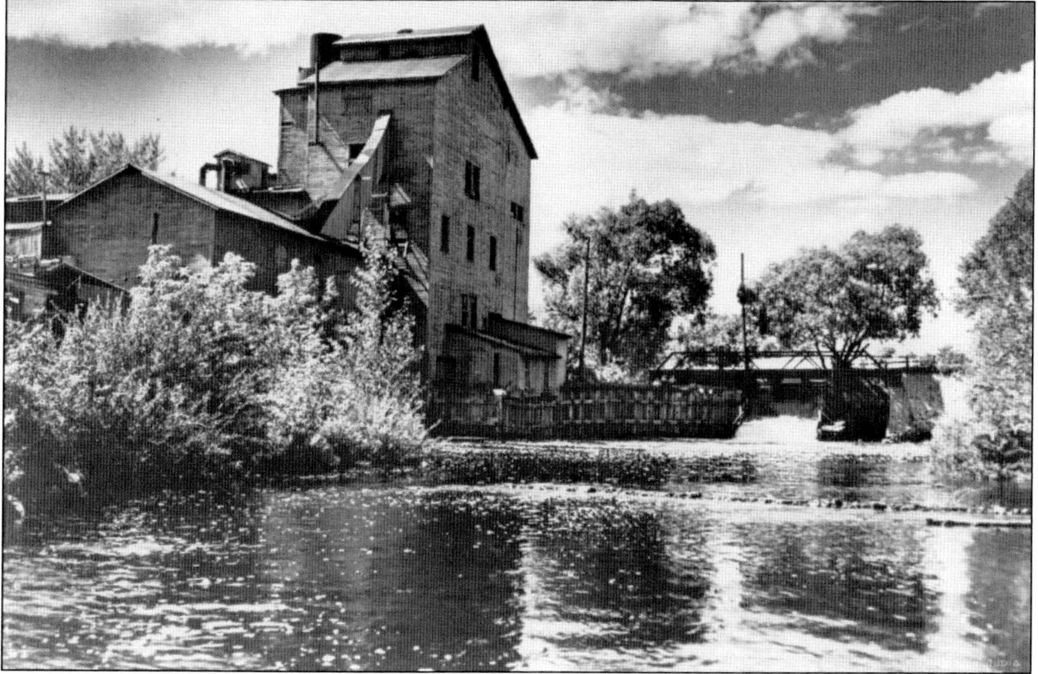

The John Strange Paper Mill was infamously known as the "Stink Mill" because its paper-making process used sulfate, creating a rotten smell. The mill was built around 1916 by Strange, and he operated the Stevens Point Pulp and Paper Company out of it. The mill was purchased by newer owners when Strange died in 1923 and operated until 1954. This mill was located on the Plover River where the current baseball field of the Lower Whiting Park is today.

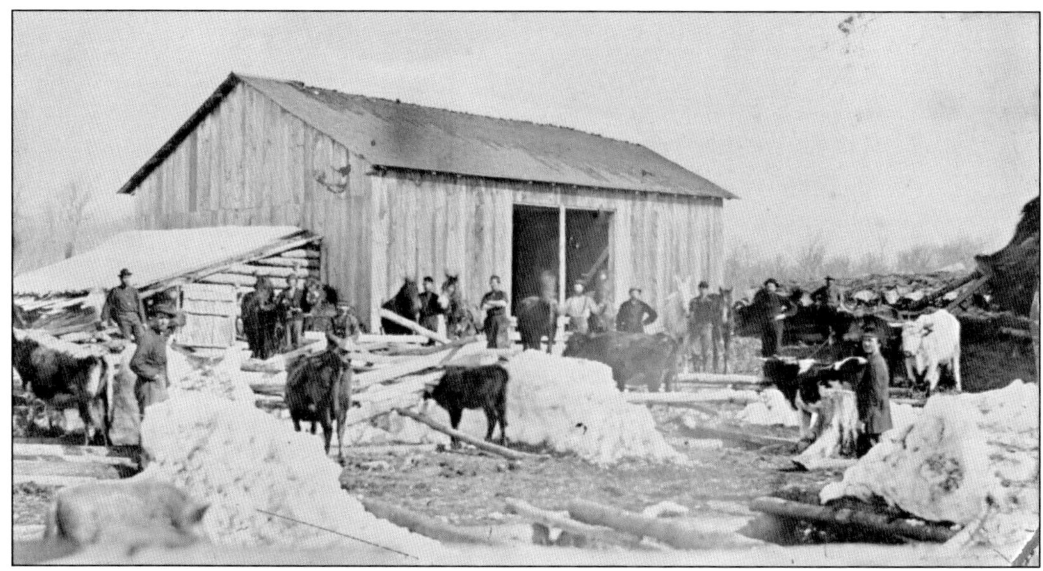

This is a late 1860s tintype of the Meehan mill that was built by brothers Patrick and James Meehan. Although located on the north side of the Wisconsin River in the Town of Linwood, the settlement known as Meehan was established on the south side of the river in the Town of Plover. A ferry provided transportation across the river from the Green Bay & Western Railroad spur on the south side of the river to the mill.

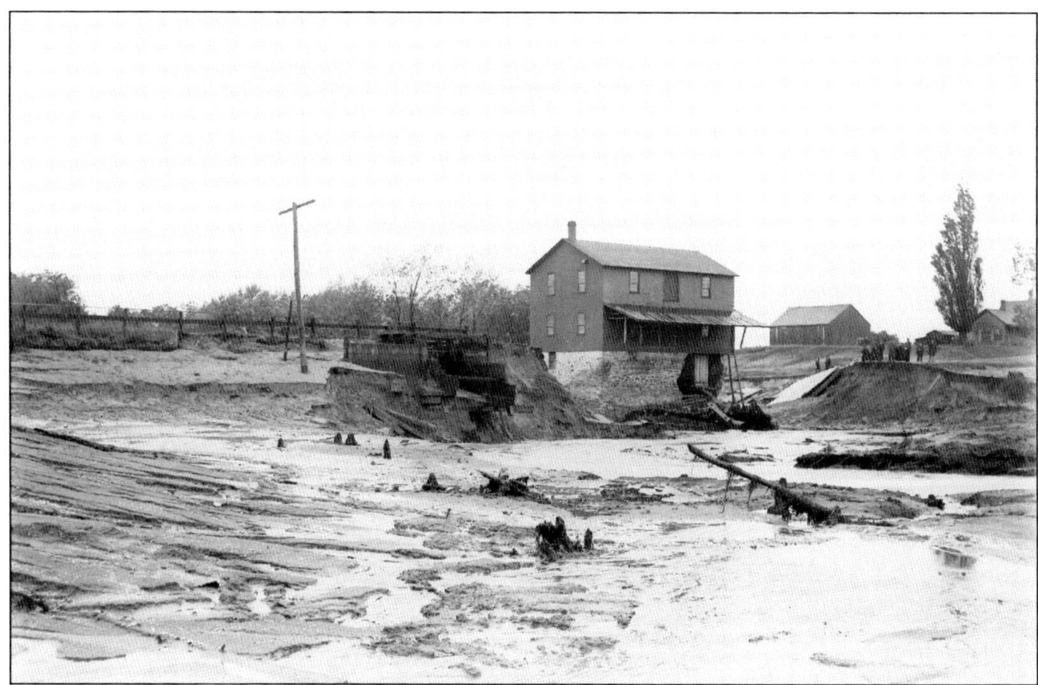

The Springville roller mill/flouring mill is pictured after a 1910 flood that destroyed the mill's dam. Located on the Little Plover River, the mill was built under a partnership of E.H. Rossier and James C. Eilertsen. Rossier owned the mill for 30 years and sold it in 1923 to E.A. Oberweiser. During this time, it produced ground feed and sold farm products.

Seven

AERIAL VIEWS

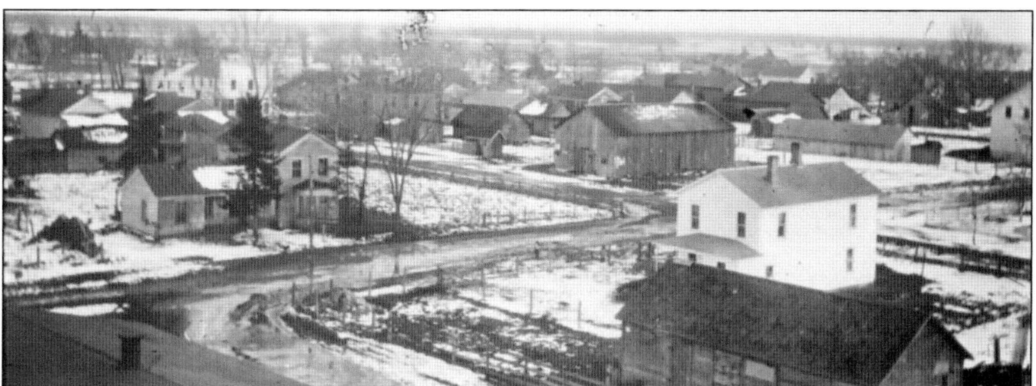

This is a bird's-eye view of the village of Plover during the early 1900s. The photograph was taken from atop the Green Bay & Western water tower, which was located near what is today the western end of Walnut Street. It looks southeast toward the downtown of Plover. The intersection in the center is Second Street (currently Earhart Avenue) and Willow Street.

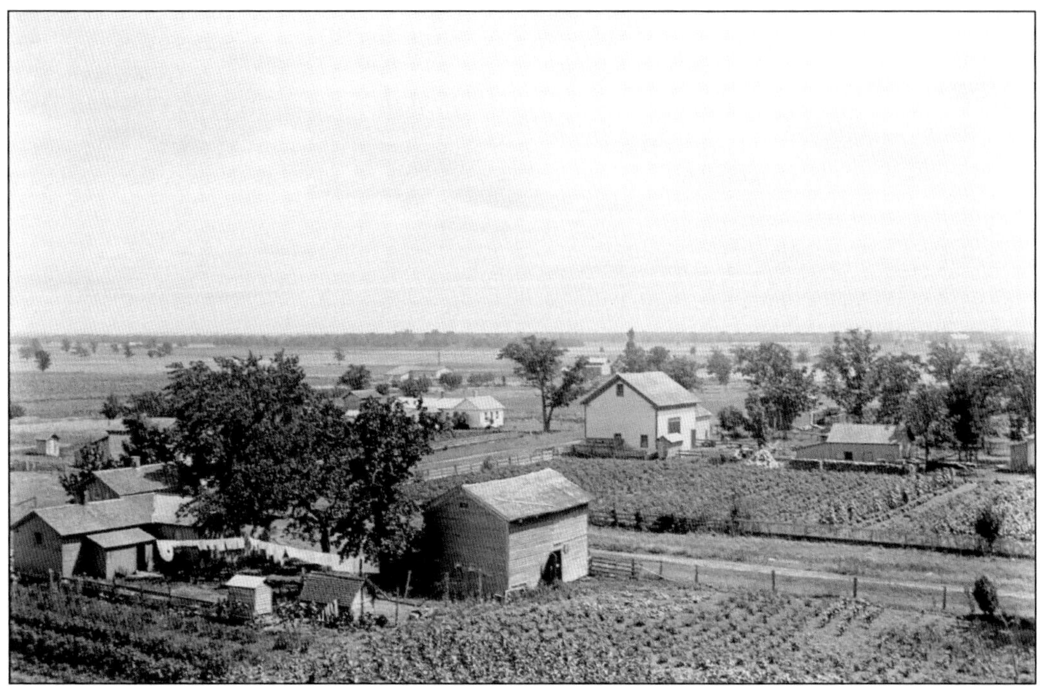

This early bird's-eye view of Plover from the top of the Plover Methodist Episcopal Church looks southeast over the intersection of Willow and Washington Streets toward Plover Road. This photograph is commonly misidentified as looking northeast, but the Plover Creamery Company is visible at center left at the edge of town.

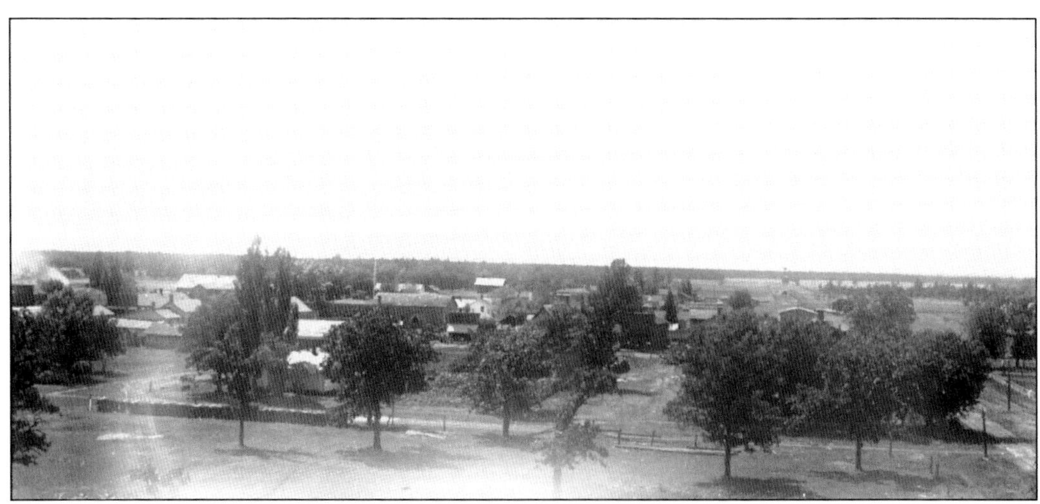

This bird's-eye view of Plover looking west, which was likely taken from atop the Plover Methodist Episcopal Church, was captured during the early 1900s. The land in the foreground was originally platted to be the town square. Although difficult to make out, the businesses on First Street are visible at center, as is the Tremont House.

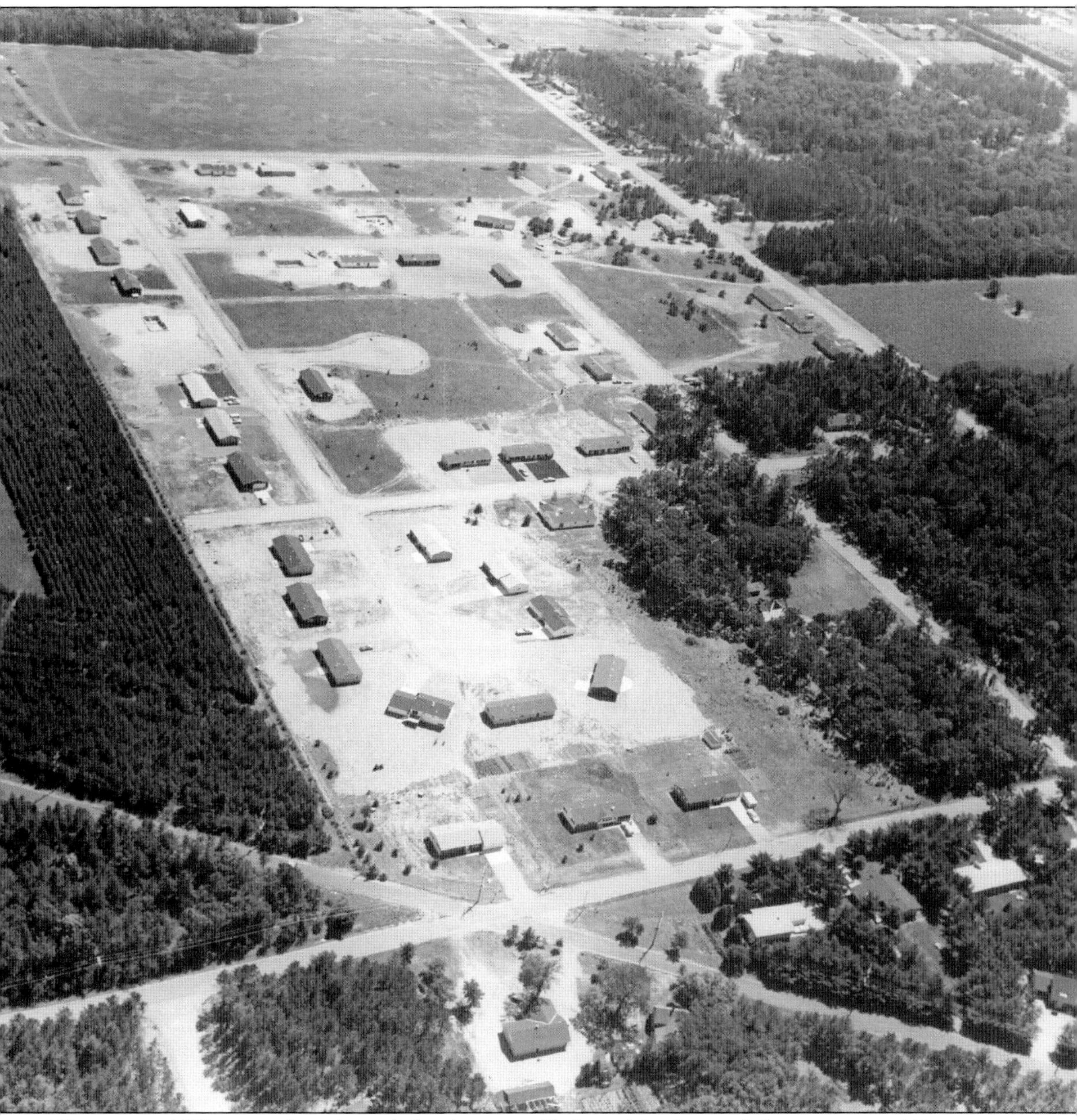

This is a c. 1977 view of residential development Hickory Meadows subdivision around Porter Road, Airline Road, Hickory Drive, and Ashwood Drive. Advertised as a parade of 33 custom built three- or four-bedroom ranch homes, these brand new homes started at $34,000.

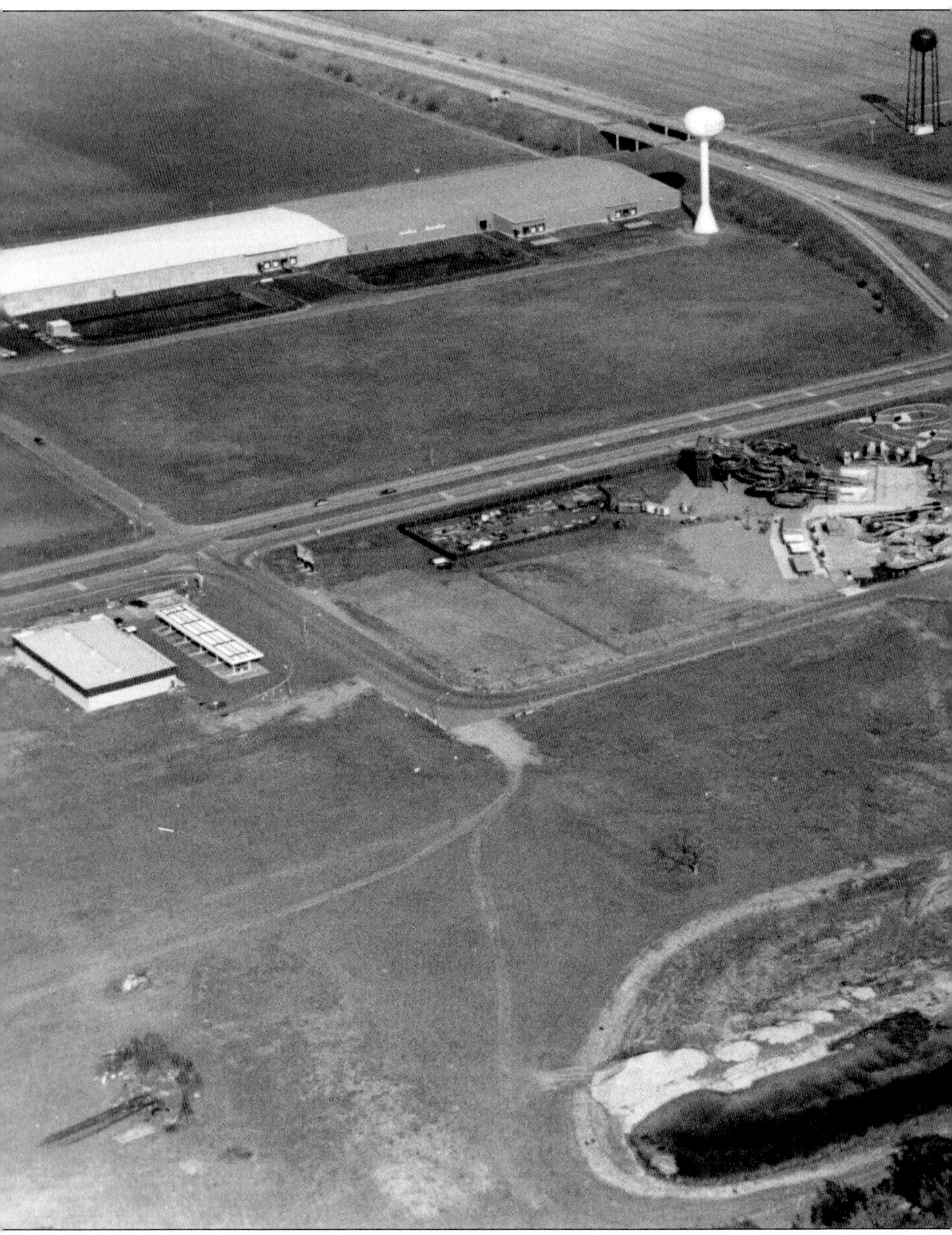

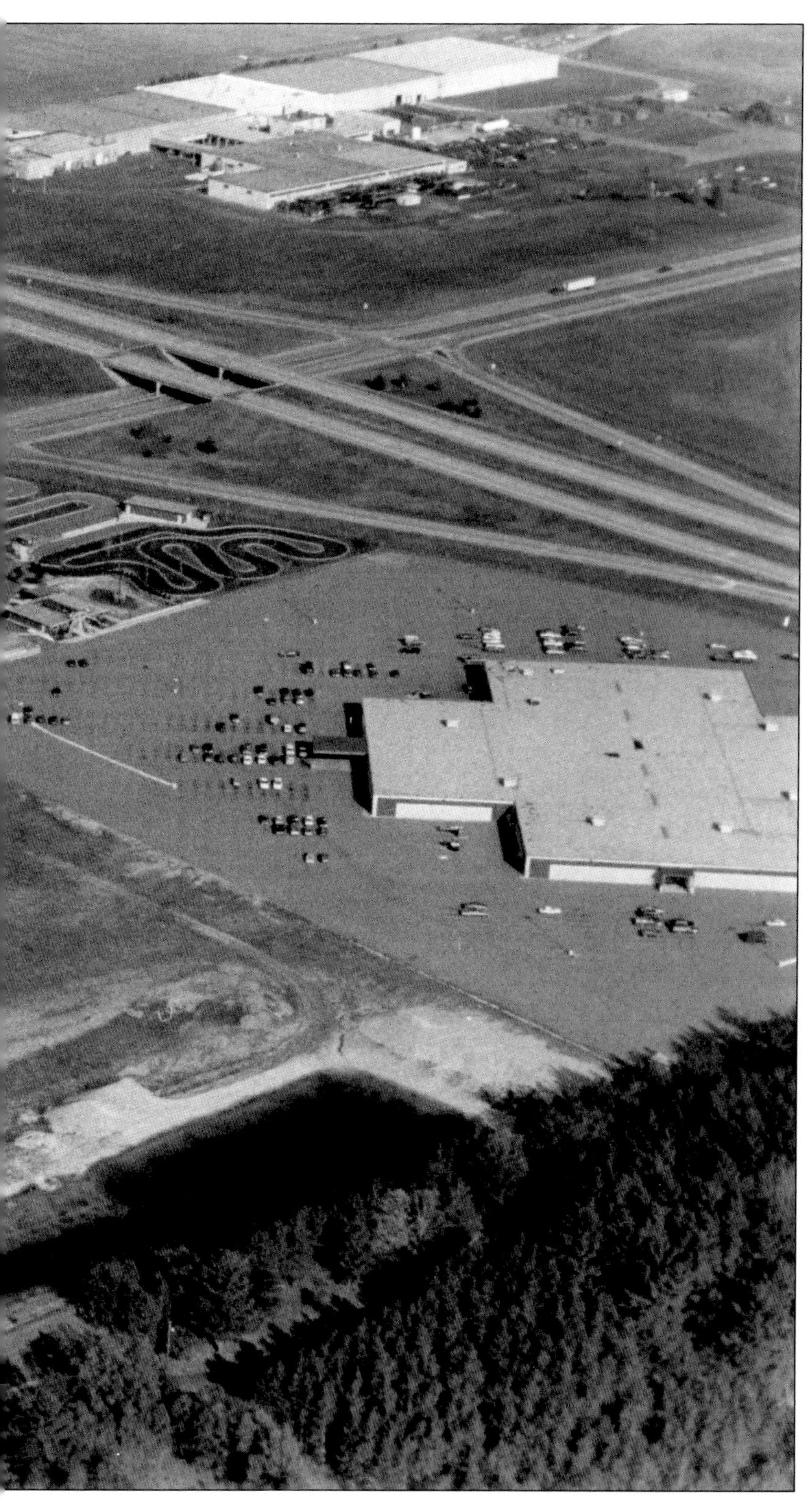

Taken on November 1, 1990, this aerial view looks northeast toward Del Monte and the Manufacturer's Direct Mall and the intersection of Interstate 39 and Plover Road. Rainbow Falls is seen at center before the construction of the Wave Pool and River of Rainbows.

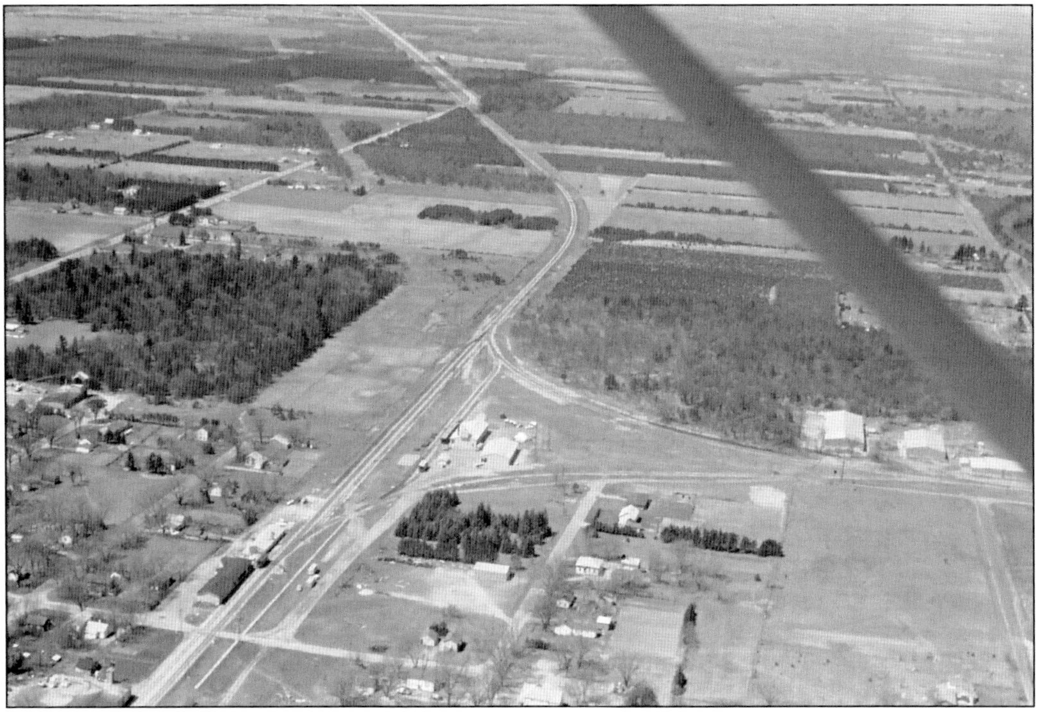

This 1966 photograph shows the Green Bay & Western wye, which is situated just to the west of the intersection of Earhart Avenue and Walnut Drive. (UWSP Archives.)

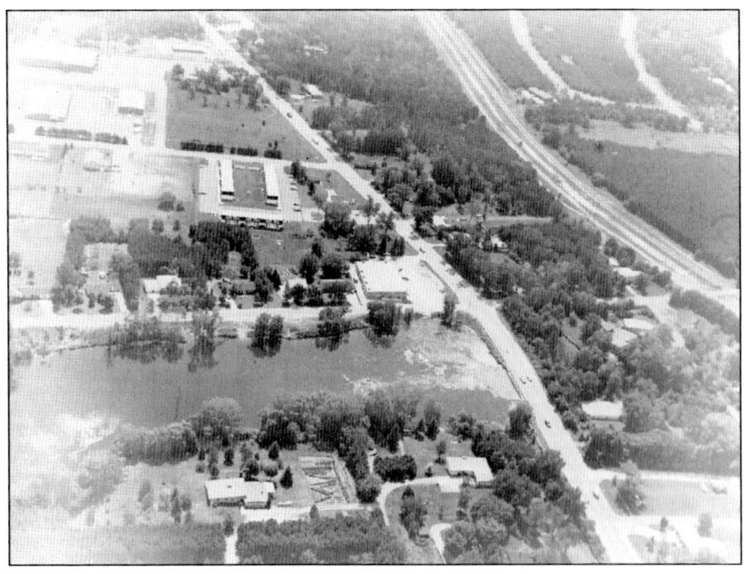

This 1981 aerial view looks south at the intersection of Springville Drive and Post Road, with the Springville Pond in the foreground. At the center is the Springville Wharf just south of the Springville Pond. The Iber House, designed by Frank Lloyd Wright and Marshall Erdman, can be seen on the right between Post Road and Okray Avenue.

INDEX

Consistent with our mission to preserve history on a local level, this book was printed in South Carolina on American-made paper and manufactured entirely in the United States. Products carrying the accredited Forest Stewardship Council (FSC) label are printed on 100 percent FSC-certified paper.

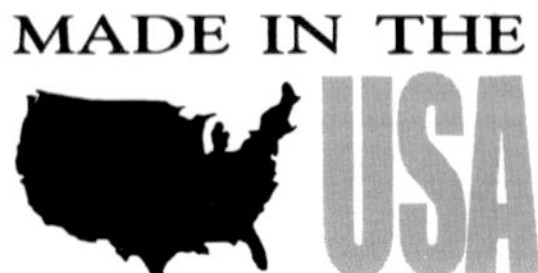